D0209278

PRAISE FOR

LIVING

═══ ON THE ═══

FAULT LINE

"Managers who have wondered whether today's seemingly irrational competitive and capital market behavior might become 'normal' again need to read *Living on the Fault Line*. Moore shows convincingly that technology and capital market efficiency have fundamentally changed not just the reality that all managers face, but have changed the way they need to define, measure, and manage success. This is a great book."

—CLAYTON CHRISTENSEN, AUTHOR OF *THE INNOVATOR'S DILEMMA: WHEN NEW TECHNOLOGIES CAUSE GREAT COMPANIES TO FAIL*

"Cisco is committed to creating unprecedented value and opportunity for our shareholders, customers, partners, and employees. Geoffrey Moore's new book, *Living on the Fault Line*, reveals his understanding of fast growth industries and offers insight to help us manage shareholder value in today's Internet economy."

—JOHN CHAMBERS, CEO, CISCO SYSTEMS

"When you live on the *fault line*, you have to reinvent yourself every single day. In the past year we have been incorporating ideas from this book into the strategy training portions of our executive development program, and the feedback has been tremendous."

—BOB HERBOLD, EXECUTIVE VICE PRESIDENT AND COO, MICROSOFT

"*Living on the Fault Line* cuts through the hype of the Internet economy. It gets at where real benefits lie, which is in applying our premium resources directly on increasing our competitive advantage and taking waste out of the total value chain. Now Geoffrey Moore tells us how to navigate the river to real sustainable value creation."

—ERIK FYRWALD, VICE PRESIDENT, E-COMMERCE, DUPONT CORPORATION;
CEO, CAPSPAN

"Having lived on the *fault line* as a senior executive at IBM, BBN, GTE, and now Akamai, I must say that this book, unlike any other I have ever read, clearly lays out the blueprint for how old-economy franchises can make a full transition to the new economy. It is also a great guide for those of us leading new-economy companies as we chart our paths forward."

—GEORGE CONRADES, CHAIRMAN AND CEO, AKAMAI

"As CEO at both Sybase and Commerce One, I can attest to the power of what Geoff Moore calls the *fault line* to disrupt existing markets and reset the rules of competition in a flash. Geoff's new book, like his prior ones, gives executives in the middle of the fray a frame of reference for setting new strategies and changing old ways."

—MARK HOFFMAN, PRESIDENT AND CEO, COMMERCE ONE

"Every executive I talk to is confused about how to build shareholder value in the Internet economy. Geoff Moore explains what's going on, why it's happening, and gives you a road map you can take to your board! This is a must read for everyone who cares about the future of their business."

—PATRICIA SEYBOLD, CEO, THE PATRICIA SEYBOLD GROUP;
AUTHOR OF *CUSTOMERS.COM*

"Geoff's book provides both vocabulary and guidance to help our company and its associates leverage the power of the new economy."

—THOMAS G. STEMBERG, CHAIRMAN AND CEO, STAPLES INC.

"New economies require new rules. If you don't read this book, you're not going to be the billionaire next door. And it will be your fault, not Geoffrey's or mine."

—GUY KAWASAKI, CEO, GARAGE.COM

"At NEON managing for shareholder value is a way of life. We have experienced the extremes of the *fault line* as we and the global capital markets work to find a consistent and enduring basis for shareholder valuations. In the process Geoff's models have brought clarity and insight to both our internal and external communications. Going forward we see them as key to shaping our strategy for the new economy."

—RICK ADAM, CHAIRMAN AND CEO, NEW ERA OF NETWORKS (NEON)

"From the epicenter of technology, Silicon Valley, comes another 'must read' from Geoffrey Moore, the man who crystallized the challenges of marketing high tech in *Crossing the Chasm*. *Living on the Fault Line* will compel executives to examine the core value of their organizations under the harsh light of the new economy and guide them with sound strategies for surviving the onslaught of the dot-coms."

—TOM KENDRA, VICE PRESIDENT, SOFTWARE, ASIA PACIFIC IBM CORPORATION

"At Viant we help companies of all kinds build new economy digital businesses. Most traditional companies are greatly challenged in transforming their cultures to support the new Internet business model. Geoff Moore's new book offers a practical blueprint for building a culture of innovation and execution so vital to establishing enduring success in the Internet age."

—BOB GETT, PRESIDENT AND CEO, VIANT

"Geoffrey Moore once again demonstrates his ability to take a complex set of business dynamics and forge them into a clean, coherent model. He outlines the effect that the transition from a traditional economy to the new 'e-conomy' has on companies—their internal behavior, their interactions within and across industry lines, and their perception by Wall Street. I found it an enormously helpful and engaging read."

—AART J. DE GEUS, CHAIRMAN AND CEO, SYNOPSYS, INC.

"Geoffrey Moore looks beyond today's e-buzz to help executives understand the fundamental changes needed to morph from the old economy to the new. Time is more valuable than money, assets don't matter, and market cap counts more than your P&L. Geoffrey gives hope for bricks and mortar companies, but the changes required will make most CEOs' hearts beat a little faster."

—BOB PEEBLER, PRESIDENT AND CEO, LANDMARK GRAPHICS CORPORATION

"This book is a must read for CEOs and their executive teams who are wondering what e-business is all about. According to Geoffrey Moore, you had better start shedding noncore activities quickly or your company will become a victim of the new economy. Geoffrey develops a model that provides the organizational flexibility and speed to navigate the choppy waters of the Internet age."

"At HP, we set a three-year business plan that was adjusted annually. At Bay Networks, we set an annual business plan that was adjusted quarterly. Now, at Alteon Websystems, we set a multiquarter business plan that is adjusted almost every month! In *Living on the Fault Line*, Moore details a prescription for a company to mutate its corporate genetic makeup in order to effect all these changes with a single company confine. . . . He hits the nail on the head, again."

"Using the Internet, someone is revolutionizing your industry. It's either you, one of your traditional competitors, or a dotcom you've never heard of until it's too late. Since the Internet fault line is going to be part of the landscape, you better find out how to survive on it. And there is no better person to teach you about it."

LIVING

ON THE

FAULT LINE

Books by Geoffrey A. Moore

Crossing the Chasm
The Gorilla Game
Inside the Tornado
The Gorilla Game Revised

LIVING

ON THE

FAULT LINE

Managing for Shareholder Value in the Age of the Internet

GEOFFREY A. MOORE

HarperBusiness
An Imprint of HarperCollins*Publishers*

HarperCollins books may be purchased for educational, business, or sales promotional use. For information please write: Special Markets Department, HarperCollins Publishers Inc., 10 East 53rd Street, New York, NY 10022.

FIRST EDITION

Designed by Nancy Singer Olaguera

Printed on acid-free paper

Library of Congress Cataloging-in-Publication Data

Moore, Geoffrey A., 1946–
   Living on the fault line : managing for shareholder value in the age of the internet / Geoffrey A. Moore.—1st ed.
      p.   cm.
   Includes index
   ISBN 0-88730-888-0
      1. Industrial management. 2. Information technology—Management. 3. Internet (Computer network) 4. Stocks—Prices. 5. Competition. I. Title.

HD31 .M625 2000
658.15'5—dc21   00-026312

00 01 02 03 04 ❖/RRD 10 9 8 7 6 5 4 3

To George Moore,
who has spent his entire life putting
his humor, intelligence, and compassion
in service to others,
and
to Peter Moore,
who has the gift of inspiring others
to be their best selves.
Thanks for all the love and encouragement.

CONTENTS

ACKNOWLEDGMENTS

This book had its beginning in a moment of customer dissatisfaction. It was back in 1996, and I was consulting with the Boise divisions of Hewlett-Packard using the models laid out in *Crossing the Chasm* and *Inside the Tornado* and was placing particular emphasis on how the technology adoption life cycle created a unique marketing challenge. Specifically, what I said was: *At every stage of the life cycle, the strategy that causes success in that stage causes failure in the next.*

It was then that I began to hear the grumbling. *Wait a minute. We are a global company. We are managing offerings at every stage in the life cycle all at the same time. Indeed, in some countries the offering is at one stage of adoption, and in other countries at another. We have teams around the world trying to work together from a common basis. You cannot just switch strategies every ten minutes. So now what, smart guy?*

Now what, indeed. How could a large enterprise manage the amount of change that technology-enabled markets demand? Start-ups, by virtue of their small size, could perhaps make the adjustments I was calling for, but what could global organizations hope to accomplish? The more I thought about it, the more it came down to a single question: *What could management do to overcome the inertia of large organizations?* If I could answer that question, clearly it was time to write the next book.

But before I could find that answer, my agent, Jim Levine, suggested I write a different book, this one on high-tech investing, and that in turn led to a collaboration with Tom Kippola of The Chasm Group and Paul Johnson of Robertson Stephens called *The Gorilla Game*. That intervention was fortuitous because it brought to light a connection between stock price and competitive advantage that became the basis for tackling the problem of corporate inertia described in Chapter 2 of this book.

So at the outset I would like to acknowledge my dissatisfied clients in the Boise divisions of Hewlett-Packard—thank you, for without your prodding this book would never have happened, and sorry for it being so late. And I would like to thank Jim, Tom, and Paul for the wonderful detour into the realm of high-tech stock valuations and the value that has added to this book.

To these I need to add several people who made direct contributions to the ideas and models that populate these pages. On coming to grips with stock price and the valuation of technology stocks, Michael Mauboussin of Crédit Suisse First Boston has been a continual inspiration and help. He continues to write some of the best essays on this subject, and I encourage interested readers to track them down. On the issue of value disciplines and their impact on competitive advantage, I continue to profit from the work of Michael Treacy and Fred Wiersema as described in their book *The Value Disciplines of Market Leaders*. And on the issue of culture, I am deeply grateful for and dependent upon the work and assistance of Bill Schneider, whose work I cite and whose models I have taken more than a few liberties with. I am also indebted to Brad Spencer, an organizational development consultant and friend, who helped me bridge the thinking between Schneider's work and Treacy and Wiersema's.

Those are some of the most explicit influences I can acknowledge that supported the development of this book. But there is also the implicit influence of colleagues, and here I am blessed with two sets. For the past decade I have been a part of The Chasm Group along with Mark Cavender, Tom Kippola, Philip Lay, Mike Tanner, and Paul Wiefels, all of whom, like myself, spend most of their days consulting with high-tech executives on the challenges of developing technology-enabled markets. The result has been a community of intellectual exchange that has contributed to every idea on every page of this book. At the same time, for the past two years I have been a venture partner at Mohr Davidow Ventures. Here my colleagues include Bill Davidow, Jon Feiber, Nancy Schoendorf, Rob Chaplinsky, George Zachary, Michael Solomon, Randy Strahan, Donna Novitsky, Mo Virani, Jim Smith, and Erik

Straser. What they have all brought to my thinking is a continual focus on shareholder value—what creates it, what enhances it, what destroys it—all of which has been instrumental in the development of this book.

Then there have been the readers of this manuscript in its earlier drafts. These brave souls deserve special acknowledgment, particularly because they were able to get comments back after a ludicrously brief interval in order to influence the final draft. Needless to say, they should not be held accountable for any defects therein, but instead be acknowledged for contributing to whatever coherence there is. These include Michael Eckhardt, Chris Meyer, Jim Fawcette, Greg Ruff, Dennis Hunter, Russell Redenbaugh, Stan Leopard, Tom Kendra, Al Magid, and Mel Lemberger. Two additional readers I would like to especially acknowledge. The first is Nicholas Carr at *The Harvard Business Review* who rightly took me to task for flaws in an early version of Chapter 2. I don't know that they have all been addressed, but the chapter benefited greatly from his critique. And the second is Bill Meade, a friend and colleague at Hewlett-Packard, who, in addition to managing the on-line investment chat community that has formed around *The Gorilla Game*, has continually participated in and helped shaped the ideas that frame this book, including giving me mini-lectures via e-mail on the work of Joseph Schumpeter.

That leaves a small cadre of people without whom any author is hopelessly adrift. These include my literary agent, Jim Levine, my editor, David Conti, and my business manager and aide-de-camp, Angelynn Hanley. All three of these individuals live with me behind the scenes where the work is anything but polished. Yet all three retain a cheerful optimism in the face of any number of pending calamities, reminding me of the character Henslowe in the recent movie, *Shakespeare in Love,* who when faced with similar circumstances repeatedly asserts, "It all works out. I don't know how exactly, but it just does." Thanks to all three of you for keeping the faith.

And that brings me to one final person to acknowledge, Marie, who has kept her faith in me for more than thirty years of marriage and has been "the wind beneath my wings." (There is a story about that line, but I will leave it for another time.) It is hard to explain how much I draw from and depend upon our relationship. On the surface our careers appear so different—she teaching third-graders, me high-tech executives (well, perhaps not *that* different)—but at the core we come together in common values and in a common strategy for living. And so we continually exchange ideas and perceptions, anecdotes and incidents, laughter and love, and in so doing come away so much the stronger. To the degree that there is balance in this work, that there is any stability beneath its constant dealings with change, it has its roots here. For this and so much more I am deeply and forever thankful.

INTRODUCTION

In picking up this book, I sincerely hope you are more interested in its subtitle than its title. There is precious little here that relates to actual earthquakes or how to achieve preparedness for them. Rather it is a book about managing for shareholder value, a discipline that has been widely endorsed but rather poorly described. Specifically, it is intended to answer one question that is haunting numerous management teams at the turn of the century: *What should a public company that rose to prominence prior to the age of the Internet know and do about its stock price now that the Internet is upon us?*

Now to be sure, the metrics are clear: *Just make the stock price go up, stupid—what else do you need to know?* Well, for starters, it might be nice to know which management actions actually affect stock price, and which don't. Indeed, it might be nice to know, given the gyrations of the stock market, what forces of any kind affect stock price. Then it would be good to understand why so many actions taken to raise stock price in fact lower it, and why some actions that you think ought to lower stock price in fact raise it.

All these bits of knowledge would be wonderful indeed. But I venture that the executive teams at more than a few *Fortune* 500 companies would trade in all these chits in return for the answer to just one question: *What in the world are we supposed to do about these (expletive deleted) dotcoms?*

And that brings us to the remaining phrase in our subtitle, "in the age of the Internet," seemingly so benign when considered from the consumer's point of view, but striking terror into the boardrooms of established firms everywhere. What indeed can management do when its home markets, territory it has nurtured and served for decades, come under direct assault from companies whose investors appear to have repealed the law of profitability?

It is the intent of this book to answer that question in depth and in detail. It is, if nothing else, a timely topic. With the release of Clayton Christensen's book in 1997, *The Innovator's Dilemma: When New Technologies Cause Great Companies to Fail,* executive teams everywhere were put on notice that their whole approach to management might be fundamentally flawed. Specifically, Christensen shows with example after example how companies that commit to strategies of continuous innovation and incremental improvement will almost always fail to embrace the next wave of technology in their markets and thus, over time, will fall from positions of market dominance to also-rans. It is a tale as chilling as any that has ever been told because it calls into question so much that for so long has been so thoroughly taken for granted.

Christensen's book, then, may be taken as the definitive ringing out of the alarm: *The dotcoms are coming! The dotcoms are coming!* Neither by land nor by sea, as it turns out, but over our own phone lines, these new institutions are invading every segment of commerce, overturning established relationships, reengineering markets, attacking long-established price points, and disintermediating long-standing institutions. At first it was just an isolated instance, an Amazon.com attacking a Barnes & Noble, an Autobytel inserting itself between car buyers and established dealerships, an E-Trade enabling on-line trading. But then on-line retail began to take off, and soon it became clear that no company's position was really secure—not Toys "R" Us from an attack by eToys, not Safeway from an attack by Webvan, not Wal-Mart from an attack by Amazon. And more recently still it has been declared that the business-to-business sector of commerce, some ten times larger than retail, is the new hunting grounds for dotcoms, with sector after sector promising to be transformed into digital marketplaces, whatever those might be. *Is no one safe? In this new economy, is nothing sacred?*

The answers to those questions appear to be no, and no. We live in a Darwinian world, and either we adapt to change or we get left behind. Those are the rules. So we had best get over it and then get on with it.

This book consists of six chapters, each of which takes some element of the title and attempts to set forth the relevant under-standing needed. Chapter 1 is entitled "The Age of the Internet." It dissects fundamental changes that collectively represent the transition to the new economy in order to show how radically sources of competitive advantage are shifting away from their traditional moorings. These shifts call into question the traditional operations of established corporations and demand that executive teams drastically rethink what their core value is. In so doing, they will discover that the overwhelming bulk of their current activity has no direct impact on creating shareholder value, and this in turn will create ever-increasing pressure to outsource this work so that the company can focus more energy where it can make a difference.

Such calls, of course, are nothing new. Traditional corporations have heard them before and have learned painfully that, despite the seeming rightness of these arguments, corporate inertia is not a force to be trifled with. What, indeed, could one bring to bear against such massive weight to truly change its course? It turns out there is one force that may indeed be equal to this challenge: *stock price*. Thus to find a lever to move this world we turn to the second chapter, "Shareholder Value."

The goal of this second chapter is to create a common understanding within the management team about the nature of shareholder value and to provide a specific set of tools for converting stock price into a kind of management information system. With respect to shareholder value, the key point is that stock price directly equates to sustainable competitive advantage. Managing for shareholder value, thus, becomes synonymous with managing for competitive advantage. The corollary here is that stock price, a metric of shareholder value, is indirectly a feedback mechanism regarding value creation and competitive advantage. What core activities should your company be focused on? Why, those that can increase your stock price! That is what defines core, and if you are not sure whether you are hitting the mark or not, let your stock price be your guide.

This notion, in turn, creates a need for a set of tools to decode not only your own stock price but that of every other competitor in your environment. Total market capitalization, price/earnings ratios, and price/sales ratios all come into play here as well as a new metric called "price/vision" ratio. By the end of the chapter, readers should be comfortable incorporating stock market data into their own strategy development as well as their analyses of the competition's.

At the end of the day, it all comes back to competitive advantage and how it is changing in the age of the Internet, and that is the topic of our third chapter. Here, there is already a plethora of models and work to draw upon, and my goal is merely to update this body of material with new learning specific to technology-enabled markets. The single biggest source of competitive advantage in these markets is simply catching and riding the next technology wave. Within this general context, the next biggest source comes from joining the winning value chain and achieving a leadership role within it. After these two, which are both somewhat peculiar to technology-enabled markets, the chapter looks into three additional sources of competitive advantage that work across all markets—market segment leadership, execution focus, and differentiated offerings. By the end of the chapter, readers have a five-layer model for competitive advantage to bring to the management challenge of living on the fault line.

"Living on the Fault Line" is the title of Chapter 4. The metaphor refers to the way in which shifts in underlying technologies create destabilizing effects on the markets above them. In the high-tech sector, these shifts have become so frequent that we have learned how to take them for granted. In the rest of the economy, however, they are still sufficiently novel that executive teams are likely to be unfamiliar with their dynamics. The goal of this chapter is to address that problem.

The fundamental model that explains the dynamics of technology-enabled markets is the technology adoption life cycle. Under its influence, markets evolve through a series of four distinct stages, each characterized by different customer behavior and different value-chain priorities. As a result, at each stage different forms of competitive advantage are privileged, with different kinds of companies gaining ascendancy, which in turn gets reflected in stock price appreciation. The chapter dissects each stage in terms of all these variables so that executive teams can understand when and where they should strike and when and where they should be content to take a backseat role.

One key take-away from this chapter is that no one company can hope to optimize its operations for all phases of the life cycle. But there is actually a darker side to the story, one that is examined in the fifth chapter of the book, "Triage." This is the chapter that speaks directly to the innovator's dilemma. Using the life-cycle models, it shows exactly how and where new technology causes traditional corporations to fail. Specifically, it shows that these companies spontaneously reject discontinuous innovations, regardless of their source, even if that source is their own laboratories. As such, they have a problem we label "recrossing the chasm," a reference to an earlier book, *Crossing the Chasm*, that addressed how to deal with this problem in the external marketplace.

Here the challenge is the internal marketplace. *Triage* in this context translates into a set of prescriptions for the board of directors, the executive team, and each of the major line functions, all focused on temporarily deconstructing the resistance to innovation sufficiently to allow the company to get on the next technology wave. As the metaphor of triage is intended to convey, there is nothing particularly elegant about these actions, and indeed many of them are truly painful. That observation, in turn, leads to the sixth and final chapter, "Building to Last."

The problems that the triage operation encounters can ultimately be traced to a failure to manage culture appropriately. That is, unmanaged, culture in established organizations defaults to behaviors that proliferate noncore activities faster than core and that suffocate innovation. The argument of the chapter is that this need not be the case. Indeed, it argues that there are at least four different cultural models that can sustain long-term vibrant success and that perhaps the greatest contribution executive management can make to shareholder value is to choose one of these models and manage to it. To that end, the chapter dissects the four models to point out their strengths and weaknesses, show their natural alignments with one or another of the traditional line functions, how they prosper or suffer depending on what stage of the life cycle the market may be in, and in general how they can create a foundation upon which one can build to last.

Taken all together, this set of six chapters can be thought of as material for a sequence of six workshops intended to provide executive teams with the understanding, the tools, and the vocabulary for navigating technology-enabled or technology-impacted markets. The material comes from more than twenty years of working and consulting within the high-tech sector. Heretofore, these effects were largely confined to that sector, but with the emergence of the Internet as a world-changing force in the economy, they are now being felt by virtually every type of business on the planet.

In this context, if you are already part of high tech, I hope this book will confirm lessons learned and add insight going forward. And if you are coming to technology-enabled markets for the first time, I hope that these chapters can ease your transition and allow you to benefit from the experience of others instead of having to learn it all on your own nickel. In either case, what I wish most of all is that this book generates a clearer understanding of what it really means to manage for shareholder value in the age of the Internet, and that we can use that understanding to create new wealth for all the constituencies we serve.

LIVING

ON THE

FAULT LINE

1

THE AGE OF THE INTERNET

Living on a fault line causes one to take an interest in what geologists call plate tectonics. These are the forces under the earth that create the conditions for recurrent and severe earthquakes. In the case of the new information economy, the emergence of the Internet is demonstrating itself to be just such a force.

In this chapter, we are going to examine how what used to be bedrock for our economy, the foundation upon which most established companies "built to last," is now in fact shifting beneath our feet. This in turn will call us to put a new focus on information technology, require us to manage to a new resource equation, and demand from us a new level of commitment to focus our resources increasingly on core processes only.

By the end of this chapter, we will see that in the new economy strategies that heavily leverage outsourcing have a distinct competitive advantage. At the same time, we will acknowledge that the inertia within established organizations resists moving to such strategies. In the search for a lever to move our companies forward, we will hit upon shareholder value and stock price, which will transition us smoothly into the next chapter.

It is a known disease of writers and editors to declare the era they live in "the age of . . ." something, and for the present "the age of the Internet" seems reasonable enough. But why should any self-respecting manager or executive fall prey to this vice? The answer is, only if it will help you to manage for shareholder value better. In this case I think it will.

The claim that we are entering a new age is based on the notion that over the past decade a series of subtle but profound changes in the nature and structure of business have fundamentally changed the game we are playing. At one level, we see the impact of these changes in the unprecedented behavior of our stock market: It appears to overvalue the new and speculative and undervalue the proven ways—*dramatically*. At another level, we see line functions that used to be the heart of our businesses—like manufacturing—now being outsourced while other disciplines that used to be staff functions—like computer systems—have come to the fore. Looking elsewhere, we see the graduates of our finest business schools uniformly agreeing that a *Fortune* 500 corporation is the last place they would want to work—*even when that corporation is footing the bill for their schooling!* What makes this last observation even more chilling is that it is not based on the corporation being boring, slow-moving, or lacking in advancement opportunities. No, the big beef the new crop of graduates has with the *Fortune* 500 is that they think going forward, these companies are going to be *losers*! (Heaven only knows what they think is in store for all the other corporations out there.)

So in the words of the Buffalo Springfield, "Something's happening here, though what it is ain't exactly clear." The job of this chapter is to bring that something to light and to assess what it means for the management agenda.

BACKFIELD IN MOTION

The forces that are reshaping business are for the most part happening in the background and not manifesting themselves directly in events happening in the foreground. As a result, they don't get reported in the *Wall Street Journal,* do not come up on quarterly conference calls with the investment analysts, and are not raised by customers in advisory board sessions. Thus, not surprisingly, they do not tend to register on the executive team's radar screen.

These forces are best understood in terms of a series of remarkable transitions, of which we will look at six. In each case, note that power is shifting away from something that has long been a trusted source of value creation and toward something that heretofore was considered secondary, derivative, or tangential.

FROM ASSETS TO INFORMATION

In *Being Digital*, Nick Negroponte describes how value in the age of the Internet has migrated from *atoms* to *bits*. The implication for the new management agenda is that *information about an asset has become more valuable than the asset itself*. It is now more profitable, in other words, to own information about oil than to own oil, information about airline flights than to own an airline, information about a nation's currency than to own the currency itself.

This is bizarre, so let's take a moment to see why it is true. Suppose you own 100 barrels of oil worth $10 each. In other words, you have $1,000 invested in oil. Suppose the price of oil goes up $5 per barrel. You make $500. But suppose for $1 per barrel you could buy *the option* to buy oil at $10 a barrel at some future date. You wouldn't own any oil; you would just own "a position" in oil. Now you could take your $1,000 and instead of buying 100 barrels of oil you could buy the option to purchase 1,000 barrels. Once again, the price of oil goes up $5. Now you can call in your option, buy (virtually) 1,000 barrels of oil at $10 and sell them (again, virtually) at $15. Instead of $500 you make $5,000 minus the $1,000 you paid for the options, or $4,000.

Ah, you say, but what if oil prices had gone down $5? Where would we have been then? Well, if you had owned the 100 barrels of oil, and the price went down, you just lost $500. Worse still, if you had bought 1,000 options at $1 per barrel, you just lost $1,000! But here's the real kicker—if you had used that same $1,000 to buy options for $1 to *sell* oil at $10 a barrel, then once again you would have *made* $4,000!

The difference in leverage is huge. That is, the ability of capital to create more capital has been magnified by a factor of 8. How is this possible? The answer is, none of the capital was tied up in atoms, all of it was attached to bits. These transactions were not about the value of oil. They were about the *variability in the price* of oil. The value was in either insuring against or speculating upon *change*. It made no difference what the change was in—the options could have been in pork bellies or Barbie dolls and they would have served the same function. This represents a whole new world.

In this new world, information is king. The more information you have, and the better (and faster) your analysis, the greater the probability that you will make winning investments. That is why speakers and authors continually note that we are living in an information age—information is not only more plentiful, it is more valuable. It is also why companies in the information technology sector have taken over the stock market, causing a massive transfer of wealth from the NYSE to NASDAQ. But why now? one might ask. Why didn't this happen ten years or one hundred years or one thousand years ago?

It turns out that for information value to exceed asset value you need relatively efficient markets that are free from intimidation and corruption. If markets are not efficient, then you cannot capitalize on information advantage because by the time you seek to execute the trade, the information has become more broadly disseminated, and your knowledge is no longer differentiated. In such cases it is better to just possess the asset. Similarly, if your environment is war torn, if it is dangerous to expose your goods to potential customers because it also exposes them to risk of theft or confiscation, or if trades can be thwarted or taxed by unlawful authority, then again, holding the asset is likely to be a better strategy. And finally, if information systems are relatively primitive, then you cannot garner sufficient information to diminish the risk in any trade of making the wrong decision, and so once again, the better play is to hold on to the proven asset.

Thus it is only in recent years, with the rise of efficient and increasingly global markets, the relatively low level of warfare, and the dramatic progress in information technology, that an information-value strategy has come to the fore. The question now is, so what? What are the implications of this change going forward?

FROM PRODUCTS TO SERVICES

The first implication, and perhaps the most profound, is this: In an information age, *products are less valuable than services*. This is just the opposite from an asset economy, and the amount of havoc this change is wreaking is astounding. Start with accounting procedures. Today virtually nothing of importance is on the balance sheet and everything of importance is off it. As executives managing knowledge-based businesses—and pray tell, what business these days is not?—we have long understood that our people and what they know are at the core of our competitive advantage. But there is no way to acknowledge any of that on our books. Instead, we can dutifully record our factories and equipment—the keys to competitive advantage in an asset age—all the while having no place to list even something as obviously valuable as our patent portfolio. It's absurd.

But forget about accounting. Let's just think about core strategy. It used to be that product companies got much higher multiples than services companies. And even today, if the comparison is made between a product company and a project-oriented professional services firm, that valuation ratio can hold—although the Internet services firms are currently giving the product folks a run for their money. But it is a whole new ball game when you bring *transaction services* to the table—recurrent revenue streams from delivering subscriptions, clearing transactions, connecting phone calls or data links, booking reservations, or advertising or selling to consumers. These are all things at the core of the new Internet market where the bulk of the market capitalization has gravitated to the service providers. Indeed, the fewer the atoms in your business plan, the more it is devoted just to bits, the higher the valuation investors are giving it. Services have fewer atoms than products.

From a strategic point of view, the relation between service and product is intriguingly interchangeable. A long time ago, there used to be a professional service called an *answering service,* which was then replaced by a product called an *answering machine,* which in turn was replaced by a transaction service called *voice-mail.* At the outset for many companies, computing used to be a transaction service rented from a *service bureau,* which was then replaced by the acquisition of a suite of *computer* products installed by a professional services firm called a *systems integrator,* which are now poised to be replaced by a new category of transaction service provider called an *ASP (application service provider)* whose offerings are accessed over the Internet. The French have a saying—*La plus ça change, la plus c'est la même chose*—the more things change, the more they remain the same.

Thus the advantaged form of delivery can shift back and forth between product and service. If there is no widespread infrastructure in place, then the advantage goes to product, but if the infrastructure is already in place, if all you have to do is send bits over an existing array of atoms (what else is a TV program, for example), then the advantage goes to service. And that is where we are today. The Internet represents an inflection point in the deployment of global communications infrastructure. Before its emergence, inertia was on the side of the status quo, and new offerings had to overcome it. Now inertia is on the side of change and new offerings have only to ride the wave. That is why even the most product-centric of companies—automobile manufacturers, factory equipment vendors, raw materials providers—real atoms guys—are now assigning their best and brightest to the task of differentiating on services.

Consider the example of Ford. CEO Jacques Nasser has announced he wants to transform the company from an automobile manufacturer to the premier provider of consumer services in the automotive industry. Nasser recognizes that for every dollar spent buying a car, there are four dollars spent on financing it, insuring it, fueling it, and maintaining it. And that's just today. In the future the car, among other things, is destined to become a second media center, a mobile node on the Internet, with all the e-commerce implications that entails.

Or consider the example of Hewlett-Packard (HP). Nick Earle, corporate strategist, has announced that the company's future does not lie in *computers* as much as in *computing*. Earle recognizes that computer power delivered over the Internet is an anonymous commodity, like electricity, and that what will differentiate it in the future is the services attached to it.

To put this as bluntly as possible, in the age of the Internet, product is more likely to be a liability than an asset. And there is nothing that is a product that cannot be delivered as a service. Clothing? Rent the tuxedo. Car? Take a cab. Camera? Hire a photographer. Stove? Dine out. All products have benefits, to be sure, but it is the benefits, not the product, that you want to buy. I don't want to own a one-inch drill, I want to buy a bunch of one-inch holes. Once I have the holes, what would I want the drill for? Once you have your directory on your phone, what do you do with a phone book? Once you outsource your manufacturing successfully, what do you need a manufacturing plant for?

FROM VERTICAL TO VIRTUAL INTEGRATION

This leads us to the next change driven by the age of the Internet—the move from *vertical* integration to *virtual* integration. In the 1970s, the exemplary high-tech companies were Xerox and IBM, both vertically integrated corporations that developed everything from their core technology and their base systems to the software that ran them and the service organizations that supported them. These companies sustained their competitive advantage by *hoarding the value chain*. The advantage to the customer was superior systems integration and unambiguous accountability—everything end to end came from the same vendor. The advantage to the vendors was greater share of the customer's mind and wallet, current expenditures, and future plans. There are downside factors in this model as we now know—namely, high cost and vendor lock-in—but at the time neither was a great concern: Customers were capturing productivity gains that more than paid back their investments, and as long as the technology was relatively novel, being locked in didn't feel bad—in fact, it felt sort of good.

All that changed with the arrival of the PC and the UNIX computer, each of which spawned an *open architecture value chain* in which third parties are encouraged to make best-of-breed contributions to a given specification. In this new world, the companies that make the microprocessors (Intel, Motorola, MIPS), the people who make the memory (Toshiba, Micron, Samsung), the people who make the terminals (Sony, Matsushita, Samsung), the people who make the disk drives (Seagate, Quantum, EMC), the people who manufacture the subassemblies (Solectron, Flextronics, GE Harris), the people who distribute the systems (Ingram Micro, Merisel, TechData), the people who sell to the end user (CompUSA, Fry's, and a host of value-added resellers), and the people who support the systems going forward (EDS, Unisys, Honeywell)—all are different.

The learning from these two market models is that virtual value chains scale much faster and are more cost-competitive than vertically integrated ones. Frankly, they do not compete well on quality of integration or accountability—and in niche markets this still gives the advantage to a vertically integrated company—but they get to "good enough" quickly, so that in mass-market deployments they have a distinct advantage. Thus the UNIX-based servers systematically eroded the proprietary minicomputer business at the high end, while the PCs and local area networks eroded it at the low end. *Virtual* successfully trumped *vertical*.

Such effects are hardly confined to the computer industry. In pharmaceuticals biotech start-ups are providing much of the R and D to global corporations while bio-information companies are providing maps or genomes and genetic sequences. In the automotive industry modular architecture has laid the foundation for outsourcing a wide range of subassemblies from interiors to climate control to suspensions. Again we might ask ourselves why now—why is any of this particular to the age of the Internet?

The answer is that virtual trumps vertical only in the presence of effective and responsive communications. It does no good to outsource something if the product or service cannot be delivered on time and in coordination with the rest of the system. But when it can, then outsourcers gain the benefits they need without having to dedicate scarce internal resources to achieve them. The Internet has created a true information highway here where any company in any country can post and buy goods and services today, without (at present) additional taxation, and for the most part with very few restrictions. It has thus become the backbone of the open architecture value chain, and it is attracting newcomers at unprecedented rates of adoption, in part because it is simply so valuable, in part for fear that if they don't get there before their competitors, they are going to lose out in a big way.

This is the point of transition at which we stand today. It is a hugely challenging one for traditional *Fortune* 500 corporations because it asks them to abandon their long-standing competitive-advantage strategy of value-chain hoarding and to embrace its dead opposite. A heritage of suspicion must be replaced with a propensity to trust. The instinct to compete must be modulated by the ability to collaborate. The passion to control must be complemented by the willingness to cultivate. And worst of all, there must be a willingness to see at least initial (and probably permanent) deterioration in accountability and quality of service provided—open architectures, as noted, do not compete well on this vector—which runs counter to every value and instinct in the culture. In short, life is a mess.

This is the landscape depicted by Clayton Christensen in *The Innovator's Dilemma*, the essence of which is that disruptive technologies like the Internet force changes in strategy and behavior that are deeply counterintuitive to established companies and are normally not embraced. As a result, over time these companies become less competitive, their relevance and influence marginalized, their stock price depressed, their core constituencies defensive, their futures dim. It is a grim scenario, not the least so because it is so damnably familiar.

FROM COMMAND AND CONTROL TO SELF-ORGANIZING SYSTEMS

As the underlying market model migrates from vertical to virtual integration, the old management model of command and control is becoming increasingly obsolete. It is just barely possible to command and control the activities of people who report to you (or at least to think you are). It is absolutely impossible to do so with resources that don't belong to you at all. A whole new model for management is needed.

At the heart of the new model is a realization that markets, specifically the value chains of companies that interoperate to make up an open architecture market, are *self-organizing systems*. Self-organization describes how anything organic grows and develops. It stands in direct contrast to *planned assembly*, which is how most inorganic artifacts are created. In self-organization there is no master planner, no scheduler, no bill of materials, no work orders, and no quality assurance (except for Darwin). Even our DNA is just a list of suggestions. Change the environment significantly, and some suggestions get overruled, others get reinforced, with the resulting organism looking and behaving in ways very different from its parents. But at no time can you point to anyone or anything that is in control of this process. Nonetheless, every year plants grow, calves are born, and humans develop—all without a manual, and most without adult supervision. The same holds true for markets.

In the age of the Internet, new markets are coming on-line faster than ever before, and as each one goes through its development stages, it gives power to those companies that "get" what is happening and takes it away from those that do not. To traditionalists these rapidly emerging worlds look—and indeed literally are—*out of control.* That was the point of Kevin Kelly's book of the same title. Self-organizing systems do not yield to command-and-control approaches. Instead, like grass growing through concrete, they simply outmaneuver them.

So rather than relying upon externally imposed controls under threat of sanctions, the winning approach seeks to elicit an internally generated alignment given voluntarily. This requires a new approach from management in which the head of collaboration—the business development officer—has become at least as important as the head of competition—the vice president of sales. It also reconstructs our understanding of how competition plays out in an evolutionary context. Essentially it takes place in two phases. The first phase is *market versus market,* during which the new value chain tries to make a place for itself in the world. During this phase, when anybody wins, everybody wins—the category is gaining validity—and thus *collaboration* is the critical strategy. On the other hand, once the category gets momentum, then the locus of development shifts from the chain to its constituent links. Now it is a *company versus company* context to see who can emerge as the market leader. This is a zero-sum game, and so *competition* is the core strategy.

Winning companies, then, must be able to field both cooperative and competitive teams with the right timing. That, in turn, requires sensitivity to market development dynamics, evolutionary forces that cannot be planned or assembled but that can be influenced, sometimes even orchestrated. Companies that are doing this orchestration well are said to "get it." They build their plans backward from the market's behavior instead of trying to push them forward from an internally driven financial agenda. In traditional companies with powerful silos built around line functions, this approach never gets traction, and inevitably their programs falter. Meanwhile, more nimble competitors are getting themselves designed into the very fabric and standards of the new market, such that when the traditional competitor finally does get its act together, it finds itself competing on a playing field that is permanently tilted against it.

FROM MONEY TO TIME

The key to managing within emerging self-organizing systems is timing. In the development of a fetus, the heart and lungs have to form at exactly the right time, as do the head and limbs, the circulatory system, and the rest. Markets are the same. The initial customers, the initial solution set, the open architecture, the key service providers, the killer application—all these things must come on-line within a given window of opportunity or they will never come on-line at all. It is in the gestation phase that market leaders and followers are determined—more or less permanently. To not be present at that time is virtually to guarantee a follower position in the market during its mature phase.

Therefore, in emerging markets, in the trade-off between money and time, time wins hands down. You would buy time at virtually at any price. Conversely, no short-term profits could ever match the lifetime value of getting "designed in" to the market leader position. It is this principle that underlies the fundamental shift in stock market valuations over the last half decade. Enormous amounts of private and public capital are being thrown at a one-time opportunity, the emergence of Internet-based markets, in an effort to secure long-term leadership positions that can be exploited more or less permanently. In the course of this influx of capital, the current valuation equations do not balance—this is *not* about money. But they are not irrational, they are simply time based. The urgency of a one-time opportunity in a potentially winner-take-all market that has global ramifications overcomes all—this *is* about time.

In this context, one of the elements of the new management philosophy is to *go ugly early.* Of course your 1.0 product sucks, but it is in the market, and customers and partners are explaining to you just how it sucks, and more important, what you should do (and by implication what you do not have to do) to fix it. Competitors are gleeful that you got bad reviews, but they miss the point, which is that you *got* reviews in the first place. And you got talked about. So when you release your 2.0 product, which hits the market about the time a "proper" 1.0 would have, both it and you are actually much farther ahead of the game than your competitors think.

So even though it looks ugly, you actually are winning. Now to be sure, neither the 1.0 nor the 2.0 product makes any money, and that can throw off your management team if you aren't careful. But the truth is, profits don't matter at this stage at all, and revenues matter only if they accurately reflect customer uptake. The pertinent issue is the competition to generate, influence, and perhaps even gain control of an open architecture value chain. The other players in this game have only a finite amount of patience to participate in this experiment, so it is critical to engage now, regardless of how well prepared you are, and regardless of how pitiful the short-term returns.

Needless to say, taking delight in bad reviews and cheerfully disregarding appalling returns on assets are not the strongest suits of mature management teams. This is the innovator's dilemma once again. Indeed, wherever the best strategy is to swap money for time, traditional organizations are typically hobbled because their systems force the trade-off to go in the opposite direction. Corporate budgeting, that is, is based upon allocating fixed amounts of money across standard units of time. But markets do not develop according to a calendar. They do not move according to standard units of time but rather to standard stages of development. So corporations would be far better served by tying resource allocations to market development milestones rather than to accounting periods.

That is how venture capital works. Neither the amount of the funding nor the rate of its expenditure is tightly defined—both are allowed to float. The focus instead is on winning a dominating position before someone else does. The target market, the metrics for dominance, and the competitive set are all tightly monitored. If you hit your target in the market-allotted time window, and it took twice as much money as you originally thought, no one will blink. But if you fail to win the competition, regardless of how well you executed your plan or stayed within budget, you'll be sent packing.

In sum, building shareholder value in emerging markets is a game of timing and as such puts an enormous premium on flexibility. It is a continual exercise in start, stop, start again, stop again. Traditional organizations simply are not set up to tolerate this kind of inefficiency. (Of course, from an emerging market's point of view it is *they* who are the inefficient ones, showering resources when they are unusable and withholding them when they are desperately needed.) What offends the traditional organization's sensibility is the waste of money. What it is not registering is the optimization of time—not time by the corporation's watch, that's being wasted too—but market time, catching the market at just the right time. So while more competitive organizations accept the need to replan, rebudget, and reprioritize every 90 to 120 days just to stay close to an emerging market's dynamics, traditional organizations treat such efforts as rogue processes that need to be shut down and rebooted.

What traditional organizations are failing to register is the opportunity cost. Strategically, as we have noted, it comes from not participating in the new category in time. But tactically there is another more frustrating cost—wasting the progress one has already made. For all those fits and starts that looked like no progress could in fact have represented true progress, progress as it happens in chaotic circumstances. That is, even though all the normal metrics of the organization imply failure and loss of control, the effort could in fact be on course. Shutting down such efforts, given their long-term implications for shareholder value, is close to criminal.

However, to keep all this in perspective, let us remind ourselves that making a practice of accommodating chaos is for emerging markets only. Mature markets do not reward this constant jiggling of the handle. They have their own Darwinian selection under way, one that has generated the *Fortune* 500 as we know it today. And all the confining traditional mores and metrics we have been chafing against work to ensure survival of the fittest in that context. This is the fault-line problem: All the behaviors that look so wrong at one phase of the technology adoption life cycle become mission-critical success factors at another.

So it is not that the current management team is brain dead. It is just that they are out of phase. The problem, as we go forward into the age of the Internet, is that the bulk of wealth creation and the leverage for creating shareholder value have shifted from generating earnings in established markets to capturing market-share leadership in emerging markets. Nowhere is this more visible than in our stock markets.

FROM PROFIT AND LOSS TO MARKET CAP

This will be the final shift in business fundamentals we will examine in this section. It has been signaled by a curious change in the answer to a very familiar question: *How's business?* It used to be you answered by saying, "Great—sales are up and we're making a ton of money" (an answer you would give pretty much regardless of how sales and earnings were actually doing). But now what people really want to know is, *How's your stock price?* Why the change?

We're going to dig into the topic of stock price more deeply in the next chapter, but for now the short answer to the question is that stock price—or rather, to be precise, total market capitalization—has become the new scorecard for business competitions. That is because it unambiguously ranks every publicly held company versus every other publicly held company, regardless of industry or geography. There is no other universally common ground. Oil companies like to measure their success in proven reserves, financial institutions in revenues under management, manufacturers in product sales, media companies in the number of subscribers—but all of them also measure their success in terms of stock price. It is the common denominator, literally.

But why isn't the P&L statement in the annual report a proxy for stock price? The CEO's letter presumes it is. The analysts who quote P/E ratios act as if it is. And indeed in mature markets it *is* a good proxy. But not so for emerging markets. In an emerging market the primary objective for creating shareholder value is to stake out the largest sustainable market-share position you can. This gives you a powerful position in the market going forward and builds an installed base of customers you can sell back into long term. Only after the market has fully emerged should enterprises settle down to focus on optimizing revenues and earnings. Think of this as an exercise in imperial expansion—first you capture the land, then you farm it. Yield per acre is indeed the ultimate goal—it's just not a good metric during the military phase of the action.

Accounting as it is traditionally practiced does not "get" this, or rather it does not provide the tools to register it properly. It is fundamentally trapped in a P&L view of the world. It has no mechanism, for example, to represent the notion that making a profit could be bad. But consider the case of a hypergrowth market where you are frantically competing for market share. In this context profits represent residual capital you were unable to apply to your prime agenda—market expansion during a brief window of hypergrowth—and that's bad. Even revenues, which usually do equate to success with market-share capture, can be the wrong metric in cases where a bigger sustainable market share could have been captured by free offers, as exemplified by the successes of Netscape, Hotmail, Critical Path, and Yahoo!. It is hard to "get" any of these companies from a traditional accounting point of view.

But investors do get them. To be sure, they don't always get them right, at least not at first. But over time, as lessons are learned and captured, they become reflected in market capitalization. Incessant buying and selling, in other words, leads to a Darwinian selection of the fittest—the flow of capital to its highest risk-adjusted return. Thus, despite our initial impressions to the contrary, it was Yahoo! and not Netscape that truly won the initial battle for sustainable market share. We didn't get that at the time, but we do now. How do we know this for sure? Because Yahoo! has a market cap of $57 billion as of this writing and Netscape got acquired by America Online. Stock price, as we said, has become the common denominator.

Needless to say, this drives traditional established companies nuts. When Priceline's market cap exceeds that of any airline, when Amazon's dwarfs that of Barnes & Noble, when Charles Schwab's passes Merrill Lynch's, when Microsoft's market cap exceeds the sum of the market caps of the entire U.S. automobile industry, people just shake their heads. This cannot be. We enter a state psychologists call *denial* because not to do so would mean having to forsake so much conventional wisdom that we are afraid to go there.

But of course we must. And we know that. We know we have to get a grip on this new world somehow. What makes it all so bewildering, as we pointed out at the beginning of the chapter, is that these changes that have proved so cataclysmic have been happening in the background, not in the foreground. But now they are upon us, and now that we have called them out, what are we, specifically the we who are directors, executives, and managers in successful publicly traded corporations, supposed to do about them?

THE NEW IT

I think it was Clara Bow who in the early twentieth century was the new "It Girl," where *it* was sex appeal. It says something about our national values that at the end of the century, once again we are all concerned about "IT," but now the reference is to *information technology.*

The first thing we must register is that every one of the shifts we have been tracing thus far has a direct impact on our traditional information technology systems. Let's list the shifts one more time just to test this point:

1. Atoms to Bits
2. Assets to Information
3. Products to Services
4. Vertical to Virtual
5. Command and control to Self-organization
6. Money to Time
7. Profit and loss to Market cap

Atoms to *bits* is the biggest shift in the background, the one that is driving all the others, with these bits, of course, existing only in information systems. Thus IT is not just an enabler of information exchange, it is the natural host of information itself.

In effect, the computer becomes the factory and the warehouse and the distribution center, all in one. Production is now a computer task, and IT has become a line function.

This is a natural consequence of the next shift we discussed, wherein the greatest leverage comes not from owning *assets* but owning *information* about assets—a strategy that works only if you have great information systems. The key word to rethink here is *owning*. As in the parable of the talents, information that is buried in the ground generates no returns. One of the great struggles of the past decade has been the largely unfulfilled mission of *Fortune* 500 IT departments to dig up that corporate-owned data and get it to the point of decision in time to impact that decision. Smaller, nimbler companies do not have this problem, and that gives them a major competitive advantage.

The shift from *products* to *services,* further exemplifying the flight of capital out of atoms, has also put new pressure on information systems. You cannot manage service offerings with the same information systems that you use to manage product offerings. In particular, they need to become much more customer-centric, as reflected in the current shift in emphasis in enterprise software from back-office ERP (enterprise resource planning) systems to front-office CRM (customer relationship management) applications. *Customer service,* which used to be thought of as a post-sales support function, is being recast as *customer interaction,* occurring before, during, and after the sale, while the sale itself is being recast as a *series of sales* with the profit coming from *customer retention.* All this information is kept in and served up by computers, so here again IT has become ground zero in the battle for market share and profit margins.

The move from *vertical* to *virtual* integration further expands the pressure on information systems to change by resetting the boundaries of the system across an entire value chain of companies. We are just beginning an era of negotiating a new generation of XML-based protocols for these bidirectional exchanges, in support of which corporations must get their internal systems in line so they perform accurately in unaided transaction processing. Working against this outcome in well-established corporations are generations of systems that were never designed to operate unaided and that throw up a seemingly endless stream of road-blocks to this effort. By contrast, companies like Dell Computers that have built to this goal from the ground up are enjoying an extraordinary competitive advantage.

The transition from *money* to *time* is all about claiming a position in an emerging market at the time the market demands it. This is primarily a problem in value-chain coordination, and the pressure to come up to speed quickly in this arena is forcing the convergence of *computing* and *communication* systems. This melding began with a reorganization in the late 1980s that moved the telephony and fax group out of the facilities department and into the IT department, specifically into the networking group, where voice and data have begun to work out their uneasy marriage. External market forces, supplemented by the efforts of voice/data vendors like Cisco and Lucent, are driving these two reluctant spouses toward each other, and the companies that are first able to put their customer- and supplier-facing systems on the new integrated platform will enjoy a compelling differentiation over their competitors.

And finally, as we move from *P&L* to *market cap* as our base metric of success, management teams need to track metrics that are not to be found in our traditional accounting systems—indeed, are not to be found in any traditional corporate information system. Instead, going forward we should be looking to the trader workstation of Wall Street for the new model. There, active transactions are hosted in a central window or windows, with programmed trading in the background, and both are surrounded by streaming information from a variety of sources with monitors and alerts for any breaking news that would impact current decisions. In corporations we'll end up calling this the *enterprise information portal* and will customize it for each workstation to match the manager's role and personal preference.

To sum up, regardless of exactly what vision of the new information system we espouse, it is certainly not going to be the old one, not if it is to cope with the economic shifts we have been tracing. And that means there is a gigantic pile of work in store for the information technology department. And that raises a whole class of new issues in itself.

THE NEW IT DEPARTMENT

It is not just workload that is at issue. To execute on the agenda we have been describing requires a fundamental change in the status of the IT function in corporations. When I first engaged with high tech back in the 1970s, IT was a *staff* function. Initially it was a department called *data processing*, and in that role it was perceived as the automator of clerks and was housed (usually) in the basement of the building where pale and somewhat odd-looking individuals worked barricaded behind stacks of unburst, unread reports under the supervision of a data-processing manager.

During the early 1980s, the function got a promotion of sorts, achieving the status of an organization with a new name, *Management Information Systems*. Now it was seen as the keeper of transaction history, the provider of reports, and the supplier of data to analytical applications for graphic and spreadsheet analysis. Individuals in this era wore white shirts (well, at least the ones who were allowed to see the light of day), worked in cubicles that might even occasionally display a clean desk at night, and were looked after by the MIS director.

Then in the 1990s, the age of reengineering led to a wholesale replacement of mission-critical systems, initially for manufacturing and the back office, eventually for customer relationship management and the front office. The bulk of this software came from packaged applications from independent software vendors, and the head of what now became known as the IT department garnered the title of CIO (chief information officer). The CIO in visionary companies took on a new kind of power as for the first time software was installed to revamp business processes, overriding the history and preferences of many of the user groups ordered to adopt it.

The emergence of this new power heralded the shift in IT from essentially a *staff* function, a resource that provided information *about the business,* toward that of a *line* function, something that *defines the very nature of the business.* In the age of the Internet, that transition must be completed. IT must become a true *line* function, and the CIO must undergo one more transformation to become the CTO (chief technology officer), an unequivocally executive position qualifying its holder for promotion to CEO.

We are not yet there today. Indeed, it is the great irony of our current era that at a time when IT systems are becoming truly mission-critical, the IT organization is being shunted aside in favor of boutique consultancies and Big Five project teams. We will look into the reasons for this in a moment. For now we should simply register that it is a huge mistake. Here's why.

In this new age, IT is not *about* the business—it *is* the business. What is a bank other than a computer with a marketing department? The vaults are for show—there is no money in them. That wonderful image of Scrooge McDuck diving into a room full of money? There are no such rooms. Indeed money itself is becoming a curious artifact, a holdover from the world of atoms. It's all bits.

What is insurance, brokerage, cable TV, telephony, e-mail, fax? What are Amazon, Yahoo!, eBay, Priceline, America Online? What is the Web itself? It is all just IT of one sort or another with a business coating. The software has shifted from being a *recorder* to being an *enabler* of transactions—it embodies, enacts, and enforces management policy. It is not that people don't matter in this new world, it's that IT does matter, and matters in a way we have never seen before.

And there's the rub.

For now when IT "can't get to something," when a development schedule slips, that means there is a serious gap in the company's strategic deployment. Again, the pain here is felt most acutely in emerging markets where the structure of the future is being incubated in the present. So when you can't connect up with a supplier in time, and they go with someone else, the risk is that the value chain forms around their coalition, not yours, and you are marginalized in the new market, potentially forever. All because your IT department couldn't get to something.

A CLARIFICATION: IT "R" US

This argument has been developed thus far under the fabrication that information technology systems are solely the responsibility of the IT department. That, however, is like saying that quality is the sole responsibility of the quality department, customer service of the customer service department, or financial management of the finance department. Like all significant functions, IT is in fact everyone's job.

Indeed, IT systems are nothing more than preprogrammed decision trees. Once the decision rules have been set, then it is indeed the IT department's job to encode, deploy, and maintain the systems that execute them. But the real bottleneck here is not the code, it's the message. Just what rules are we living by, after all? When we go to the Web, what are our pricing rules? When our current reseller channel complains, what new rules will we need to put in place? When the margins begin to fall below budget, now what rules apply? When competition undercuts our already unprofitable pricing, now what? When our best customers refuse to use the system, what then?

These are the very decisions that affect the core operations, growth, and profitability of the company. In the new economy, they must be implemented in IT systems. The IT department is swamped for its own reasons, but it is doubly swamped when it finds itself shuttling back and forth among other functions trying to pin down a stable set of decision rules. To the outside world, this behavior looks like nothing more than management indecision and paralysis. It annoys customers, delights competitors, frustrates partners, and disturbs shareholders.

In short, to put this as bluntly as possible, the ability (or lack thereof) to execute crisply on an IT agenda has become a prime determinant of stock price—all too often, sadly, in a negative way. If nothing else, that should lead you inexorably to embrace the need for a new resource equation.

THE NEW RESOURCE EQUATION

In the new resource equation, there are three scarce resources against which companies can balance three plentiful resources, as follows:

Scarce Resources	Plentiful Resources
Time	Money
Talent	Computing
Management attention	Service providers

The three resources that are in critically short supply are *time, talent,* and *management attention.* The issue of time is most obvious in those industries where established companies are confronting the dotcoms. The only way to compete against these new entities is through the new information systems. You have to be on the Web, have to handle transactions, have to do the customer service. That makes for a lot of *have-to's* to process through an IT organization that is simultaneously burdened with maintaining a mountain of legacy systems.

Beneath this surface of Web enablement, however, lies an even deeper series of challenges. Business processes that worked well enough when we filtered them through individuals break down when they are exposed to the self-service pressures of the Web. Thus both our customer-facing service initiatives and our supplier-facing supply-chain initiatives are painfully hobbled, and that means even more work for you and your IT department, taking even more of both your time. Meanwhile the market is not waiting. It is spinning itself up around those suppliers and vendors who are there to serve it. Those who arrive late to the game get the leftovers.

Adding to this challenge is the brain drain that is sucking the *talent* out of corporate IT departments to fuel the very dotcoms that are mounting the attack. What bright young person wants to join a restructuring Old Guard when the siren lure of start-up freedom and stock options is singing in his or her ear? And how could one afford to pay these people a competitive wage even if they were interested in coming? Indeed, how are we going to hold on to the talent we have? It is a huge challenge.

Finally, given the foregoing pressures of time and talent loss, the scarcest resource of all becomes *management attention.* Who is doing all the reengineering and recruiting and retaining? There are only so many things one can make happen in any given period, and the number of things on the IT department's plate far exceeds that limit. Of course, this has always been the case, but in the past it was not a mission-critical issue. Now it is.

It is here that established companies show themselves at their most profligate, for nothing is wasted more in a *Fortune* 500 corporation than management attention. And it's not just the IT management I am talking about here, it's everyone. I don't have to make the case for this point—just look at your own engagement calendar. You are trying to fight a war, and you are scheduled to be in a meeting. It's not even your meeting, by the way, it's somebody else's meeting. And the subject of the meeting is not anything external to the corporation but something internal. And the reason you are there is to protect the resources and prerogatives you have accumulated so that, with any luck, they can get the jobs done that you have committed them to do.

Well, guess what, your dotcom competitor isn't at that meeting nor at any of the other meetings you have scheduled for this week, or the next, or the following. No, he or she is out in the marketplace cheerfully hacking off your head and handing it to you. Why? Because in a dotcom they don't have these meetings—they aren't big enough yet to need them. And you *know* this—nothing I am saying here is news—and *still* you find yourself going to these damned meetings. And it is not just you, it's everybody you know, so if for some reason you did break away from this corporate gravitational field, *you* would be the weird one, and worse, your absence might become the occasion for some redistribution of resources that would cause you to lose capability at a time when you need it most.

(It is now time to put down this book, give a silent scream, curse, hit something, or just sigh or laugh maniacally—whatever you do to release stress—then we'll talk when you get back.)

In this new world, where can one turn for help? It turns out that for each of the scarce resources we have just called out, there is a corresponding plentiful resource that can be brought to bear. They are *money, packaged software,* and *service providers.* Unfortunately for traditional corporations, the dotcoms are playing this game as well.

Let's start with money. To be sure, for anyone who has ever struggled to make a payroll, to say that money is a plentiful resource comes somewhat close to insult. But in the Internet economy, there's been an unprecedented influx of capital, and it has created classes of investment that were never before possible. At one end of the spectrum are the start-ups, where two bright people, a bright idea, and a business plan are getting funded at valuations that make seasoned venture capitalists blanch. The only resources these folks have to bargain with really are time, talent, and management attention, and it is a testimony to their scarcity to see how much money they can move.

At the other end of the spectrum, however, companies like Cisco, American Online, Yahoo!, and Microsoft are leveraging their own extraordinary market valuations to acquire companies that have already developed what they cannot wait to build. As John Chambers noted upon the acquisition of Cerent, a $10 million revenue company acquired in 1999 for $6.75 billion, Cisco plans to turn that product into a $1 billion market in two years. More important, if Cisco didn't buy Cerent, perhaps its archrival Lucent would, and then the company would have lost a step in the critical battle for time.

The big losers in this battle are those traditional corporations whose management, and more painfully whose shareholders, still hold that money—specifically, earnings—is the only valuable resource. These institutions are sitting out the battle for market share on the Internet or else are trying to buy into the game on the cheap. On paper (specifically, on the profit and loss statement) this does not look like a bad strategy. But on Wall Street these companies lose. Their existing investors approve their prudence but see no reason to accord the stock a premium for *not losing* money on the Internet, so they are in a HOLD mood. The rest of the investment community, seeing the company staring blankly into the onrushing headlight of the Internet train, discounts its future dramatically. They are in a SELL mood. And no one is in a BUY mood, nor could they be until such time as the Internet, as a category, proves itself to have been a bad investment, at which point the economy presumably would crater so badly it is hard to imagine anyone coming out a winner. Traditional companies, in other words, by treating money as more valuable than time, are effectively *shorting the Internet*. This is a hugely risky strategy that ironically is being conducted under a banner of risk avoidance.

We'll look more deeply into this matter in the next chapter on stock price. For now, let's turn to the second element in the new resource equation, the substitution of packaged software for talent. Here we are on less controversial ground. Specifically, the opportunity is to substitute standard packaged software for custom or customized software to perform IT functions that do not differentiate the company's marketplace offerings. In the 1980s, we learned to do this for financial analysis, word processing, and graphic presentations—but not for corporate computing. In the 1990s, we learned to do it for electronic mail, accounting, and human resources—but not for mission-critical process automation. In the coming decade, we must learn to do it for *every conceivable process that does not directly differentiate our company's offerings*. Specifically, we must learn to recognize when a process that *used to differentiate* no longer does and to proactively replace the old custom software that does it "our way" with off-the-shelf software that does it "the standard way." Not to do so is to shackle the time, talent, and management attention of the IT department to a maintenance task that cannot add to shareholder value.

And that leads us directly to the third and final element in the new resource equation—*outsourcing*—the substitution of the plentiful resource, service providers, for the scarce one, management attention. This is not an exercise in cost reduction. Indeed, it may be more expensive. It is instead part of the battle to recapture time, talent, and management attention. Wherever another company can come in and take some chunk of the task load off our plate, management should champion that effort. And the more standardized the offer, the more likely the service will satisfy, and the less likely someone will have to pull scarce internal resources off whatever they are doing in order to straighten out the outsourced piece.

This is most obviously true for IT, the function at the core of the new economy. Going forward, however, we are going to suggest that the IT department is simply a microcosm of the corporation at large, and that to the degree that your corporation needs to recapture mobility, initiative, and energy to pursue new markets, it must take the same approach to all its processes and all its departments. The new mantra will be, if it can't improve our stock price, why are *we* worrying about it? Why aren't we letting somebody else—someone whose stock price *does* depend on doing this particular process right—do our worrying for us?

To put this all in perspective, let's return to the IT function and ask ourselves, what benefit do our shareholders gain from our IT department running our corporate e-mail? Most IT departments do, of course. Time, talent, and management attention, in other words, are being spent on it today. Why? Why, for that matter, do we run our own payroll systems? HR benefits? Fixed assets?

There are only two reasons why shareholders might applaud this choice:

1. Our industry is characterized by a mature market that is not under technological attack, one where every penny of cost we can squeeze out of the mix is a penny of hard-won earnings. In this context keeping work in house in order to save money is a sensible strategy.

2. Alternatively, we do live in markets under technological attack, so we are looking at outsourcing everything that is not strategic, but in our strategy this particular system *is* strategic, *is* something we differentiate with to gain competitive advantage, and so we are keeping it in house.

Those are the two legitimate reasons for keeping such systems in house, but for most of us, neither one applies. Instead, we keep maintaining our old systems out of inertia, saving a bit of money in a world that wants us desperately to change our ways to save a lot of time. And so our IT organization's plate is full of work that not only is not strategic but that is also blocking its ability to take on the work that is. That is why we have become so dependent on outside consultancies to take care of our truly important IT systems. We do not have the resources to do the critical work because we have not freed ourselves from the noncritical work. In short, we are failing to respond to the new resource equation, and we need to get back on the right track.

CORE VERSUS CONTEXT

The problem facing the IT organization, which is in microcosm the same as the problem facing the corporation as a whole, is that too much time is being spent on tasks that are *context*, too little on tasks that are *core*.

A task is core when its outcome directly affects the competitive advantage of the company in its targeted markets. This is the ground upon which companies differentiate, and the goal of core work is to create and sustain that differentiation. To put it in terms of a very simple litmus test: *Any behavior that can raise your stock price is core—everything else is context.*

For core activities, the goal is to *differentiate as much as possible* and to assign one's best resources to that challenge. By contrast, every other activity in the corporation—and this is the overwhelming bulk of all activities—is not core. It is context. The goal for *context* tasks is to execute them effectively and efficiently in as standardized and undifferentiated a manner as possible.

Differentiating on context is the single biggest waste of resources in *Fortune* 500 operations. In the case of tasks that used to differentiate, it is the result of our failing to intervene now that they no longer do. But in many other cases, we differentiate on tasks that never could increase shareholder value. This is the natural result of people wanting to make the best contribution they can and to get recognition for it. The problem is, differentiation soaks up time, talent, and management attention with no opportunity to impact stock price. If the goal is to manage for shareholder value, then such an expenditure of scarce resources is simply wrong, and management needs to put an end to it.

In so doing, of course, we need to be careful not to throw out the baby with the bath water. In any given category of business, one company's core may well be another company's context. In the pizza business, for example, Little Caesar's differentiates on price, Round Table on quality of ingredients, Domino's on time to deliver, and Chuck E. Cheese on entertainment devices in the restaurant. For Chuck E. Cheese the actual pizza is context, for Round Table it is core.

In the car business, the new Volkswagen Beetle is all about design. Everything else in the car is context. The same holds for the new Apple Macintosh in the computer industry. In both cases, the differentiating value is in the design (the bits) and not in the manufacturing (the atoms). For both, therefore, manufacturing is context, not core. The difference is, Apple is able to outsource its manufacturing whereas Volkswagen is not. In the age of the

Internet, that bodes well for Apple shareholders, poorly for Volkswagen's.

Now let's be clear here. If some contract manufacturer introduces a widespread defect into Apple's computers, that *can lower* the company's stock price. That is, failure to execute context tasks properly can undermine a company's competitive advantage. Nonetheless, because such tasks cannot raise Apple's stock price, they are not *core*. Instead one might think of them as *hygiene*.

Hygiene refers to all the things that the marketplace expects you to do well but gives you no credit for doing *exceptionally well*. Do you bathe consistently? Good. If you didn't, someone might have to speak to you. But even if you bathe constantly, no one is going to give you a promotion. The same goes for companies who ship what the customer asked for, send them a bill that actually corresponds to what they ordered and received, and answer the phone when a customer calls for support. If they fail to do these things, they will be in trouble, but once they achieve a certain level of consistency in them, they get no premium for doing them better than that. In short, context tasks add value but do not contribute to competitive advantage.

Core and context, therefore, interoperate to create quality, and both are fundamental to every organization's effectiveness. The interaction between core and context determines how much core value gets through to the marketplace. Without careful management to the contrary, however, *context always gets in the way of core*. It is simply a matter of absorbing time, talent, and management attention.

To test the degree to which your organization has the problem, ask yourself how much of your week is spent in context meetings. How much of your time, in other words, is spend on *hygiene*? Now apply that ratio to the company as a whole. In a start-up, the ratio is typically 80/20. Eighty percent of the resources are being deployed against core tasks. In the typical *Fortune* 500 company, it is closer to the opposite, 20/80. That means the latter would have to allocate four times the number of resources to an initiative just to gain the same throughput.

But the actual situation is much worse than that. We focused on the 20 percent that was actively trying to do the core work.

What about the other 80 percent? Well, they are hard at work on context tasks. What are they doing? Trying to add value, of course. How do they do that? By differentiating their work, making it stand out, making it special. What does that take? Time, talent, and management attention, of course. Whose? Now here is the nasty part. It doesn't just take *their* time, talent, and attention—it takes *everyone else's* as well! Wherever differentiation occurs, that is, it requires widespread interaction to make sure the desired novel effect is achieved.

Now we can see why failing to outsource context is so debilitating. This is where all those meetings that you don't really want to attend come from. Of course, there is a theoretical alternative. One could hire people and give them a mandate *not to differentiate*. But that is a hideous charter to give any human being, and even people who overtly agree to it—I am thinking of assembly-line workers in particular—will subvert it over time, consciously or unconsciously. And so whether we intend to or not, as we add context function after context function to our payroll, we spin a cocoon that eventually enwraps and immobilizes us all.

Now we might justify this course by saying we are creating jobs, and we are. But let's look a little more closely at the people in these jobs. They're not stupid. They know in the back of their minds that these jobs are not core and thus could be eliminated. So what kind of behavior does that perception generate? Conservative behavior, of course. Don't rock the boat, you might tip the boat over. Resistance to change inside established companies, in short, is primarily a function of too many resources deployed in *context* as opposed to *core* activities.

It is what one might call the Dilbert problem. Dilbert cartoons parody an organization that has become 100 percent context—it has no core. It is the contemporary version of theater of the absurd, an ongoing production of *Waiting for Godot* in cubicles. In such a world, individuals know their jobs are meaningless but struggle valiantly to retain them anyway for fear they can find nothing else. And so when some new disruptive technology comes to town, when aggressive change is clearly the order of the day, it runs headlong right into a *business-as-usual coalition*, not in any one department specifically, but in every department generally.

Nothing can get done quickly, and in many cases, nothing can get done at all.

CLIMBING UP THE DOWN ESCALATOR

Where, we begin to wonder, is all this context coming from? Here is the ultimate irony. In technology-enabled markets, where technology itself is the basis of differentiation, core *becomes* context over time! That is, by virtue of competition, whatever differentiated last year's offerings is likely to become hygiene by next year. This is simply the inexorable progress of the technology adoption life cycle.

Management teams in such markets find themselves perpetually climbing a down escalator, as recent developments in e-commerce will illustrate:

E-Commerce Escalator

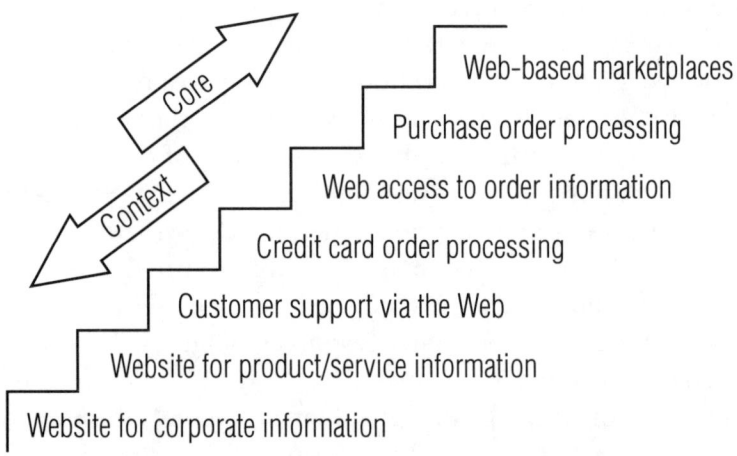

Figure 1.1

In 1995, Netscape shipped Navigator 1.0. Having a corporate Website to present information about your company in 1995 was differentiating. It meant you were "in." Today my limousine driver has a Website (www.phl-limousine.com; his name is Sam, and he is great).

By 1997, as companies were getting on the Website bandwagon, the rage was the intranet, not the Internet, but even then marketing was working to get its offers presented to prospects over the Web. If you could do that in 1997, you were differentiated. Today every dotcom on the planet bombards you with this stuff.

In the same time period, technology-based companies were driving their customer support operations to the Web, thinking to lower costs, not realizing they were also increasing customer satisfaction. (As ATM banking has taught us, often the best service is self-service.) Cisco was a leader in this effort. At the turning of the millennium, every significant company in high tech does it.

And so it goes. Each of the lower steps on this escalator *was* core and then *became* context. And it does not take too much imagination to see that even the highest step in view—Web-enabled digital marketplaces, the rage of venture capitalists at the turn of the millennium—soon will be next. Thus all the work we put into differentiation—because it was core—will someday come to haunt us because it has become context. It just doesn't seem fair, but this is Darwin at work, improving the species by perpetually raising the bar.

This forced migration to higher orders of behavior has two dimensions we must address before we are done with this book:

1. Once they cease to differentiate, most custom processes are too complex to maintain given the value they add. That is, as context, they require too much ongoing application of time, talent, and management attention. We need to find some way to dispose of them.

2. Executives who excelled at managing core processes in their day won promotions and are now running the company. Their greatest expertise, however, may now lie in what have become context functions. When met with an emerging competitive challenge, their instincts and experience may therefore lead them to push the wrong agenda, with the corollary that if the company fails to make progress, they are likely to push all the harder.

The second of these issues lies at the heart of a widespread critique of command-and-control management that has characterized the past ten to twenty years. Hierarchical organizations centralize decision making in senior executives at the top, the very people most at risk of mistaking context for core. By contrast, people competing face-to-face in the marketplace on a daily basis have all such illusions stripped from them. It is critical that the seasoned judgment of the former be infused with the recent experience of the latter if good decisions are to be made. Going forward, therefore, companies in the age of the Internet must explore alternative management cultures and styles, a subject we will address at some length in the last chapter of this book, "Building to Last."

In the meantime, however, we need to attack the custom process maintenance problem right in front of us: How are we going to get out of going to all these meetings?

OUTSOURCE THE CONTEXT, INSOURCE THE CORE

Fortunately, in the new virtually integrated economy, there are an increasing number of resources that address this very problem. Indeed, the great discovery of the age of the Internet is that *there is no context that cannot become someone else's core.*

You make the hamburger? Great, I'll make the bun. Oh, the bun is core too? Great, how about the condiments? How about the coffee? How about keeping the bathrooms clean? How about the uniforms, the hiring, the payroll, the benefits administration, the promotions, the marketing, the advertising, the facilities construction, the real estate planning, the financing? You decide what you think is core, and then let's talk about everything else.

This is the world of outsourcing. In the age of the Internet, with more and more of our business processes going on-line, we have an exceptional communications infrastructure to support the coordination of such efforts. Moreover, there are phalanxes of new service providers lining up outside our doors anxious to do this kind of business. The question to ask is, why should these people do any better at our context work than we would ourselves?

The simple answer is, this is where they are putting their A team. It's context to you, but it is core to them. Take your copy room. What is the career path for someone working in it? What kind of a player are you going to recruit? But outsource that same copy room to Ikon or someone like them, and now the person running the operation can aspire to become president. Why? Because that's what Ikon does for a living. Who's going to attract the better person to do the job—you or Ikon? Who is going to come up with more efficient procedures, additional value-adding service offerings, higher-quality processes?

Well, maybe they are, you grudgingly reply, but I bet it will cost a bundle. Will it? Will *the marginal cost* of that company adding another customer truly exceed *the total cost* your company must bear if you do it in house? The service economy bets the opposite way. It says we can not only do it better than you, we can do it cheaper than you. Why? Again, it's our core, it's what we do for a living—give us some credit. If we think about this all day every day, and you try to think about it never at all, don't you think we might be able to outperform you? Moreover, it is a competitive economy. If you don't like our price performance, take the other guy's bid.

But suppose, nonetheless, that for some class of context work the company cannot find a qualified outsourcer. Suppose, for example, that you want a specialized kind of condiments, or a particular approach to recruiting, hiring, or training—something you have been doing in house for some time, in a differentiated way. Now, despite its attractive features, you realize it is not core, but as it is also not standard, no service provider wants to touch it. Now what?

SPIN-OUT CONTEXT, NOT CORE!

Now is the time to call together the internal organization that is responsible for this body of work and make them an offer they can't refuse. And that offer is to create their own service company, independent of your company, with your company as their first customer and with a guarantee of some period of business and a promise to be an active customer reference. The alternative to this offer is that the company will go with a standard outsourcer, eliminating the in-house function anyway, but with nowhere near as happy an outcome for either the group or the company.

If the group goes forward with your offer, now when it differentiates, it will be doing the right thing, because it will be improving *its* competitive advantage, and thus such changes will deserve *its* time, talent, and management attention. To be sure, these same resources will now also start serving your competitors. That's why it is important that you be sure this is context, not core, that you are outsourcing. But if it is context, then just as you don't mind your competitors using your plumbing contractor, you should not mind them using this team either. Of course, it is always possible your competitor will stick with its own internal team, which means they will not use the new service and instead continue fighting you with less than their own full complement of time, talent, and management attention. That's when you gain the outsourcer's advantage.

Please note that this spin-out strategy is the dead opposite of much of the current practice in the age of the Internet. Far too many companies, that is, believe it is better to spin-out their dotcoms and hold fast to their context-laden traditional business models. In so doing, they distance themselves from a disturbingly unfamiliar future and embrace a comfortably reassuring past.

This is a huge mistake. The justification that it is done in the interest of shareholder value is appalling. To be sure, in-house dotcoms at their outset are saddled with liabilities that their fresh-minted venture-capital-backed brethren are not, not the least of which is risk-averse investors, and so it is true that in the beginning they will not garner high valuations—nor should they. But if the management team can realign its traditional business so that the bricks-and-mortar side can create synergy with the Internet side—the so-called "bricks and clicks" strategy—then competitive advantage should shift to the company with the established brand, logistics, customer service systems, retail sales outlets, supplier relationships, and industry knowledge.

To put it bluntly, when you see the dotcoms coming, the correct strategy is not to turn tail and run!

The best companies in high tech know this and are already aggressively pursuing a context outsourcing strategy. HP, long reputed as one of the best manufacturers in the sector, is now driving as much of its manufacturing to outsourcers as it can. At the same time they are aggressively pursuing Web-based business opportunities where their relationships, skills, and heritage can create competitive advantage. The value in their brand, they have rightly concluded, lies in the bits, not in the atoms, and that is where they are assigning their best resources. The same holds true for Cisco, which brags that over 50 percent of its products ship *without ever being touched by a Cisco employee*! The company creates value across the Internet by shipping design and test information to its supply chain partners and by turning its customer service site into a digital marketplace.

If you need further encouragement to aggressively pursue outsourcing context, look at the supply side of this equation, and specifically at what Wall Street thinks of the emerging outsourcers. Ariba and CommerceOne, both of which promise to outsource noncore procurement, are trading at 77 and 45 times revenues at the time of this writing. Critical Path, an e-mail outsourcer, is valued at the time of this writing at $1.7 billion on revenues of less than $10 million. Wall Street is weighing in on the side of the outsourcers, which means investors think they know where competitive advantage lies. Why would we want to disagree?

Well, actually, there might be one good reason. This whole outsourcing trend sounds an awful lot like what the reengineering gurus were preaching a few years ago, and where are they now? So before we bring this chapter to a close, let's make sure we are not reopening a can of worms that we just spent a decade putting back in the can.

REENGINEERING REDUX?

To begin with, there is a key distinction to make: Outsourcing is about *distancing the company from context*; reengineering is about *taking a new approach to core*. The former is much less ambitious than the latter (and thus potentially much more likely to come about). Here's why.

Companies do not set out to overcommit resources to context tasks. It happens for the most part during hypergrowth markets, periods of accelerated market development during which demand far exceeds supply, the company and its competitors are all growing like weeds, and the prime directive is *Just ship!* During this period, the company takes in more revenue that it can spend, so resources are plentiful. Moreover, it is under huge time pressure to capture market share. As a result, whenever any glitch shows up, or could show up, management's knee-jerk response is simply to throw additional resources at the problem. That's when we hire in all these troops that we are now trying to spin out.

Then the market goes to Main Street, supply once again returns to its normal state of exceeding demand, competition increases, prices decline, margins decline, and cost cutting sets in. This is the period when we look to downsizing to reset the balance of resources in the company. It is a perfect time to invoke the core-versus-context exercise. Moreover, at this time the context resources are not so thoroughly entrenched as to be hard to dislodge. It ought to be a relatively straightforward project.

So why are we not more successful in doing so? The truth is, outsourcing, like reengineering, goes against the grain of organizational politics. At the end of the tornado the organization is in a self-congratulatory mood. It wants to hand out rewards all around, and one set of rewards is, in effect, empires. The more people in your empire, the higher your reward. Reducing head count reduces the "reward account." Moreover, the need to reduce head count is not quite yet upon us—there are several years of coasting we can still get away with—so why fight the tough battles now?

Unfortunately, by the time we do decide to fight them, they have gotten a lot tougher. Now the organizations are entrenched. That is, people in positions of power now owe lots of favors to lots of people, in both core and context functions, and they find it difficult to betray those relationships. As a result, when the need to cut comes, rather than call out context versus core, the company opts for across-the-board cuts instead. This form of cost-cutting is deeply damaging, for it trades a permanent loss in core resources, plus zero progress in disengaging itself from the context resources that are holding it back, all just for a temporary improvement in the bottom line. Which means it is going to do this again. And again. And again. Until it gets permanently dismantled to be acquired at a fraction of its once-proud valuation.

The path out of this maze does *not* require reengineering core tasks. It does require a thoughtful review of what is core versus what is context, what directly contributes to the company's competitive advantage in the marketplace versus all other work. This effort must not be allowed to degenerate into an exercise in self-justification. All the context work is likely to be justified—well, most of it, at any rate—so the question is not *should* it be done but rather *by whom* should it be done.

Nor is this an exercise in reengineering or simplifying context tasks. That too would absorb too much time, talent, and management attention. The goal instead is to get the entire task suite off of your plate and on to some service provider's instead. You are buying your way out of jail. At the outset, you will probably think you are paying too much from an immediate cost-comparison point of view. Think of this expense instead as bail money. You're getting out. Once out, then you can start worrying about costs, and over time, you can engineer a market competition to get them down to where you want them.

The litmus test for evaluating a true outsourcing offer as opposed to a reengineering project is called the *monkey test*. Consider any particular set of context responsibilities as *the monkey*. The question is, at the end of the day, *Who has the monkey on their back?* The fundamental value of any outsourcing offer is to move the monkey from your back to theirs. If the monkey stays on yours, you have not won back any of the scarce resources needed in the age of the Internet—you still are allocating time, talent, and management attention to managing the monkey. That's a bad deal. But conversely, if you can truly free yourself from the monkey, then regardless of whether there is an immediate cost reduction to take to the bottom line, you have won the key battle of recapturing scarce resources to refocus on core activity.

The key to successful "monkey management" is to construct effective service-level agreements. This is a much easier task in the world of context than in the world of core. When you outsource a core process, you put yourself in harm's way. Now your interests are at odds with the outsourcer's, for you are seeking *differentiation* while they are seeking *standardization*. No service-level agreement can bridge this gulf. But when you outsource context, then you and the provider are on the same page, and service-level agreements work well. The management challenge is to ensure going forward that whatever improvements are made, they are done at the expense of the plentiful resources, not the scarce ones.

In sum, outsourcing context is doable. The real question is, can we decide to do it?

SEEKING A LEVER THAT CAN MOVE THE WORLD

I hope by now I have made a persuasive case for outsourcing context as a fundamental element of corporate strategy in the age of the Internet. Given the new pressures on time, talent, and management attention, not outsourcing context tasks is, I believe, a fatal mistake. Thus the great challenge of the new millennium is not reinventing our core business processes—that, I believe, management teams are both willing and able to do—but rather clearing the decks for these management teams to get on with it. In other words, the winning teams in this new age will be those that *manage context in order to make room for core*.

Outsourcing context represents a dramatic change from the status quo and thereby inherits the problem of inertia. To be sure, inertia can be a positive as well as a negative force. That is, going forward, once this process gets under way, competitive dynamics are going to play more and more in its favor, and we will find it attracting increasing support and eventually creating its own momentum. It is getting it going in the first place that is the challenge.

This is the problem that Archimedes understood so well. He said, "Give me a lever long enough, and a fulcrum to place it against, and I can move the world." To this end, we need to place a powerful force in our hands, a lever that can overcome the inertia of political alliances that holds the old system in place. That lever is *stock price*. And the fulcrum upon which it is placed is the *stock option*.

Stock price works as a lever because investors are on our side. They want to put their money to work on core tasks that create competitive advantage. They know that for their investment dollars to grow, they must be deployed at the point of attack. If they think instead that their capital is going to fund context, they will withdraw it in a heartbeat and put it somewhere else, causing the company's stock price to go down. By contrast, where they see a well-focused strategy and an organization aligned to execute it, and not a lot of other stuff getting in the way, then they want to put more money to work there, and stock price goes up. That is why outsourcing, at the outset, does not have to be cost-cutting to be successful. Just the fact that you are doing it can raise your stock price because it communicates to investors that you are putting your time, your talent, and your management attention to work on core issues. Because stock price is the lever with which we are going to drive change, we are going to have a lot more to say about it in the next chapter. To close this chapter, it is simply important to see that stock options—making management into shareholders—is the best way of getting the entire organization on the same page. If we all commit to manage for shareholder value, and if we are all significantly compensated as shareholders to reinforce that commitment, then in our own self-interest we will work through the core-versus-context issue successfully and guide our corporate boat back into the market's mainstream.

That, at any rate, is the premise of this book.

SUMMARY OF KEY POINTS IN CHAPTER 1

1. The age of the Internet is characterized by six transitions occurring across the entire economy, as follows:

From:	To:
Assets (atoms)	Information (bits)
Products	Services
Vertical integration	Virtual integration
Command and control	Self-organizing systems
Money	Time
Profit and loss	Market capitalization

2. All six transitions are driving corporations to give priority to a new center of operations, the information technology department.

3. The IT department in most cases is woefully unprepared and underresourced to succeed in this new role.

4. Complicating its ability to rise to this occasion, the IT organization is enmeshed in a large web of tasks and responsibilities that are not core to the business. In this it reflects the corporation as a whole, which also finds most of its resources going to context, not to core.

5. To break free, both the IT department and the corporation as a whole must undertake a massive outsourcing of context in order to focus scarce resources on core.

6. The good news is that the age of the Internet is poised to support this outsourcing with an outpouring of capital, computing, and service providers.

7. The bad news is that all organizations resist change via inertia; the more dramatic the change, the greater the resistance.

8. The lever by which this massive inertia can be overcome is stock price, and how that lever can be used is the subject of the next chapter.

2

SHAREHOLDER VALUE

Living on the fault line calls for drilling foundations deep into bedrock. In the absence of a recent quake, however, the population gets caught up in other goals. The same thing happens in business. To get our companies' focus off of context and onto core, we need to create earthquake awareness. That awareness comes from attending to stock price.

Fortune 500 corporations are built on the premise of accountability to shareholders, and this makes stock price the single most powerful lever for motivating change. Moreover, the increasingly widespread use of stock options as a major component of compensation has the potential to align management decisions with shareholder interests. Thus any initiative predicated on improving stock price has the potential to grab the attention of the entire corporate ladder. We are going to leverage this potential to gain commitment to the change initiatives advocated in the final two chapters of this book.

For the initiatives proposed there to be effective, however, executives and managers need to thoroughly overhaul their understanding of stock price and shareholder value. Much of what we always thought was true about valuation is, in fact, only situationally true and, indeed, is untrue in the age of the Internet. We need to recast our thinking, in other words, to meet this new challenge. That is the function of this chapter and the next. Here we will look at the mechanics of shareholder value, with a focus on stock price. In the following chapter we will look at the dynamics of shareholder value, with a focus on competitive advantage.

• • •

The theme of this chapter—that a management team will per-form much more effectively if it centers and focuses its efforts on increasing shareholder value—is one that currently sets the busi-ness culture in the United States to some degree apart from those in other countries. Many European and Japanese writers and executives are quick to criticize America's apparently unqualified endorsement of making shareholders wealthy. They are particu-larly uncomfortable when the amount of that wealth is stagger-ingly huge and the preponderance of it ends up in the hands of the management team itself. So much wealth going to so few people in such a self-serving way strikes them as symptomatic of a cul-ture out of touch with personal discipline, social responsibility, and spiritual balance.

Personally I share these concerns. From the time I came of age, American culture has been struggling on all of these fronts, and I do not see it achieving resolution or breakthrough anytime soon. Moreover, I believe as a society we risk paying a terrible price if we do not change, and I am not at all surprised when citizens of other coun-tries actively distance themselves from some of our practices. All that being said, however, I believe that this is more a problem with being an American than a problem with managing for shareholder value.

Similarly, many shareholders themselves have their own qualms about executive and management compensation. In particular, when stock prices crater and management re-prices stock options to ensure it can continue to recruit and retain talent, shareholders cry foul, rightly arguing that they are now paying twice for the "same" appre-ciation in value. The grumbling, however, rarely reaches the action-able stage, in part because the argument is not quite fair and in part because the remedy is worse than the disease, since not re-pricing would put the company in an untenably uncompetitive position.

Finally, executives at high-flying dotcoms themselves express concerns about stock price becoming a major distraction to their work force. They well know how volatile their markets are and, therefore, seek to keep their teams focused on the long-term goal of building a great and lasting company. When feathers ruffle at every fluctuation in price, or when talent flees at the first real cor-rection, it just makes everyone's job that much harder.

Yet despite all these legitimate concerns, aligning management with shareholders in a joint quest to create sustainable increases in stock price is the foundation of the new economy. Here's why.

STOCK PRICE IS AN INFORMATION SYSTEM

Stock price is a consequence of an impersonal force—*investment*—supplying capital to the sources of greatest risk-adjusted return. Investors in the aggregate are representatives of that force. As such they will never lie. They may get confused in the short term, but as soon as the true lay of the land comes clear, they will adjust their investments accordingly. In other words, you can trust investment to be unflaggingly self-interested.

More important, however, you can trust investment to be right. To be sure, as individuals, investors are often wrong, but *collectively over time*, they cannot be. That is, because investing is an inherently Darwinian exercise, poor investors lose capital and lose the ability to raise more, whereas good investors increase the capital they have under management and get pressed into investing additional capital as well. Over time, capital ends up in the hands of those most fit to generate more capital. (As a society, we may choose to enforce redistribution of that capital—that's a decision that lies outside the purview of this book—but regardless of that decision, it is in everyone's interest first to accumulate it.)

These successful investors pursue a single, simple end: to gain the best risk-adjusted return on capital they can. As we shall explain in more detail shortly, this is primarily a function of investing in entities that demonstrate the strongest competitive advantage in the markets they serve. Capital, in other words, *flows to competitive advantage* and *abandons competitive disadvantage.*

When we are on the winning end of this exchange, we praise the wisdom of our shareholders for seeing our true value. When we are on the losing end, we grouse about disloyal or impatient investors who are too short-term in their orientation. Neither reaction is truly appropriate, however, because both *personalize* the transaction. It is not personal. Capital is like water—it does not flow uphill against the gravity of competitive advantage. It can be pumped uphill, to be sure—that is what governments do all the time—but that is not its natural tendency. Therefore, wherever capital is allowed to follow its natural course, you can count on it to point out where competitive advantage lies.

This has huge implications for all kinds of executive decisions. Because stock price is in effect an information system about competitive advantage, it can help you sort through which markets to attack, which strategies to pursue, which partners to endorse, and which tactics to execute. It can teach you to abandon the familiar and embrace the strange—or vice versa. It can tell you where to invest and where to divest—or to put it in Kenny Rogers's vernacular, it can let you know when to hold 'em and when to fold 'em. In short, investors, by where they put their capital, will tell you over and over what is *core* and what is *context*.

Capital in this sense functions like a canary in a coal mine. It is your best leading indicator about your future competitive advantage as well as that of your partners and your competitors. It is thus a great counselor. Now to be sure, there are times when true leaders, like great chess players, do choose to go against the wisdom of others and disregard the advice of counsel. It is not the goal of this book to make you or your company a slave to capital's dictates. But it is a goal that you should learn how to take counsel from capital markets, and to that end, the first step is learning how to decode stock price, beginning with your own.

DEFINING SHAREHOLDER VALUE

What is a share of your stock worth? By definition it entitles its owner to a percentage of the future returns of your business. Owning all the stock entitles one to 100 percent of these future earnings. What would that be worth?

The challenge lies in the word *future*—how to value what is essentially a bird in the bush, not a bird in the hand. Investors and analysts must find some way to understand your business and its future trajectory so that, at any given price, they can decide whether to buy, sell, or hold your stock.

This has led to something of a consensus around the following as the fundamental valuation formula:

> The total value of a company, its market capitalization,
> is equal to the present value of its forecastable future
> earnings from current and planned operations,
> discounted for risk.

Let's parse this sentence one phrase at a time. We're interested in the **present value** because the initial competition for all investment is cash—investors keeping their cash in hand and not parting with it to anyone. How much of this cash in hand is your company really worth? Only a buyer and a seller agreeing to trade shares for cash at a given price can truly testify to that amount, each new trade bearing witness to a new act of valuation. The stock market continuously reports on the fluctuations in this ongoing stream of cash-equivalent valuations in the form of a running series of stock price quotes. Multiplying any given quote by the number of shares outstanding, you can calculate your company's current total value, or **market capitalization,** at any time.

The price of the last trade sets the *historical* value for your company. It is a benchmark for the next trade, but it does not set the value of that trade. Instead, future considerations do. Specifically, investors focus on **forecastable future earnings** for the following reasons.

- It is *earnings*, not revenues, that are tracked because that is what an investor is entitled to a share of.[1]

---

[1] I am thoroughly indebted to Michael Mauboussin of Crédit Suisse First Boston for guidance in writing much of this section, although he should not be held accountable for any errors I make in trying to translate financial theory into everyday management language. As a case in point, take the sentence footnoted here. Technically, it's not earnings but cash flow that the stock market tracks. For most technology companies, the numbers are similar—but not always. The challenge is that earnings can be defined by accounting practices in multiple ways, not all of which are of interest to or in the interests of investors. Cash in and cash out, on the other hand, leaves an unmistakable trace of value created. Nonetheless, I will continue to use everyday language and concepts despite their susceptibility to technical correction.

- They are *future* earnings because investors are not entitled to past earnings, only those coming up. When these earnings move from a future promise to a present achieved reality, they can either be distributed to investors in the form of some kind of a dividend or they can be reinvested in the company. If they are reinvested, the investor defers their reward in hopes of future additional earnings that such reinvestment might generate.

- And finally, they must be *forecastable* earnings because investors need some current foundation for incorporating the future into their present calculations.

Forecastability is fundamental to investability. The higher the probability of the forecast, the lower the risk of investment. Companies with high forecastability are typically market leaders in robust markets, such as Cisco in network hardware, Microsoft in PC software, and Intel in microprocessors. When a company is a market leader in a weak market, such as American Airlines or United Airlines, or when they are in a strong market but not the market leader, such as Barnes&Noble.com in the Internet retail market for books, then forecastability becomes a much greater challenge, and stock price suffers.

The forecastable future earnings investors focus on must come from the company's ongoing **current and planned operations**. That is, although investors are entitled to a percentage of any bonanza earnings the company gets—say by finding gold on its corporate site or, perhaps more likely, by investing in a strategic partner whose stock subsequently goes through the roof—they have no practical basis for incorporating the chance of such gains into their valuation of the stock. Thus, although Adobe made over $300 million when it sold its investment in Netscape, the windfall had no appreciable impact on its stock. Moreover, although a company can indeed create earnings outside of operations—say, via the actions of its corporate treasury, by investing in derivatives, for example—it will not please its investors by so doing because it is inherently changing the risk to which the earnings stream is exposed. Indeed, in recent years the CFO of Dell Computers was taken to task precisely for such actions. If investors want to take derivative risk, they would like do so on their own time; they don't want someone else to do it for them.

And that leads directly to the last phrase, ***discounted for risk***. This discount is what compensates investors for the use of their capital. After all, in committing their capital to your company, investors are taking a risk that it may be consumed without a return, or that it may generate a substandard return, or that had they invested it somewhere else they could have earned a better return. You pay for that risk by promising to return them more money than they invest. The question is, how much of a premium would be fair?

Risk is the true wild card in all investment decisions. It can never be known, only probabilistically assigned. Moreover, perceived risk changes dynamically with new information about any of the myriad of variables incorporated in its view. So rather than try to calculate it, free markets use the mechanism of many investors buying and selling to let the price seek its own level. That is why the stock market is so jittery. It is continually rebalancing its equations to account for streams of information that may have bearing on the risk factor. The market does this not through some grand mathematics but rather through the simple expedient of free exchanges, some right, some wrong, but all having the effect of automatically rebuilding the new equation. We may never be able to write this equation down, but with the ticker tape we have its output before us at all times.

To recap then, your market capitalization is equal to the present value of your company's forecastable future earnings from current and planned operations, discounted for risk. That's the definition, if you will. But it is one thing to define a concept and another to really get it. To really get shareholder value I think you have to visualize it.

VISUALIZING SHAREHOLDER VALUE

To put all the foregoing words into a single picture, consider the following figure:

Valuing Future Earnings

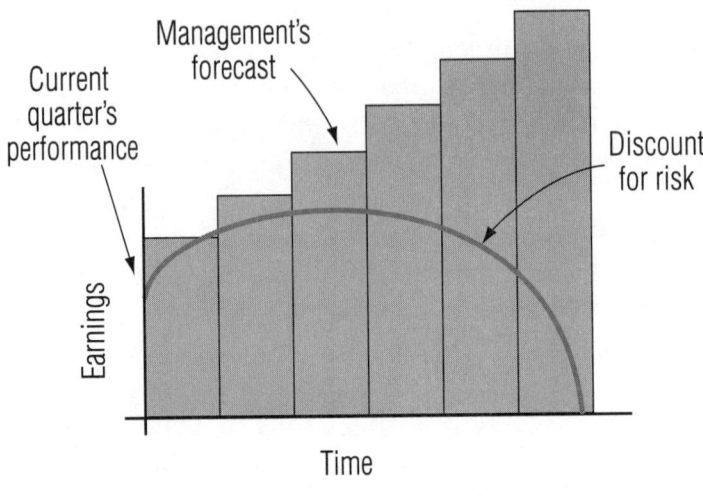

Figure 2.1

The *Y*-axis in this graph represents earnings. It is benchmarked by the operation's latest earnings report—that sets the value of *Y* on the left side of the curve. The *X*-axis represents future time. The bars represent management's forecast of future earnings over the next several years. The curve represents an investment analyst's attempt to "factor" management's forecast to incorporate an appropriate discount for risk.

Every quarter this graph gets redrawn based on a new benchmark and a new forecast. That is, you can think of each of the bars shifting one space to the left, the leftmost bar now being replaced by the new quarterly report, and a new bar appearing on the right representing a future quarter just coming into view. This results in the projection of a new curve, representing a revised assessment of the present value of future returns discounted for risk.

Any point on the curve is to some degree speculative, and the farther out to the right it is, the more so it becomes. That is, earnings forecasts near the *Y*-axis tend to track closely to management's guidance. That is because sales pipelines, work-in-process, and backlog all help make the next few quarters more visible and predictable. As a result, this part of the curve is not subject to significant discount for risk unless management's credibility is at stake.

Farther out on the curve, however, it is a different story. Forecasts that extend beyond the sales pipeline are necessarily little more than extrapolations of investments and trends. The risk in these forecasts increases directly with time, and thus the discount for risk must also increase over time as well. Thus, even though future earnings forecasts increase indefinitely, the present value placed on them decreases. Eventually this value is set to zero—at the far right of the curve where it meets the X-axis—meaning that beyond this point in time no forecasts of any size will alter the valuation investors are willing to support.

Each unit of time on the X-axis, therefore, implies an increasingly larger discount rate applied to management's forecast. Where $X = 0$, the discount rate $= 0$, because that's the quarterly report's figure and that money is in the bank. Where $Y = 0$, the discount rate $= 100$ percent. At every point in between, the effective discount rate is set by the judgment of the investor or investment analyst.

Now let's assume for the moment that the operation we are forecasting represents the total revenues of the company. Then we can make the following claim:

Market Capitalization

Time

Figure 2.2

The *area under the curve* represents this company's *market capitalization*. That is, it is a direct visualization of the present value of forecastable future earnings from current and planned operations discounted for risk. This is the pie that investors are buying a piece of. A share of stock, therefore, is valued as a percentage of this pie.

Now let's stop for a moment.

While there are still a number of additional modifications needed to make this figure actually correspond to any real-world situation, we can make one key point using the market capitalization figure simply as it stands. The job of the executive team of any corporation from an investor's point of view is to *grow the area under this curve*. Period. So how would you do that?

CREATING SHAREHOLDER VALUE

To enlarge the area under the curve, you must move the curve itself either up or to the right. Effectively this means:

1. Make the forecastable earnings line go higher, or
2. Make the forecastable earnings line extend out farther, or better still
3. Do both.

The way to do either or both is to *increase your competitive advantage in your target markets:*

Competitive Advantage

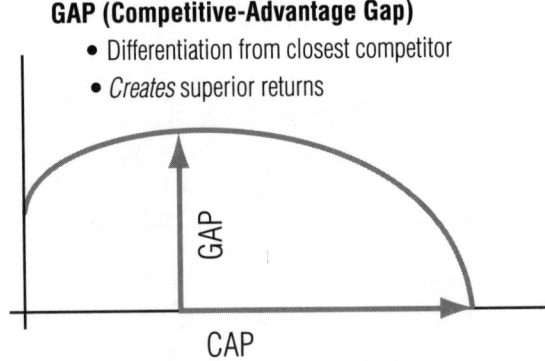

GAP (Competitive-Advantage Gap)
- Differentiation from closest competitor
- *Creates* superior returns

GAP

CAP

CAP (Competitive-Advantage Period)
- Barriers to competitor entry, customer exit
- *Sustains* superior returns

Figure 2.3

Competitive advantage has two dimensions—somewhat analogous to space and time. The domain of space has to do with the *competitive-advantage gap*, or *GAP* for short. This is the distance (metaphorically) between your company's offerings and those of your closest competitors. You can increase this distance by any number of tactics—coming out with a new product, cost-reducing a current offering, building a coalition to add value to your existing offers, enhancing the service component of your current offer, and the like. When you do this, and your competitors do not, you increase the value gap between your offer and theirs.

Improving GAP shows up primarily on the vertical axis because it directly impacts both sales revenues and gross margins. That is, a larger GAP allows your company's offer to win a greater share of sales away from your competition, or it allows it to earn a higher price premium than it did before, or in many cases, both. Such increases in sales volume and gross margins, assuming they are made within your existing cost structure, go straight to the bottom line to create increased earnings, thereby pushing the curve higher on the *Y*-axis.

Competing on GAP is familiar to virtually all management teams. Every time Ford introduces a new car, J. Crew a new line of shirts, or Compaq a new computer, they are competing on GAP. Every time your company rolls out a price promotion, adds a new feature, or cost-reduces a component assembly, it is competing on GAP. The intent in every case is to increase competitive advantage in the short term by differentiating the offer.

That is how securing a new competitive advantage changes the height of the curve. Now let's see how it can change its length. Here the question investors must ask is, how long can your company sustain the competitive advantage it has just created? We call this length of time the *competitive-advantage period*, or *CAP*. CAP represents the *sustainability* of GAP—the length of time your company can hold on to your competitive advantage once the superior returns you are generating attract additional competition.

A long CAP is typically a function of high barriers to entry for competition seeking a piece of your market, or high switching costs for customers and partners who might wish to defect to such a competitor, or both. Long CAPs contribute to a higher stock price by increasing the length of the forecastable period for advantaged returns. In effect, they represent a reduction in long-term risk, which leads to a reduction in the discount rate applied for that risk, which in turn allows the projected earnings curve to extend farther out to the right before it finally touches down on the X-axis.

Let's look at the impact of improving GAP and CAP in visual terms:

Increasing GAP and CAP

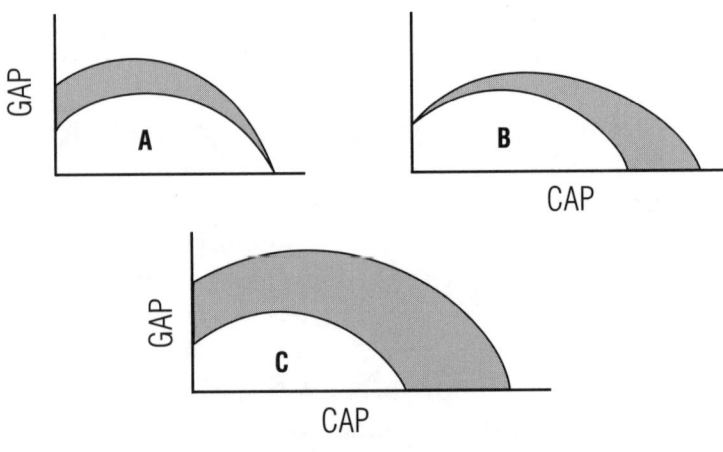

Figure 2.4

Thus it is that *tall GAPs* and *long CAPs* become the focal point for the rest of this book. Or, to put it another way, time and management attention spent engineering *strong sustainable competitive advantages* (GAP times CAP) is the essence of what we mean by managing for shareholder value.

LOSING SHAREHOLDER VALUE

While there are no laws of gravity in financial space, nonetheless it often happens that what goes up on occasion comes down. So before we launch into our discussion of how management can raise stock price by increasing GAP and CAP, it behooves us to understand what can cause it to go the other way. The simplest instance is when stock price goes down after the release of a quarterly earnings report.

Recall that quarterly earnings represent a kind of variance report on last quarter's projected earnings, a rolling forward of the calendar one quarter that tests whether the quarter's actual earnings lived up to their promise. Effectively, this roll-forward resets the starting position of GAP at the Y-axis, placing it either higher, lower, or equal to the expectations implied by the pre-report curve.

Impact of the Q2 Quarterly Report

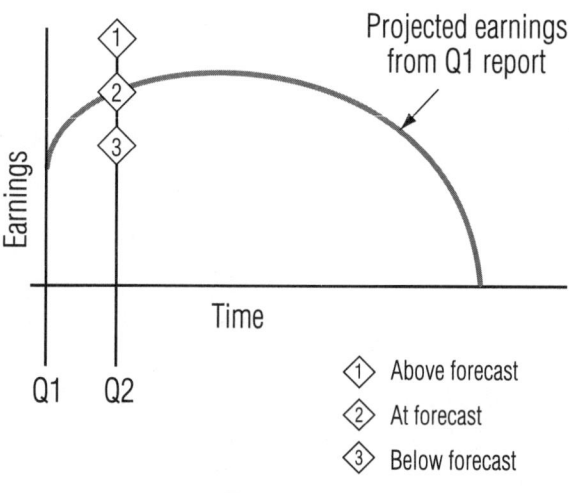

Figure 2.5

Depending on that outcome, investors then decide whether the company's value has increased, decreased, or remained the same, and the company's stock price moves accordingly.

The significance for the investor of reported quarterly earnings—indeed their only meaningful impact on stock price—is based on whether or not they confirm the market's existing valuation of the company. Did management execute its stated strategy and did it work? If the numbers confirm it did, the company's stock price will continue to move in lockstep with its category, keeping pace with its comparables as the market weighs the relative value of that category against other investable categories. If they do not confirm expectations, however, the market uses the occasion of the quarterly report to adjust the value of the company's shares, often dramatically.

In making these corrections, the market performs a curiously asymmetrical operation. If earnings exceed estimates by a few cents per share, the stock price might get no rise at all (it could even fall a bit). By contrast, if earnings miss those same estimates by a few cents, the company's stock could easily lose half its value in a single day. This seems neither rational nor fair, but in fact it is both. Here's why.

When actual performance exceeds estimates, these are typically the ones that appear in print. They are known to be conservative, if for no other reason than that it is in the interests of both management and investment analysts to keep them that way. This gives rise to a second estimate, sometimes called the whisper number, which savvy investors use as the real standard against which to calibrate the upcoming report. In an efficient market, valuation moves to accommodate this later projection and adjusts to the actual report from that vantage, hence the possibility of management beating its numbers and having its stock price go down. It may be that the whole category is off, but it may also be that the company missed its whisper number.

In either case, however, when earnings exceed published estimates by a few cents, the adjustments are modest. This is not the case, by contrast, when companies miss on the downside.

CORRECTIONS TO THE DOWNSIDE ARE SEVERE

Investors know how hard management teams work to set expectations that they will not miss. So when that does happen, it means the team has exhausted all its reserves, activated all its safety valves, and still has come up short. This does not bode well for the future at all.

When companies miss their numbers, it usually reflects problems that are several quarters old or older and that are likely to take several quarters or longer to correct. That is, although the team has made its numbers in all the preceding quarters, we can now surmise that they applied increasingly heroic efforts to do so. When the team eventually fails to pull out the quarter, investors infer, usually quite rightly, that there has been a long-term erosion in the company's competitive-advantage position. Worse, this situation can be expected to worsen over the following quarters. Here's why.

Short-term problems are always attributable to GAP. The company's offers, for whatever reason, are no longer as compelling as they once were. Sales or gross margins or both are down. If the company could magically restore its GAP overnight, then all would be well. Sometimes this actually happens. For example, when a company is transitioning its product line from an old platform to a new one, they almost always have at least one bad quarter as customers stop buying the old in anticipation of getting the new. In that case, as soon as the new product line comes out, the backlog is released and a great quarter makes up for the previous poor one.

But in other cases the problems are not as fixable. New entrants may have confused the market. Some company may be trying to buy market share at ruinously low prices. Some other company may be able to give away the product in order to garner a lucrative service contract or perhaps the company's offerings may be getting a bit long in the tooth and a competitor has come up with much better ones. In each of these cases, the company's GAP will be impacted for some time to come, perhaps even permanently. A reduced GAP projected forward in time creates a lower market cap.

But that's not the end of it. Consider what a deteriorating GAP does to CAP. As a company's overall power in its marketplace weakens, the other members of its value chain begin to reexamine their allegiances, pulling back some of their commitments to the company and reallocating them to other vendors. Observing this, competitors sense an opportunity and move in, often offering sweetheart deals to gain market share. Their gains in share undermine the company's previously secure position, leading investors to reduce their estimates of the company's CAP. Now a reduced GAP is being projected forward over a shortened CAP, further reducing market cap.

Worse still, that action, in turn, further reduces GAP! As stock prices go down, partners retreat farther, and competitors increase their attacks. None of this is lost on customers. They experience an increase in their negotiating power and begin to press the company for better prices. This diminishes the company's ability to achieve differentiated earnings, thereby shrinking its GAP. And so it goes, decreases in GAP creating decreases in CAP, and vice versa, in a truly vicious circle.

When a company misses its forecast by a few cents, the market assumes that it may have lost its edge and it recalculates not only the height of its projected future earnings curve but its duration as well.

Impact of Missing Expectations

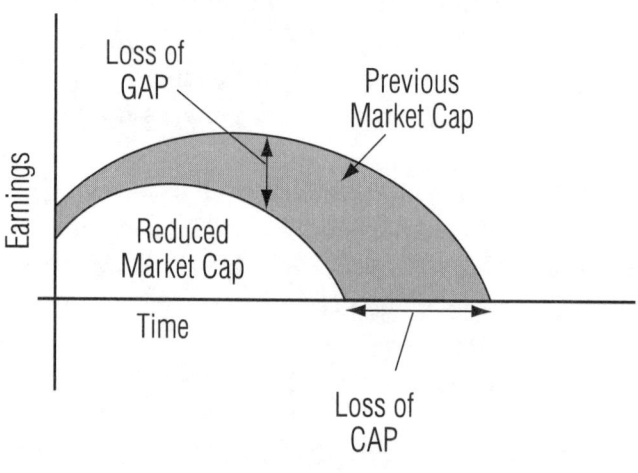

Figure 2.6

When GAP and CAP are corrected simultaneously, the area under the earnings curve is drastically reduced, as the diagram illustrates. This is the visualization that correlates to a 50 percent decrease in market cap, the sort of thing that happens in high tech routinely when quarterly numbers are missed.

Why is this effect largely confined to high tech? Actually severe market cap collapses—effectively, fault-line behavior—is an artifact of any market in which securities are being valued primarily for their long-term future growth opportunities rather than their near-term earnings. When the bulk of the value of an investment is based on the company's expected ability to dominate *the future acquisition of new customers*, the market is very sensitive to any changes in that company's current competitive-advantage position. This is where the volatility of the fault line comes from. It is just part of the lay of the land.

But because these effects are so violent, they galvanize investors to demand that management take immediate and drastic action. Management interprets this to mean get your grades back up—show us a better financial report immediately. Unfortunately, all too often that is precisely what is *not* called for, and thus what is sometimes thought of as managing for shareholder value can in fact result in a permanently depressed stock price.

SO WHAT IS MANAGEMENT SUPPOSED TO DO?

The fifty-thousand-foot answer to this question is that management is supposed to focus scarce resources on core tasks that create competitive advantage. That was the whole point of the first chapter, which argued that until management clears the decks of a whole lot of context, it simply will not be able to get traction on core.

If we descend to ten thousand feet, we can add that management should focus first on CAP, then on GAP. In part this is because CAP, the effects of which are more far-reaching, has a bigger impact on stock price than GAP, which tends to be short term. CAP is the realm of strategic marketing. There, the goal is to align forces in the marketplace to create barriers to entry for competitors and barriers to exit for customers and partners. The end result is a tilted playing field that gives the edge to the market leader not in one or two transactions but in every single one.

Of course, CAP without GAP is meaningless, and just as important, so is strategy without execution. If companies do not execute on their advantages, they lose them to weaker positioned but more aggressive competitors, with the ultimate result that the playing field begins to tilt the other way. So focusing scarce resources to create distinctive differentiation at the point of sale is the recurrent theme of day-to-day management in any successful venture.

Despite the best of intentions, even good management teams make fundamental mistakes in managing for shareholder value. We are going to look at the classic expression of this problem when we take on the innovator's dilemma in Chapter 5, "Triage." There we will see an entire management team trapped in a system of their own making with no apparent exit. In order to appreciate that dilemma, however, we are first going to have to build a better understanding of competitive advantage in technology-enabled markets (the function of Chapters 3 and 4). But even before we have done this, with an understanding of just CAP and GAP, we can call out a raft of typical management behaviors that need adjustment.

Just so we don't pick on any one group unfairly, we'll take a look at challenges facing each of the major line functions in a *Fortune* 500 company—from sales, marketing, and professional services to research and development, operations, and finance— and then we'll look at the executive team as a whole as it faces fundamental issues with its P&L statement. In every case, the goal is simply to point out how easy it is to think you are doing the right thing when in fact your actions are detracting from, not adding to, shareholder value.

MANAGING SALES FOR SHAREHOLDER VALUE

From a shareholder's perspective, a sale has value in two dimensions. In the immediate present, it represents revenue commitments that fulfill the company's current competitive-advantage potential. At the same time, a sale can also help construct an even stronger competitive advantage in the future. This happens when the new customer is added to others in the same market segment to create a majority of customers dedicated to a single vendor—in other words, when the sale contributes to market leadership. Such sales represent *good revenue* because they move the shareholder agenda forward.

Even among good revenues, there are gradations of shareholder value. In a high-growth marketplace, only revenues representing significant new commitments from new customers truly reflect increases in power, so these are the true indicators of changes in shareholder value. As a result, high-tech-sector analysts grill management regarding how many new accounts were gained in the quarter and how big a commitment each customer made. In the enterprise software domain, for example, they will always ask how much of the quarter came from license revenue (representing a strong new commitment) versus service revenue (revenue from maintenance contracts that represents a low commitment from existing customers) and how many deals were in excess of $1 million (strong commitments) as opposed to, say, under $100,000.

Implicit in all this quizzing is the notion that there is such a thing as "neutral" revenue and, as we shall see in a moment, even "bad" revenue that can put the shareholder engine in reverse. It is a rare salesperson who is willing to entertain such a thought, and indeed the management team as a whole is hardly likely to welcome it: *Good God, man, do you know how hard revenue of any kind is to come by? Come down from that ivory tower, boy.* But from an investor's point of view—and thus from a managing-for-shareholder-value point of view—both concepts unfortunately make sense.

Neutral revenue is income from outside the domain of market competition, typically the result of opportunistic sales. It adds to working capital, but it does not represent any gain in marketplace power, so it adds to GAP but does not add to CAP. Neutral revenue may also come from outside operations—say from selling an investment, for example, or making money on currency exchanges, or capturing gains from a tracking stock. In addition, from time to time changes in accounting rules may create changes in the P&L that reallocate revenues or expenses. The SEC's handling of pooled-interest transactions is an example of this. In all these cases, however, the revenues in question have nothing to contribute to the question of current or future competitive advantage. So, whether their impacts are positive or negative, Wall Street tries to "look through them" to the basic dynamics of the enterprise. Its primary interest is to track transactions that create leading indicators of change in the balance of power in the marketplace.

Bad revenue is something else altogether. It is income from outside the domain of market competition that has been earned at the expense of scarce resources and it puts the shareholder engine in reverse. That is, while it adds to GAP, it actually *subtracts* from CAP. Typically, bad revenue results from a big deal well outside your normal market space. Such deals are bad for two reasons. First, they require a continued future diversion of precious resources simply to continue to serve this customer. If the company is not making a market commitment in this direction, then all subsequent work here is at best neutral to its market power position. This revenue amounts to context, not core. Second, these deals reflect a lost opportunity to put those same precious resources to work in the critical competitive space. A better-focused company would have used this chance to make progress where it counts, where a sale today would help create multiple sales tomorrow. A better company, in other words, keeps its resources invested in core. By taking this deal this company has actually jeopardized its shareholder value.

Bad-revenue deals are rarely criticized in the quarter in which they are earned. Indeed, the stock market typically is not able to ferret out all the neutral and bad revenue in any quarter's performance. As a result, in the short to medium term, management teams can normally claim credit for all their revenue as forward revenue—that is, revenues that indicate increasing market share.

Here, however, is where it's important not to kid yourself. Simply understand that once bad revenues have been counted as good, once they have been aggregated into the forward-looking category, they establish a market-share growth-rate expectation for revenues within that category that becomes harder and harder to live up to. Next quarter, to keep up with the rate you portrayed last quarter, the company not only has to sell more of its good business faster, it also has to sell additional good business beyond that to hide the fact that there was bad business in the old numbers. And, of course, having some portion of current resources deflected to supporting the old bad business does not help. One does not have to look very far down the track to see that this is a losing game. Sooner or later the company must miss big, and when it does, correction comes with a vengeance.

So what is a sales manager to do? Three practices stand out:

1. Find a way to compensate generators of good revenue over neutral revenue, thereby encouraging your people to make the extra effort to focus on the markets where your company can gain a leadership position.

2. Do not imply that neutral revenue is undesired. No company can make its revenue commitments without a large complement of opportunistic sales. And winning a sale on a playing

field that is not tilted in your favor is no mean feat. So hats off to that accomplishment.

3. Do not approve bad-revenue deals. The way to block them is to deny access to the scarce resources needed to close them. If the deal closes anyway, then it is neutral revenue, and all is well.

The tough choice falls between taking bad revenue or missing a quarter. But the answer here is actually very straightforward. You now have no chance of not missing a quarter—the only question is, which quarter are you going to miss? If you take this deal, you put yourself even farther behind the eight ball in future quarters. A classic expression of this problem was the case of Informix in the late 1990s. Quarter after quarter they pulled out the numbers through diving catches in the end zone. When they finally missed, however, they missed by over $100 million, and the restatements of revenues that ensued over the following year revealed just how grisly bad revenue can be.

MANAGING MARKETING FOR SHAREHOLDER VALUE

The single most important strategic role of marketing is to help the company target markets where it can gain a sustainable competitive advantage. In so doing, it typically reviews a large set of possible targets and then winnows them through a set of selection criteria. One of these is market size, where the assumption is the larger, the better. Not so.

True, a large untapped market is always terrifically attractive, especially when no other company has a head start in going after it. That in essence is one of the core mantras of venture investing. But these opportunities are few and far between unless you are spawning a truly discontinuous innovation. Consider instead the much more typical choice between the following:

- Market A: A very large market served by any number of vendors that has significant opportunities developing within it. The market as a whole has been tapped but the new spaces opening up are untapped.

- Market B: A neglected niche market ineffectually served by market leaders. The market as a whole has never really been tapped.

Which of these opportunities is more attractive? Market A is preferred if you are already one of the vendors that serves it, you have reason to believe you can get to the new opportunities ahead of the others, and the current market leader (if it is not you) cannot muscle in and take away your momentum. But Market B is preferable if you do not have a preexisting position of strength. Remember, the goal is to pick markets based on the size of their *untapped potential,* not their total size, and to factor in the probability of your company gaining dominant market share—essentially what is required to sustain competitive advantage.

By these criteria, narrow vertical markets often bring higher rewards than broad mass markets. In general, they are attractive to investors because they lend themselves to creating very strong GAP and CAP positions. Vendors who specialize in a single market can create highly differentiated offers for the targeted segment. This gives them a very high GAP, which results in increased segment share. As the vendor's share of segment increases, complementary vendors in the segment begin to operate more intimately with them, creating higher barriers for a competitor and higher switching costs should the partner defect to the competitor. Over time, the risk of the company losing its competitive advantage decreases substantially. All this results in a longer CAP, resulting in increased ability to forecast advantaged returns and thus higher valuation.

It is almost always in a company's interests, therefore, to limit its targeted markets to spaces that it has the power and reach to dominate. A strong position in a small market is much more valuable as a source of future advantaged earnings than a weak position in a large market. Of course, if that small market is also growing rapidly, the position becomes even more valuable. By contrast, however, overreaching into marginal market positions diminishes competitive advantage and creates stock weakness.

Why, then, don't companies pursue vertical markets more aggressively? Why are they more likely to pursue weak positions in large markets at the expense of strong positions in smaller markets? Their answer is that their investors demand greater returns than can come from any particular vertical market. That is, as companies become larger, investors expect increasing growth in both the top and bottom lines, management teams begin to view target market size as increasingly important because they are looking to achieve growth over increasingly larger numbers, and even dominant positions in small markets do not generate the numbers they are hoping for. At this juncture, management tends to shift its focus to larger markets where gaining even a small amount of market share, perhaps only a few percent, can generate the expected revenue gains and thus meet their investors' expectations and sustain their stock price. This is a mistake.

Whenever your goal is to get a small share of a large market, you are typically conceding that other companies already have a larger share. The market has already formed GAP and CAP structures around its existing participants. These structures work to inhibit any competitor's entry. It will cost you plenty just to get into the market. Nonetheless, at the outset you can expect success because every market has some potential customers who are dissatisfied with the current offerings and are looking for a new face.

Once you get that foothold, however, the power hierarchy in the market works even more strongly to prevent your gaining additional market share. Markets are extremely conservative about changes in their pecking orders and spontaneously self-organize to expel late entrants. After an initial jump in revenues reflecting the novelty of your new arrival, future sales will be harder and harder to come by. Worse, because you have no power in this market, your offers will be on the losing end of GAP, not the winning end. You will have to discount more and more to gain the sales you do win. This creates a negative impact on your returns line, as more and more capital chases less and less profitable deals, with the net effect of lowering your stock price, not raising it.

The mistake that led to this weak position is management thinking that investors value revenues per se. That's not quite true. Instead, what they value are competitive-advantage positions that create streams of high-margin revenues over extended periods of time. They care, in other words, about future revenue potential that has *high forecastability* and *low risk*. When you permit your company to pursue marginal positions in large established markets, therefore, you are working against, not for, your investors' agenda. Instead you want to be focusing the team on being the biggest fish in the pond.

This creates a marketing imperative to monitor *fish-to-pond ratios*, something that Jack Welch made a cornerstone of the management philosophy at General Electric when he said GE will be number one or number two in every one of its markets or it won't play. Once you determine what percentage of your revenue you intend to derive from a given market, then you must determine if you'll be number one or number two in that market. If not, then you must either commit the investment resources to change your competitive-advantage GAP until you can gain such market share, or according to Welch, you must exit the market. If you do not, you will be competing against some other company that has the market leadership advantages that you do not, and your results are bound to disappoint investors.

Now let's be clear about something here. Regardless of how single-mindedly you pursue this strategy, there will always be a large portion of revenue that in fact comes from opportunistic sales into untargeted markets where you are anything but the dominant market-share leader. It is not the advice of this chapter, nor of Mr. Welch, to turn these sales down. Rather, understand that they do not create a firm foundation of stock price appreciation. You will never make your revenue projections without them, but neither can you entrust your future to them. Instead, you must continually build that future by systematically extending market leadership positions where you can create advantaged GAPs that can lead over time to long CAPs.

MANAGING PROFESSIONAL SERVICES ORGANIZATIONS FOR SHAREHOLDER VALUE

The professional services organization represents the consulting arm within a large corporation whose offers require some level of systems integration. In technology-enabled markets, this group tends to undergo an identity crisis as it looks enviously at the success of both the large independent consulting firms, such as Andersen Consulting or EDS, and the smaller boutique firms that are riding the current technology wave—today, the Viants, Scients, Sapients, and such of the Internet. It feels its capabilities are every bit as good as theirs and it chafes against the restriction of having to drag its own company's offers into every deal. If the company would just let it compete freely, it could make a much better contribution to shareholder value.

Anyone who has ever had to bring a younger sibling along with them when they went out with their friends knows how this organization feels. But the fundamental premise that, if freed, it could make a greater contribution to shareholder value is flawed. Captive professional services organizations exist to increase the GAP and CAP of the company's core offers. True, they are also expected to generate revenue, and true, this revenue does count on the bottom line, but that is not their primary value-creating function. It is, instead, to contribute to the greater good.

The challenge facing this organization's management is to charter it correctly, to make absolutely clear what is core and what is context. For independent consulting firms, revenue is core; for professional services organizations, *revenue is context*! To be sure, if revenue is not earned, that is bad, because this organization should more than pay for itself. But earning more and more revenue will not raise stock price. Instead, the PSO's core contributions will lie in the following areas:

- Helping to sell and then implement projects that advance the company's state of the art, featuring products that are fresh from R and D. Such projects get much-needed visibility for the company's innovative offers and help start new product categories.

- Doing the gritty, unglamorous work behind the scenes that has to get done to make any system work right, the very work that the independent consulting firms want no part of. By signing up for these tasks, the organization ensures the customer gets a successful result and becomes a superior reference for the company.

- Developing domain expertise in one or more vertical markets to help differentiate the company's offerings in market-domination exercises. Such expertise enables the company to modify its offers in compelling ways that secure deep and abiding loyalty from grateful customers.

- Capturing the essential systems integration knowledge needed to implement large, complex offerings, and then packaging that knowledge and handing it over to third-party partners. This broadens the company's reach to incorporate indirect sales and support, the cost of which is off the balance sheet.

- Offering its services to long-established customers to take on a challenge that no one else will help them with. Not only does this, too, help secure long-term loyalty and commitment, but it can also lead to the discovery of new market opportunities.

In short, professional services organizations create the most shareholder value when they subordinate their own P&Ls to the greater good. This should not be taken as a license for them to be unprofitable. Skilled human resources are simply too scarce to be deployed at a loss. It should, however, be taken as a call to make every project count toward the company's core, toward increasing the GAP and the CAP of the company's offers in its primary target markets.

MANAGING R AND D FOR SHAREHOLDER VALUE

When I entered business back in the 1970s, large corporations were the bastion of R and D, and centers like Xerox PARC, Bell Labs, HP Labs, and IBM Labs were perceived as the crown jewels of their respective corporations, sources of innovation that would keep their competitive advantage alive for generations to come. Interestingly, if we fast-forward thirty years, that is not what has transpired. Instead, innovation has largely centered in venture-backed start-ups directly exposed to the Darwinian forces of a highly competitive marketplace. Many of these companies die from such exposure, but those that survive and reach critical mass become highly attractive as IPO candidates or acquisitions. If they go public in the longer term they are likely to merge into larger and larger entities, and so the function of creating R and D for large corporations is in fact fulfilled, albeit in a roundabout way. It turns out, in effect, that in the long run Darwin is a better inventor than Edison.

The only casualty is the corporate R and D labs, which, like professional services organizations, look with envy at the unfettered lives led by their outside counterparts and grumble about the lack of imagination and appreciation from within. And indeed they have much to grumble about.

If you think it is hard to get a discontinuous innovation to market from an unknown start-up, you ought to try it from a corporate lab. As Clayton M. Christensen described in *The Innovator's Dilemma*, established corporations have highly evolved immune systems that tag and reject disruptive technologies regardless of their origin. A start-up takes this for granted. A lab might be forgiven for thinking the rest of the company is on its side. Add to this the fact that the start-up can offer stock options to attract the hot new talent, and that they get a marketing budget and a sales force that has nothing else to sell but the next new thing, and you see why breakthrough R and D is much more likely to come from a decentralized, venture-funded system.

OK, so given all the above, what should R and D management do? The short answer is that the baton in large part must be passed from a corporate R and D program focused on breakthrough innovation and process innovation to a divisional R and D program focused on continuous innovation. Here's how it plays out.

- *Breakthrough innovations.* The key learning here is not to cease in these efforts but to understand it takes an uphill battle to get them through the corporation. The winning play is to kill marginal ideas early and overfund a few really good ideas to get some momentum behind them. Apple is a good example of a company that had let its corporate R and D get way out of hand, something Steve Jobs pruned back heavily when he rejoined the company. Lou Gerstner sent out a comparable but somewhat different message to the labs at IBM—stop focusing on the technologies of the future and start generating technologies for the present. John Chambers at Cisco supplements these ideas with a third view—let Silicon Valley be your lab and acquire those companies where the fit with yours is good, a lesson that has not been lost on Jobs, Gerstner, or any other high-tech CEO. Overall, the sector has come to understand that with corporate R and D you are playing a long shot, and so it is no longer assumed to be the incubator for future shareholder value.

- *Process innovations.* You don't have to work long in a corporation to see that each function operating autonomously creates an opportunity to improve productivity through cross-functional learning. As corporate functions have come under pressure to show their value, often by billing back their services to the divisions, process innovation has become a new focus. Moreover, in light of the previous chapter's discussion of how core becomes context over time, there is a process innovation that I think will contribute highly to future shareholder value—namely, *design for outsourceability.* In the 1980s and 1990s, the comparable innovation was design for manufacturability. The idea here is that, if core will become context, then you will want to be able to outsource it some day, so you should design the overall system in modules that can be readily outsourced.

  Even though I am a fan of process innovation, however, when it comes from corporate, it comes with two strikes against it. Just as the group lacks a marketing arm for taking its innovations outside the company, so does it for taking them inside. So, yes, the ideas are good, and yes, the learning is important, but no, this is not a high-probability path for creating shareholder value.

- *Continuous innovations.* These represent the bulk of the innovations that reach the market in any given year. They are the backbone of incremental improvements to GAP, and the company is highly dependent on them to differentiate its offers in the marketplace. Such work is best located in the divisions that make the products, not in the central labs. So think of this as *distributed R and D.* To be sure, centralized labs can make a contribution by investigating the basic science and technology that underlies the domain of these innovations. Thus, for example, the designers in HP's inkjet division should design the next set of inkjet cartridges, but the labs might be exploring the chaos mathematics that describe their fluid dynamics or the science of how paper interacts with ink. However, we should be modest in our expectations. The shareholder payoff from such work is very long term indeed, and there is some probability that the work could be outsourced to universities and kept off the balance sheet altogether.

The overall take-away from all this is that in the new economy start-ups have a huge advantage when it comes to breakthrough R and D, and divisions of established successful companies have a comparable advantage when it comes to incremental improvements to an established paradigm. Large centralized R and D labs, the showcase of the old economy, lack the marketplace power and the stock-option currency to compete in the new economy, at least in their traditional form. Either they need to find a new form or, from the perspective of managing for shareholder value, they need to be dismantled.

MANAGING OPERATIONS FOR SHAREHOLDER VALUE

For the purposes of this discussion, consider *operations* in its largest sense as essentially any business process that involves a fundamentally repetitive set of tasks and typically a large number of people. Thus a manufacturing line, a purchasing or personnel department, a customer support or telesales center, a shipping and receiving or warehousing function, or a facilities maintenance and security group could all qualify. Understood in this sense, when it comes to managing for shareholder value, COOs (chief operating officers) should think of themselves as chief outsourcing officers, the primary owners of the core-versus-context challenge.

That is not how COOs tend to think of themselves today. Instead, they are likely to see themselves as chief overseers of in-house business processes, chartered to make them more efficient and more effective. And to the degree that those processes should stay in house, that is absolutely correct. But if companies are ever going to implement the strategy of outsourcing context to embrace core, then the effort must be led by the team and the executive who can best testify as to which is which. And that is the operations team. Anyone else in the company may think he knows, and certainly everyone will have an opinion about what *ought to be* either core or context, but only the people who actually do the work can make the determination with any authority. The issue is, will they?

In the old economy, managers of any operation asked to downsize or dismantle itself could be expected to react defensively, taking the charter as an implied criticism of their ability to perform to an appropriate standard. So asking for their support was a little bit like asking the doomed man to help tighten the knot on the hangman's noose. But in the new economy, that is not at all the case. The winners in the new economy will be those who can craft the most imaginative solutions to managing context and then put in place pragmatic outsourcing relationships that really work.

Determining which tasks can in fact be outsourced, identifying the outsourcer that can handle them, setting up a relationship of trust anchored in a thoughtful and precise service-level agreement, supervising the transition to the new workflow including working through the inevitable glitches and complaints, and then managing the ongoing relationship toward the twin goals of improved service levels and reduced costs—all this is not the sort of thing that a "failed" management team can, or should, be asked to do. It is, in effect, the implementation of a whole new business paradigm. The venture-capital community, for its part, believes enough in this vision that it is funding scores of start-ups to play the outsourcer role wherever it can envision that one is likely to form. But at the end of the day it will be the operational management of the customer company who will make or break this effort.

What I want to make clear here is that successful outsourcing of context tasks represents the most dramatic way in which operations management can raise shareholder value. To be sure, they can also improve stock price by squeezing a bit more productivity out of their in-house teams, increasing margins and earnings per share, and garnering a stock market attaboy for so doing. In other words, it is not that the current efforts are misdirected or lacking in value. It is simply that such returns are peanuts compared to the impact operations can have wherever they are able to clear the decks of a great chunk of context work.

Perhaps the greatest challenge of all and the action that will have the greatest impact is for an operations management team to lead the spin-out of their own in-house group, taking what has historically been a cost center and converting it into an independent and profitable entity. It is a huge task and should not be undertaken without a commitment from the host company to guarantee a multiyear contract for the new entity's services to support the transition. After all, the group has never had to run itself as a company before and lacks most of the functions needed to do so. Many of these, it turns out, can themselves be outsourced in turn, but sales and marketing, to pick just two, certainly cannot. It takes real leadership, therefore, to inject entrepreneurial self-sufficiency into a group that was never recruited with such a vision in mind. But there is no question that, for those groups that can step up to this challenge, the future holds enormous promise, not only to control one's own destiny but to earn the equity rewards of entrepreneurship as well.

To close on a more practical note, any act of outsourcing context work is a step in the right direction. Indeed, simply helping sketch out the boundary line between core and context will help the corporation better target its resources. The only truly value-destroying behavior in the face of a dotcom challenge or some other wake-up call from the new economy is simply to march forward heads down along the same old paths.

MANAGING FINANCE FOR SHAREHOLDER VALUE

If there is one organization that might feel that they already are directly aligned with managing for shareholder value, it would be the finance department. As keepers of the P&L, leaders of the budgeting effort, producers of the monthly variance reports, and publishers of the quarterly report, they often see themselves as the financial conscience of the company and the shareholder's ally. In actual fact, however, a P&L orientation is not always in the shareholders' best interests. To be sure, in mature markets it is. That's because P&L statements accurately reflect earnings performance on short- to medium-term operations, the appropriate focus in a mature market. Such markets are said to be in their cash cow phase, and thus monitoring "milk flow" is the appropriate focus.

Conversely, however, in growth sectors where sustainable competitive advantage is largely a function of staking out early positions in developing markets, a pure P&L approach to strategy and planning is horribly misguided. It would be like monitoring the milk flow on a baby heifer. A proper focus instead would be on the metrics of the heifer's growth and future prospects, not on its present yield.

Success or failure in achieving a sustainable competitive-advantage position in a hypergrowth market does not show up on the P&L until well after the battle for marketplace dominance is under way, with its outcomes potentially already determined. Not understanding this principle results in *P&L myopia,* a widespread affliction not only among finance departments but whole management teams that leads to loss of shareholder value. Here's how it works.

First the good news: *P&L statements can and do detect current deterioration in GAP.* Receding GAPs show up either in loss of sales outright or diminishing gross margins as the company increases its discounts to make up for its lack of GAP or both. In any case, the P&L alerts the management team to the problem, and actions are taken. This is how and why established companies perform successfully when challenged to make continuous improvements to existing paradigms. CAP is never the issue; GAP always is. Is GAP slipping? Prop it up and get back out there for the next round of sales competitions.

Now for the bad news: *P&L statements cannot and do not detect deterioration in CAP.* Here's why. Recall that a GAP/CAP chart is the projection of a financial future. At the left side of the chart that projection is grounded in the previous quarter's financial performance. The numbers there are solid. Going forward into the next few quarters the numbers are projections, but there is enough history and momentum in the system to make them fairly reliable. But going forward from there—anything, say, beyond the next twelve to twenty-four months, the numbers themselves become fused into trend lines based not on data but on extrapolation.

We have now entered a domain where ideas and models of competitive advantage, not extrapolated spreadsheets, generate the best projections of truth. Here a strategic understanding of CAP must take over, providing a more reliable estimate of middle- to long-term prospects than any numerical tool. Unfortunately, numbers-oriented management teams miss this transition. Their vision effectively ceases at the edge of what we call the P&L window.

Numbers vs. Ideas

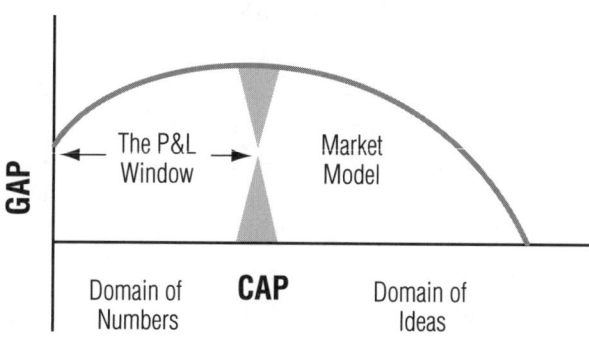

Figure 2.7

The domain of numbers functions as a P&L window. It gives visibility into the next two to six quarters, depending on the volatility of the market. Beyond that window, raw numbers offer little or no guidance. Instead one has to model the marketplace, the power of each of the players in it, and the vectors they are on, and then make a determination as to who looks to be in the best position to win and why. This is the realm of CAP analysis.

In an established market, CAP changes slowly, and so once it is strategically understood, the knowledge becomes taken for granted—effectively, priced into the market—and attention inevitably refocuses on the quarterly numbers, the latest changes in GAP. Thus over time, management teams and investment analysts in mature sectors become increasingly numerical in their approach to the market. But this approach misses the mark when confronted with the kind of recurrent disruptive change that characterizes high tech or any market that is under a technology-based attack.

What, then, should the finance team do? The first question it needs to ask itself is, what is moving the company's stock price? Let us assume it has been a traditional P/E stock for some time so that historically its own earnings have been the prime mover of its stock price. But now let us say that its marketplace has been disrupted by a dotcom or some other purveyor of discontinuous innovation and its stock price has come under an external negative influence that no amount of earnings can dispel. Shareholders are selling off its shares not because of anything it has done but because of a vision someone else has created. A pall has been cast over the company's future, and as the company's designated communications channel to Wall Street, the finance team has to dispel it.

The key learning from the high-tech sector is that there is no form of arithmetic that solves this problem. It is instead a matter of storytelling. Hostile forces have sold some portion of the marketplace on a vision of the future that cuts them in and you out. Since this dastardly deed will happen in the future, they argue, of course your earnings will be fine for a few more years, but anyone with half a brain can see you are toast in the long term. To break free from this spell, you need to weave one of your own. You need to *state your own vision*, and depending on how well you do it, you will get some of your own back from the market. Market vision is the primary price support of dotcom stocks—with little revenue and massive losses, what else do they have?—and it is not a tactic established firms can eschew.

Once your company states a credible vision and the competitors have stated their contradictory vision, then the market shifts into the second stage of competition, one that is determined by which company wins the most market share. Here we reenter the domain of the P&L, but not with a focus on earnings. Instead, it is revenues, specifically revenues that reflect gains in market share in the contested markets, that drive changes in stock price. In this contest, the faster the market as a whole is growing, the more important it is to invest in immediate and massive acceleration in revenues. Such investment is bound to wreak havoc with earnings, and investors may punish you for such effects, but that cannot be helped, and if you are successful, the effects will be temporary. Losing the market-share battle creates a far worse outcome, one in which your strategic path forward has been blocked, and you must either seek a new path or be permanently marginalized.

So when it comes to managing for shareholder value, the key learning for finance departments is that stock price is not always a simple matter of earnings per share. To be sure, *eventually* earnings are the issue with investors, but in emerging markets, especially technology-enabled markets which have a history of spinning up very fast and of having a winner-take-all outcome, *current earnings* should be readily sacrificed to achieve the sustainable competitive advantage of market-share leadership. And if your company is to receive its optimal valuation from investors, in addition to earnings in established markets and revenue growth in emerging markets, it should also be credited with additional competitive advantage coming from its vision and strategy for future markets.

MANAGING INVESTOR RELATIONS FOR SHAREHOLDER VALUE

In the new economy, winning the battle for market share in emerging markets is the primary creator of new wealth. Gaining dominant share in a single fast-growing market, therefore, creates the clearest unit of investment possible. As any number of start-ups going public can testify, such an effort is easily positioned and readily communicated. The continued need to grow, however, leads companies to expand their operations to field multiple categories of offerings that serve multiple marketplaces. As a result of these efforts, competitive-advantage positions become blurred. That is, GAP and CAP are always specific to a particular category within a single market. Change either the category or the market and GAP or CAP can change dramatically. So how should investors value a diversified company?

Actually, the first question is, should they assign any value to diversification itself? Most contemporary investors, it turns out, do not. They are not interested in individual stocks as instruments of diversification because that goal is far better accomplished by mutual funds, index funds, or similar aggregating instruments. Instead they are looking to stocks to provide returns in excess of the funds and indexes, and here the pure-play stocks have a big advantage over the diversified ones. Investors can use pure plays to invest in hypergrowth markets, ideally focusing their holdings on an emerging market leader and riding its success up and up and up. By contrast, a mature corporation comprising a portfolio of varied operations is invariably held back from such dramatic appreciation because not everything in the portfolio can be in hypergrowth at the same time.

To counter this, the management of large established companies must create a case for synergy among their various operations. Moreover, the case has to be real because in every future quarter the company's performance is going to be measured against it. In prior eras, a prime source of synergy was vertical integration. In the age of the Internet, however, with the move to virtual value chains, this strategy is becoming increasingly obsolete. Today, investable synergies are more likely to be found in shared intellectual property, shared distribution and support infrastructure, and shared customer knowledge. Regardless of where synergy comes from, however, the real question is, how does it affect the GAP and CAP of the company's various offerings in its various markets?

To speak to this question authoritatively, the company should present its operating results category by category and market by market. By so doing, it can guide investors and analysts in constructing a market capitalization model for each area by comparing its results to others in the same category. By summing up the results across all its lines of business it can present a model that should correspond to the current market valuation of the company. Indeed, this is precisely what savvy CFOs at Internet companies like America Online have been doing for the past several years. But this is not at all a common practice in the *Fortune* 500. Why not?

Traditionally *Fortune* 500 companies have withheld the kind of details needed to break out cleanly a corporation's offers for comparative purposes, primarily for two reasons. First, they do not want to reveal any more of their warts to investors than they have to. And second, they want to give as little information as possible to competitors about the strengths and weaknesses of their individual operations. In service to both these ends, traditional shareholder-reporting practice has been to cloak the corporation's internal operations wherever possible, providing financial results in as aggregated a form as investors and analysts will tolerate.

This practice, in turn, has driven investment analysts toward an increasingly abstract financial focus. They identify a set of grossly similar stocks, calculate and average the price/earnings ratios for them, and then use that ratio as a benchmark for valuing the cloaked company. Under this mechanism they put increasing scrutiny on financial statements because granting any increase in earnings is the equivalent of granting it an increase in stock price. Since accounting practices give significant leeway to how revenues and expenses are recognized, this leads to a complicated game of hide-and-seek, with the quarterly report becoming the occasion for an increasingly specialized set of questions.

In mature markets this practice, although not particularly useful, does no apparent harm. But the minute a disruptive technology emerges—in today's era signaled as likely as not by the arrival of one or more dotcoms—the entire system falls of its own weight. The dotcom threatens both the GAP and CAP of traditional market leaders. It claims it can translate the discontinuous innovation of the Internet into such high GAP offers that it will take the market away from its current owners, thereby demolishing their CAPs. On the surface, this is a very compelling story, and the market leader needs to counter it directly. Unfortunately, the very facts that would contradict it are the ones it has systematically been withholding from its reports.

Look at it from the investor's point of view. Instead of responding with specific operational break-outs, your company announces instead that it has an important Internet play, not to worry. But from your cloaked reporting all investors can see is that overall revenues are still growing at single-digit or low double-digit rates. From this they tend to infer that either you are missing the mark with your Internet offers, your Internet offers are a paltry amount of your total effort, or something else is seriously dragging your high flyer down. Your reporting practices, of course, make it impossible to determine which of these conditions actually obtains. After some thought, however, investors decide they don't much care after all which one it is: They just want out.

One emerging response to this challenge has been to create *tracking stocks* for operations that have exceptional investment attributes. This opens up a particular business operation for direct investment. Typically a controlling majority of the stock is held by the parent corporation. General Motors took this line with its Hughes Aircraft and EDS operations. Microsoft at the time of this writing is discussing doing the same with its Internet properties. And the Internet Capital Group, which specializes in business-to-business Internet companies, has effectively made its entire portfolio a loosely held set of tracking stocks.

As a practice, tracking stocks are still a work in progress. In particular, there is some confusion about the interaction between the valuation of the tracking stock and the valuation of the shares of the parent company that owns the preponderance of that stock. But there should be no confusion about the warm reception granted to decloaking the corporation. So regardless of whether literally creating a tracking stock is a good idea or not, there is nothing to stop the investor relations department from creating comparable effects—creating virtual tracking stocks, if you will—by reporting on operations less discreetly and more discretely.

MANAGING THE CORPORATION FOR SHAREHOLDER VALUE

The goal of the preceding sections, each addressing the perspective of one or another line function, has been to take the focus away from traditional rules of thumb about what creates shareholder value and put it instead on the long-term fundamentals of the markets your company serves and the competitiveness of the offerings it brings to them. The ultimate expression of this change in point of view entails a complete rethinking of the function of the quarterly report. Here, I suggest, we can all take a lesson from our personal experience with report cards.

The report card loomed large in my life as a child. A's were a good thing, B's and C's were not. When I got A's, my parents were pleased, and that was the biggest good thing in my life. That taught me how to work for a grade, a behavior that sometimes led to true learning and sometimes did not. When I grew older and became a teacher and then a parent, I came to take a different view. By then I could see that grades were not the goal but only a signpost of progress toward the goal. What I really cared about was whether my students or my children learned anything that would help them be better people. In other words, I shifted from being a CEO of my own company to being an investor in someone else's: What I cared about was whether there would be a future stream of returns from the learning gained. (Well, that's a little bit more businesslike wording than I really felt, but you get the idea.)

Now apply the same shift to yourself, your company, and your investors. Specifically, what do you think your investors really care about when they read your quarterly report? Recall that a share of stock entitles them to a share in the *future* earnings of your corporation, not its *past* earnings. In most cases, past earnings are simply reinvested in the corporation to create increases in future earnings, so shareholders aren't going to get any immediate reward for them regardless of what they are. So why are they so anxious to learn about them?

The answer, as we have already discussed, is that earnings reports are the benchmark instrument by which investors calibrate management performance versus the performance of its competition. The fundamental role of quarterly reports in this context is to adjust investor expectations regarding the company's future performance.

Now we can see why it is so important to reposition the dialogue. If the only context investors have for understanding your company is a set of cloaked financials—a report card, if you will—then getting the grades is the only thing they can evaluate. When grades are good, you win; when they are not, you lose. Moreover, when you lose, there is no basis for rebuilding confidence. By contrast, if the report is recast as a measure of progress toward competitive-advantage positions in chosen markets, then the results function more as data and less as dicta. They are not pronouncements of your fate so much as information about your progress. This is exactly the technique that savvy CFOs at Internet-based companies are using to win investor support for business plans that forecast substantial losses.

As an established company, you cannot report such losses *in your established lines of business*. There the presumption is that your competitive-advantage position has already been achieved and should now be throwing off increasingly sizable wads of cash. But I would argue you can and should report such losses *wherever you are investing in new businesses*. If you do not, if you imply that you can enter new businesses "for free," you are simply giving away competitive advantage to the dotcoms.

Of course, the challenge is not investing to win new markets. It is how to manage investor expectations when the dotcoms have attacked your traditional strongholds. Here you have to own up to a sad fact. That solid CAP that you used to enjoy in that market is no longer secure. Indeed, if you are going to save it at all, it is going to take major reinvestment in what you have been treating for some time as a cash cow. This will produce highly unattractive financial results, and investors will punish your stock accordingly. But that is fairness, not weirdness. It is not that you have done the wrong thing, it is that the world has changed, and what had higher value before has lower value now.

Essentially, this is the risk scenario illustrated over and over again in *The Innovator's Dilemma.* Unfortunately for you, technology-savvy investors are particularly sensitive to this sort of risk. They are always looking for the "next big thing," the source of the industry's *future* earnings streams. When they see leading companies underinvest in these admittedly unproven categories, they worry that management is leaving their markets open to occupation by new entrants, thereby exposing the company's current market positions to future under-mining. Investors cannot believe that the incumbent management teams could be so blind, but eventually they become convinced, and the company's stock price takes a hit.

Even now a P&L–oriented management team may respond with bewilderment. Despite increasing anecdotal evidence of com-petitive risk, the threat has yet to find its way onto the P&L, has yet to manifest itself inside the P&L window, and, sadly, is not likely to do so until it is too late. Thus it was that Novell's stock price in the 1990s was hammered due to the threat of Microsoft NT displacing Netware, even though the company had over 60 percent market share at the time and was generating record earn-ings. Imagine management's dismay.

Moreover, all along this way to perdition a P&L focus contin-ues to encourage management to stay out of the new market alto-gether. Looked at through the domain of numbers, the new market simply looks like a bad investment—market risk is very high, short- to medium-term revenue opportunities are modest at best, margins will be negative for the forecastable future, and disruptions to operations will not only be challenging in themselves but will threaten margins in other parts of the business. Why would anyone want to enter a bad business in order to cannibalize an existing good business? Through the P&L lens, management simply cannot see upside gain, only downside pain, and thus strides confidently into the jaws of a calamity.

A FAILURE IN REASONING

The failure in reasoning here is an inherited assumption from mature markets—namely, that any large market is essentially immortal. That is, there will always be an automobile market, a steel market, a beverages market, a cigarette market, an insurance market. In this context, continuous innovation will result in increased value creation indefinitely—always has, always will.

This simply is not true of markets suffering from technology-enabled disruption. As the title of this book asserts, they *live on the fault line.* That is, their fundamental underpinnings can be completely overthrown with remarkably little notice. When I joined business in 1978, for example, the word processor of choice was an IBM Selectric typewriter, the one that had the on-keyboard white-out key, and was that a boon! The Selectric cost $1,000 and was the flagship product in the typewriter industry, and the consumables after-market was every bit as lucrative, if not more. Today, there is *no* typewriter market. It isn't weak. It isn't aging. It is *nonexistent*!

What were the other big office-automation expenditures back then? Telex machines, dedicated word processors (remember when *word processing* was a place, not a product?), calculators, and cash registers. These were huge revenue-generating categories. Today they, too, simply do not exist. Moreover, in recent years the window for a given technology's life expectancy has been getting shorter, not longer. The answering-machine market did not come into existence until the 1980s and today it is virtually extinct, succumbing to ubiquitous voice-mail services. That's less than twenty years from beginning to end. Local area networks did not come into prominence until the late 1980s and now they are succumbing to intranets—fifteen years from beginning to end. Internet browsers did not come into existence until the 1990s, and now are succumbing to an expanding operating system—less than ten years from beginning to end. We're not talking about new models replacing old models—we're talking about the wholesale eradication of market categories.

In this context, management thinking needs to jettison the assumption of market immortality. This does not mean there are no more long-lived markets. HP's printer franchise looks very long term indeed—no one at present can foresee a disruptive displacement technology. PCs look long term as well, provided one is willing to take some liberties with the definition of a PC. The Internet looks to be very, very long term at this date—indeed, its ultralong CAP is at the heart of the sky-high valuation of Internet stocks—granted that it is still very young and is largely being viewed through rose-tinted glasses. The key point here is not that technology-based markets *cannot* be long lived, only that they are not *necessarily* long lived.

As soon as you accept this premise, mature market management takes on a new dimension. It is no longer simply an exercise in effective P&L management. It now becomes that, *plus* an exercise in technology-paradigm life-cycle management, which requires that management expand its arsenal of tools to incorporate an additional set of metrics.

METRICS FOR SHAREHOLDER VALUE

Ironically, one of the best tools for seeing beyond the P&L window is the stock market itself. The thesis of this chapter is that investors value companies primarily on their long-term competitive advantage, using the quarterly shareholder report as a trailing indicator of the health of that advantage. If this is true, then stock price represents the collective judgment of a large number of interested individuals as to your company's competitive advantage. How, then, can management use this stock-market data as a feedback mechanism to help guide its decision making?

MARKET CAP

Let's begin with one of the most basic tools, market cap. In the PC industry, among the relatively pure plays, the current pecking order is Dell with a market cap of $109 billion, Compaq with $46.4 billion, and Gateway with $11 billion. That is a perceived competitive-advantage hierarchy. Note that its distinctions are pretty obvious—it does not take a magnifying glass to see them, just a firm grasp of the obvious.

The market may go up or down dramatically between the time the previous paragraph was drafted and the time you read this book. What is far less likely to occur, however, is that the *relative valuation* of these three companies will change. That is, if you go check on their stock prices today as you read this sentence, my expectation is that Dell's will be highest, Gateway's lowest, and Compaq's in the middle (assuming none has been acquired), just as they were when I wrote this. Relative valuation, in other words, or what we call the pecking order, is one of the most stable elements in the stock market. Now what can management glean from that?

Whenever you have a direct competitor and its market cap is significantly higher or lower than yours, you can count on the following effects:

- The marketplace as a whole—customers, partners, employees, and investors—will give the lion's share of its discretionary resources to the market cap leader. This reflects simply a desire to go with the herd and stick with the safe buy.

- As long as no disruptive innovations come along, the marketplace will be extremely reluctant to displace this market-cap leader, even when short-term news is not in its favor. The whole point of sticking with a leader is to reinforce stability in a changing world. Swapping one leader for another undermines this objective.

- Companies in any other position in the pecking order, however, enjoy no such protection: They are subject to challenge by any other company at any time.

The management implications of these effects are two. First, you can enter almost any category and gain momentum by knocking off the weaker players in it. This will give you a feeling of increasing confidence in yourself and your future prospects. That's when you need to keep in mind the second implication. The market will not support your unseating the number one player. As soon as you approach the number two position, you must either introduce discontinuity into the category—in effect throwing the whole pecking order up for grabs—find a new category to exploit, or find a way to settle down into the number two position for the long term.

There is a limitation in using relative valuation as a tool to interpret marketplace power, however—namely, that it is often hard to find true apples-to-apples comparisons for your marketplace. The competition between McDonald's and Burger King, for example, is obscured by the fact that the latter is owned by Diageo Corporation, which buries its market cap inside a much larger diversified company. The same holds true if you are Barnes&Noble.com. Its noted competitor is Amazon.com, but that company has a lot more going for it than just bookselling, so the fact that it has a market cap of $22 billion and Barnes&Noble.com has one just under a half billion dollars, while conclusive at one level—Amazon is clearly a retail gorilla of some sort—is not useful at the next level down in the fight for control in the book industry specifically. This leads management to look to a second set of tools, the P/E and P/S ratios.

P/E RATIOS

The P/E (price-to-earnings) ratio is calculated by dividing the earnings per share into the stock price per share and is a measure of how much capital must an investor put in to get these earnings out. It makes the returns from your stock easily comparable with the interest rate earned from a bond or a loan or any other form of security with a fixed return. It also makes them readily comparable with the returns from any other stock in the marketplace. What it does not do, however, is factor in the value of growth, either market growth or market-share growth. The P/E ratio, that is, is GAP-sensitive and CAP-insensitive. It interprets only the current quarter's returns.

The P/E ratio is a useful tool for measuring company performance in mature markets, where the competition for CAP is assumed to be over and valuation rises and falls based on current GAP. Think of the retail clothing industry. If your chain has a hot fashion line, its sales take off while those of your competitors languish. As of this writing, for example, it turns out that The Gap enjoys a great GAP. But two years ago it was Banana Republic, and now it looks as if the winds are shifting to Old Navy, and who knows where they'll be by the time you are reading this book. But the stock market does not worry about this issue. It simply uses P/E ratios to rate its avenues for investment, and capital follows accordingly.

Companies of equal status within the same industry will be rewarded by the same P/E ratio. When ratios are unequal, they contain another message to management about the balance of power in the marketplace. One of two conditions typically obtains. The first is that one company is perceived as a less risky investment than the other, thereby earning a lower discount for risk and generating a higher stock price and a higher P/E ratio. The other is that one company is perceived to have significantly better growth prospects that the other, and investors are incorporating such value into that company's CAP but not the other's. In either case, if your company is being valued at a discount to your competitor, you need to decode the message in order to act appropriately.

As useful as P/E ratios are in mature markets, however, they are normally not an appropriate tool for valuing companies in emerging markets. Here true valuation depends so heavily on which company is best positioned for future customer acquisition that present earnings are simply not a useful indicator. Indeed, because P/E ratios focus exclusively on harvesting present competitive advantage and do not measure (indeed, punish) investment for future competitive advantage, they in effect lock management into the P&L window and break the connection to the technology-savvy investor.

Ultimately, to be sure, all fairly priced stocks must generate future earnings to match their current market caps, but in a high-growth market it is important to *defer present earnings* in order to *capture a greater share of future earnings*. That is, winning *market-*

share battles during the early years is the key to winning *margin-share* battles over the remaining life of the market.

To win the market-share battle now typically requires sacrificing short-term earnings by plowing them back into additional customer-acquisition activities. This is characteristic of stocks in technology-based markets where the technology itself is unfolding a vast new range of market opportunities. Technology-savvy investors believe that someone is going to take advantage of those opportunities, that the companies first into the market have a first-mover advantage, and that therefore their stocks should be awarded a premium.

All this has led technology-savvy management teams to displace P/E ratios with P/S ratios as their critical market indicator of competitive advantage.

P/S RATIOS

The P/S (price-to-sales) ratio is calculated by dividing the market capitalization of the company by its last four quarters of revenue. This is called a trailing P/S ratio. Using this ratio, high-tech stocks are often described as trading at X times revenues. In markets where the category is spinning up, there may be insufficient trailing revenues to represent the competitive-advantage competition accurately. In these cases, analysts have taken to calculating P/S ratios based on next year's projected revenues. This practice is clearly subject to abuse—hence conservative investors and analysts regard it with disdain—but there is little alternative in the case of a hypergrowth market whose long-term market-share outcome, like it or not, will be determined in the next twelve to twenty-four months.

The P/S ratio is both GAP- and CAP-sensitive. That is, the fact that a company is winning sales indicates that its offers have a current competitive-advantage GAP over alternatives. At the same time, because those sales are adding to the company's market share, they are also helping to lengthen the competitive-advantage period, in two ways. First, as more customers come into the company's camp, it gains marketplace power to attract more partners, who in turn help to institutionalize its offers as a persistent market standard. This helps increase the longevity of their value. And second, these new customers can be expected to reinforce their initial purchase downstream, purchasing additional products and services, often far in excess of their initial order. That helps increase the forecastability of future business because these sales are noncompetitive, sole-source procurements, if not in fact, certainly in spirit.

Because the P/S ratio is both GAP- and CAP-sensitive, it is a better indicator of changes in sustainable competitive advantage than the P/E ratio when power is shifting in an emerging market. Investors use the information in two ways. First they look at sales growth in the overall category to determine its value relative to other categories of investment. Think of this as *category P/S* and understand that it is inherited by any company in the category. In high tech, for example, diversified systems companies like IBM, HP, Sun, or Compaq have historically inherited a P/S ratio between 1.0 and 2.0. In the age of the Internet, however, these scores are drifting higher, and a company like Sun, which has staked out a strong competitive-advantage position in this sector, enjoys a ratio of 10.0 at the time of this writing. Needless to say, such a change has a remarkable impact on stock price, reflecting a change both in short-term execution—Sun's sales force is knocking the cover off the ball—along with a change in future trajectory—Sun's future, like Cisco's, has become unshakably aligned with the current wave of Internet provisioning.

Within a given category, relative P/S ratios indicate marketplace status, typically measured by market share. Again, this is relative valuation at work. In the database category, for example, if market-leading Oracle has a P/S ratio of 8.0, investors expect Sybase and Informix to have ratios around 2.0 or 3.0 and will price their stocks accordingly. This is not based on GAP—the competitors may be fielding the better offers in the current quarter—but rather on a mechanism for pricing CAP into the market: Over time, investors expect Oracle's market status will outweigh any temporary product advantages these other companies can gain.

When you, as a management team, are on the winning side of this exchange, it is imperative that you leverage your position, using your advantaged stock price to acquire additional companies to increase further your competitive advantage, which will increase your P/S ratio lead, which will fuel further acquisitions. Conversely, if you are on the losing side of this exchange, you must understand that you cannot execute your way out of this predicament. The market is stacked against you, and your best strategy is to change categories.

Useful as P/S ratios are to managers setting strategy in emerging markets, they too break down whenever investors become so enamored of an emerging category that they look completely beyond present performance and focus virtually entirely on a vision of the future. This, of course, represents the essence of the dotcom stock valuation phenomenon. For such situations, management needs to turn to a new ratio, one which Nick Earle of HP has jokingly defined as the "P/V ratio" or *price-to-vision ratio*.

P/V Ratios

What is management to do when it is faced with a competitor whose valuation does not appear to be affected by such mundane forces as revenues or earnings? It is as if someone had secured an antigravity device or repealed the laws of physics. How can investors be so naïve? And while they are under this spell, how can any rational communications succeed?

Although this is a matter of much joking, it is hardly a laughing matter. These valuations become very real indeed when you see the companies enjoying them using their stock to acquire other companies, thereby amassing real-world execution capability and consolidating marketplace power behind them. If your market is under attack by a dotcom and you do not respond to the challenge, there is every reason to believe that you, too, will fall victim to these dynamics. Here's what is going on.

Financial markets maintain order through the mechanism of relative valuation, not absolute valuation. Whenever investors believe that one company has a competitive advantage over another, they bid up its stock to reflect that view. When a new category impinges on an old category, they do the same thing, bidding up the stocks in that category so that, relative to the other, they reflect a higher value. In the market today investors are completely persuaded that Internet-based business models are a disruptive innovation that will thoroughly reengineer traditional business models and that the companies riding this wave will be the new market elite of the future. Thus they bid up their stocks so that, in aggregate, they carry more weight than the traditional competitors.

At the same time, however, not all investors buy into the new argument. Many still believe in the staying power of the traditional market leaders and so they continue to support their traditional market caps. This forces the new investors to assign an inflated value to the new stocks in order to maintain the relative valuation they believe to be true. That in turns leads to valuations that do not compute. When analysts calculate the present value of the future earnings from forecastable current and planned operations, even when they set the discount for risk to ridiculously low levels, they cannot get the equation to balance. Nonetheless, neither camp of investors will budge from its position.

Such a condition is not stable, and sooner or later a correction must come. When it does, all stocks in both camps will get dramatically reduced in value so that the entire market once again "adds up." But here is the kicker. Because investors rely so much on relative valuation, the pecking order that has been set among stocks is not likely to change. That is, a correction is not likely to wash away the dotcoms and leave the traditional market leaders once again standing in all their glory. It is far more likely to re-price everyone while keeping them in their same valuation relationship to one another.

If this is true (and I freely admit to using a crystal ball at the moment), then it is critical that every company in the sector manage its P/V ratio. You must have a vision, and that vision must co-opt the force of the Internet in a clear and compelling way so that your investors can place you at the upper end of the pecking order and you, too, can leverage the power of a privileged stock price. When you are on the losing end of this exchange, when a competitor enjoys an unjustifiable valuation and you do not, take that as a P/V-ratio wake-up call. Do not waste time either in complaining about or mocking the investment community. You do not have any time to waste. You must reposition yourself now or get repositioned forever.

WRAP-UP

To close this chapter on shareholder value in the age of the Internet, let us come back to its main thesis: Changes in total market capitalization represent an information system that management can use as feedback for setting strategy, particularly in emerging markets. There, small initial advantages during market formation can spin up into winner-take-all outcomes, so it is critical to get early feedback on which positions are winning or losing. If you are on the winning end, by all means pour on the coal! The market is telling you that this is core and it is your game to lose. By contrast, when you are falling behind in the market-cap race, investors are encouraging you to change the venue. Maybe you should exit the market or maybe you have found the general domain of your core but have not yet got the angle of attack just right. By reframing the competition, you could break free of the current market vision that subordinates you to another company and gain your own market leadership position. That is the essence of managing for shareholder value in emerging markets.

Finally, management of large, successful enterprises should understand that companies with diversified portfolios are at a significant disadvantage compared to pure plays when a new, hot category hits the market. Indeed, that is the prime motive for them to spin out a tracking stock. In the absence of such an instrument, management must at minimum break out its operating results in the emerging category so that it can get appropriate shareholder valuation for them—hence the importance of changing to a more open approach to financial reporting.

SUMMARY OF KEY POINTS IN CHAPTER 2

This chapter has had one and only one main thesis: Stock price is not a measure of past performance, although it is benchmarked by it; it is instead a measure of future potential based on the competitive-advantage position a company has in the present. Under that umbrella we made the following specific points:

1. Managing for shareholder value means managing for increases in competitive advantage.

2. Competitive advantage is comprised of two parts: Competitive-advantage gap (GAP), which reflects the differentiation of a company's offers in the present, and competitive-advantage period (CAP), which reflects the sustainability of that differentiation in the future.

3. In general, traditional corporations with a P&L focus have the right tools to manage GAP but lack the right tools to manage CAP. The stock market itself, it turns out, provides the missing information—if the management team is willing to listen.

4. Each individual line function—sales, marketing, professional services, R and D, operations, finance, and investor relations—needs to rethink its old metrics of success because in every case they risk clinging to some measures that actually work *against* shareholder value in the age of the Internet.

5. At the same time, the management team as a whole needs to realign itself around a broader complement of metrics to represent shareholder value, supplementing market cap and the P/E (price-to-earnings) ratio with the P/S (price-to-sales) ratio and even the P/V (price-to-vision) ratio. The goal is to use these tools to decode the feedback of the stock market to help inform the strategic focus of the company.

All these points fundamentally come back to understanding managing for shareholder value as managing for competitive advantage. As we turn to our next chapter, we are going to look more closely at competitive advantage itself and specifically at how management must reframe its understanding of it in the age of the Internet.

3

COMPETITIVE ADVANTAGE

What we learned from Chapter 1 was that to ground the corporation on true bedrock, executive teams must cut through the context to get down to the core. What we learned from Chapter 2 was that, if we listen correctly to our investors, what core equates to is competitive advantage. Now in this chapter we are going to inquire directly into competitive advantage to see how its dynamics are changed in the age of the Internet.

In technology-enabled markets, competitive advantage forms in strata. At the base lies the technology itself, the core of cores. On top of it form value chains to translate its potential into actuality. Atop this evolution lie specific markets that begin as unified constructs and then segment and separate over time, with large continents going to the dominant value chain and smaller niche-market archipelagoes going to more focused alternatives. Within all markets, companies compete against each other based on their ability to execute their strategy, differentiating primarily on which of four value disciplines they choose to emphasize. The ultimate expression of this competition, the surface stratum that is visible for all to see, is an array of differentiated offerings that compete directly for customers and consumers on the basis of price, availability, product features, and services.

In technology-enabled markets, corporations, like tall buildings, must sink their foundations down through all the strata to secure a solid footing in competitive advantage. To do so, executive teams need to understand explicitly what technologies, what value chains, what markets, and what focus of execution they are basing their strategies upon. The goal of this chapter is to provide a framework and vocabulary to support that understanding.

The classic formulation of competitive advantage is Michael Porter's five-forces model, each referring to a source of competition for control of a given marketplace: suppliers, customers, existing competitors, new entrants, and substitutes. This model is as useful today as when it was published. Its goal is to isolate the constituencies in a competition for market advantage, to determine in any given market who has what kinds of leverage, and to base competitive strategy decisions upon that analysis. Nothing we are going to say in this chapter displaces the need for this effort.

Nonetheless, the model is weak when it comes to dealing with discontinuous innovations, in large part because it takes a fundamentally company-centric view of competition, presuming no significant disruptions in technology, value chain, or market structure. In mature markets outside the technology sector, this works out all right. That is because the core technologies that drive the sector have long since been absorbed, the basic value chains long since established, and the market structure long since stabilized. The only significant variables left are company execution within its market position and differentiation of its offerings—just what the five-forces model focuses on. But this is not the case in technology-enabled markets where power ebbs and flows based on companies mastering the disruptive technologies that create discontinuous innovations.

Historically, this has been a problem unique to high tech. With the rise of the Internet, however, companies in every sector of the economy are having to deal with the "dotcom" phenomenon. This chapter is intended, therefore, to help all executives rethink their model of competitive advantage for technology-enabled markets.

In the following model, competitive advantage is portrayed as an inverted hierarchy in which each lower layer provides a stronger basis for power in the marketplace:

Competitive-Advantage Hierarchy

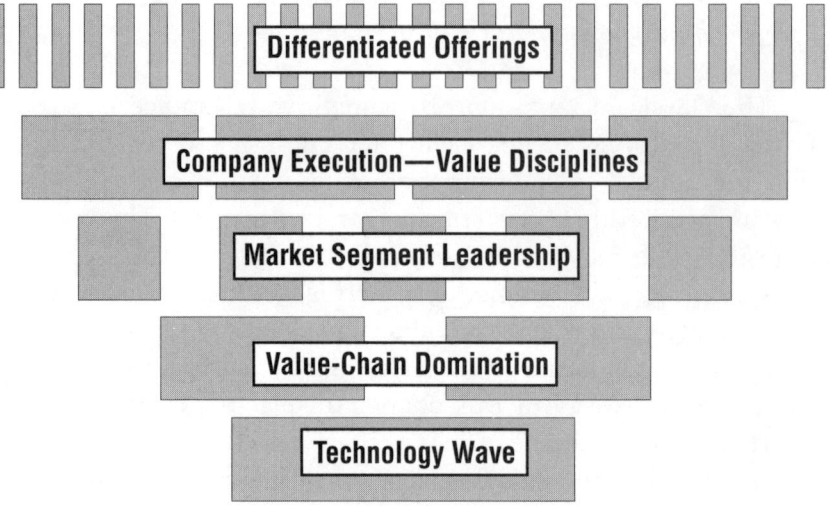

Figure 3.1

This *competitive-advantage hierarchy* should be read from the bottom up, as follows:

1. In high tech, competitive advantage begins with the categorical advantage of a new *technology* over an older one. That is, the highest form of competitive leverage comes from riding the adoption of a new wave of technology as it displaces an older paradigm. New paradigms rewrite all the rules of competition, making obsolete all market positions secured in the prior generation of technology. This is old news at IBM. It is new news at Barnes & Noble.

2. For this displacement to actually occur, the new technology must be integrated into end-to-end systems that meet existing customer needs. In the new economy, no one company is responsible for this integration; instead, it is the end product of a *value chain*, a voluntary alliance of companies coming together to create an economic benefit for customers and to share in the rewards thereof. Capturing a place in the new value chain is critical to sustaining competitive advantage during a technology shift because it enables your company to ride

with the rapidly increasing GAP and CAP of the new category instead of fighting it.

There are four phases of value-chain competition. The first is *new chain* versus *incumbent chain,* determining whether the new technology can gain a foothold for itself in the market-place. The second is *among emerging value chains*, each seeking to impose its standards on the marketplace at the expense of the other. This tends to have a winner-take-all outcome, so prudent companies will try to secure a place in every chain that has a chance of being the winner. The third and fourth competitions occur *within specific chains*, where individual companies jockey for power, both among their direct competitors for a specific role in the chain, and also with the other chain members over how profits are allocated across the chain. In these latter two competitions, the goal is to build power very much along the lines of Porter's five-forces model *while the chain is still fluid and forming.* In technology-enabled markets, once the chain has formed, it is often too late to effect changes in position as switching costs become increasingly high.

3. Initially the new value chains support a single integrated market defined simply by the new category of product—the PC market or the wireless phone market—but over time this one-size-fits-all approach inevitably compromises the unique interests of specific *market segments*. Where such compromised interests rebel, vertical markets emerge and create opportunities for companies that did not garner global value-chain power to gain local market-share dominance. Victories in one or more of these market competitions create strong GAPs and highly sustainable CAPs, but only over a limited domain of economic opportunity, and represent the third strongest form of competitive leverage, after technology power and value-chain power.

4. In competing for value-chain domination and market segment leadership, companies differentiate in their execution by prioritizing different *value disciplines*. One, for example, might choose to emphasize *operational excellence*, seeking price and quality advantage from highly efficient processes. Another might pursue *customer intimacy*, seeking higher margins

through differentiated customer service. There are a total of four of these disciplines—the other two being *product leadership* and *discontinuous innovation*—which we will explore later in this chapter. All are mechanisms for creating competitive advantage through focus. The immediate impact of focus is a higher GAP, but if it is sustained over time, it will be assimilated into the company's brand, giving it a reputation for a certain type of excellence, and thus contribute to its CAP as well.

5. Finally, none of the underlying sources of power in the competitive-advantage hierarchy can actually create shareholder value until companies ultimately transform them into *differentiated offerings*. They represent the surface of the model, the part that actually touches the customer. It is here that GAP is created through differentiation from other competing offers in the market. But no CAP can be created at this level. Thus companies that try to differentiate their offerings without building foundations in the lower strata of the hierarchy are doomed to be short-lived and undervalued.

AN EXAMPLE

Let's look at an example of how these various levels might play out in a technology-enabled market. Suppose Micron, a company that manufactures computer memory, was in competition with Samsung, another company that manufactures computer memory, for a big order at Compaq. This would be primarily an *offering versus offering* battle. Both companies would be leveraging the same technology in the same markets in cooperation with the same value-chain partners. Samsung, however, might compete primarily on operational excellence, leveraging its greater manufacturing scale to create a lower-cost offer. Micron, on the other hand, might compete on customer intimacy, promising more just-in-time delivery or special packaging that would differentiate their offer. In either situation, however, the companies would be playing the game in a mature market, which confines competition to the upper two levels of the competitive-advantage hierarchy.

By contrast, consider the history of Rambus, a high-tech start-up a fraction of the size of either Micron or Samsung, but one that has come to dominate them both. At the beginning of the 1990s Rambus proposed a discontinuous innovation—a wholly new approach to memory design that makes it operate much, much faster. Rambus decided it would not make nor even sell memory chips but instead simply license existing vendors the rights to their design. The goal was to emulate the way Microsoft licenses the Windows operating system to PC makers and by so doing to skim off as much profit while incurring as little capital outlay as possible.

The memory vendors were not amused and uniformly gave Rambus the cold shoulder. Since these vendors controlled access to the semiconductor fabrication plants, to the distributors, and to the PC makers, they assumed they could squash the little company like a bug. This is an example of an existing value chain defending its turf, and in most cases it works just as this chain had intended.

To make any headway, Rambus had to find a way to work around the incumbent value chain. Even though it had promised its investors it would go after the PC market, the first major design win for its technology came in fact from a game-playing machine. Nintendo sponsored a large special order of DRAM to Rambus specifications because it had a product leadership strategy that required a breakthrough in graphics-processing performance, one that conventional technology could not provide. Thus Rambus's first order was a *technology-based* victory. The company had no value chain supporting it, no marketplace power, no proven track record, and arguably no real product. Nonetheless, because its technology offered Nintendo an opportunity to gain dramatic competitive advantage, Rambus won the deal. The other memory vendors were not worried, however. This was a special order for a niche product and did not threaten their control over the PC market.

The next event of note was that other manufacturers in the game-machine market subsequently reacted to Nintendo's success by designing Rambus's memory into their products as well. This helped transform a technology-based victory into a *market-segment-based* victory. The company had won a sustainable position in a niche market. Again, because this was not a particularly big market and because it required significant customization to serve, it was not highly valued by, and thus not seriously defended by, the established memory vendors. But by securing a home market for itself, one that it could dominate and control, Rambus had transformed itself from a start-up with potential into a true going concern, a company that investors could reasonably expect to be in operation for years to come. A going concern enjoys a much lower discount for risk than a start-up, both from financial investors who are now more willing to provide capital at favorable rates and from partners who are now more willing to co-invest to develop future markets. So for Rambus this was a modest but world-changing event.

The really big world-changing event, on the other hand, came about when Intel realized faster memory was critical to unleashing the potential of its next-generation microprocessor. After surveying its options, Intel chose Rambus to solve this problem, largely because of its technology but also because it had demonstrated itself to be a going concern. Then, by virtue of its own *value-chain* power, Intel imposed its choice on the rest of the industry by building Rambus into the following year's reference design for the PC. Now the DRAM vendors were stuck, for the Intel reference design forms the mandate for the entire industry. So with much gnashing of teeth, they all signed up to license Rambus's technology. That is how Rambus leveraged the *value-chain* level of the competitive-advantage hierarchy (albeit using value-chain power "on loan" from Intel). The impact on the company's stock is that at the turn of the century, with trailing revenues of less than $45 million, the stock was valued at over $6.3 billion, or roughly 140 times revenues!

This story of Rambus exemplifies how the various underlying layers of the competitive-advantage hierarchy interact to create changes in the balance of power in a technology-enabled marketplace. That is, in technology-enabled markets, although at the surface the competition looks like it is between one differentiated offer versus another, in fact the outcome is decided at the lower levels of the model. In the rest of this chapter we are going to dissect these lower layers in some detail to determine how executive teams can harness them to their own companies' benefit. By the time you finish this chapter, you should have a comprehensive sense of what levers you have at your disposal to effect changes in shareholder value.

TECHNOLOGY-BASED COMPETITIVE ADVANTAGE

Technology provides the deepest layer of the competitive-advantage hierarchy because it generates the tallest GAPs and the longest CAPs. Specifically, we are talking about disruptive technologies that constitute discontinuous innovations, ones that offer an order of magnitude or more improvement in price/performance over the incumbent technology paradigm. Such technologies fall into numerous subcategories. Some, for example, never actually make it in the mainstream market—in a later chapter we will say that they failed to *cross the chasm*. These are of only passing interest to anyone except technology enthusiasts. Another subset consists of *process innovations* that are confined to a specific vertical market. These do not change the offer to the customer but dramatically reengineer the way that offer is created or delivered. As long as these are confined to a single vertical market, they are of extreme local interest but little global interest. A third subset consists of technology-based products that create whole new marketplaces all by themselves. In so doing, they call into being whole new value chains and markets to harness and commercialize this capability. Microprocessors, wireless telephony, inkjet printing, relational databases, and object-oriented programming are all disruptive technologies that have spawned new market sectors. In these cases the impact reaches across all markets as customers in virtually every sector of the economy seek to use the new technology to achieve a higher level of productivity.

The Internet combines the second and third subsets. Within the high-tech sector, the Internet challenges numerous existing market franchises, including the voice franchise of the telephony sector and the operating system franchise of the PC sector. At the same time the Internet also enables dramatic reengineering of all kinds of traditional business processes *on a global, not a segment-specific, basis*. It has become, to use the term that economist Joseph Schumpeter coined, an engine of *creative destruction*, meaning it is generating massive new wealth but at the expense of traditional sources.

Thus it is that the dynamics of technology-enabled markets are migrating beyond the realm of high tech and into the economy as a whole. As such, the lessons of Silicon Valley, which have heretofore made interesting but not required reading for managers in other sectors, now become a preview of coming attractions to a theater near you. We are all living on the fault line now.

As I enter my third decade in the computer industry, I have been witness to at least a dozen major technology shifts that have created whole new industry categories, each with its own value chain and notable gorilla leaders. They include:

1. *Mainframe computing:* IBM (360/370), MSA, Computer Associates

2. *Minicomputers:* Digital, Oracle, IBM (AS/400)

3. *Personal computers:* IBM (PC), Microsoft (DOS), Intel, Lotus

4. *Desktop publishing:* Apple (Macintosh), Aldus (Pagemaker), HP (laser printers)

5. *Local area networks:* Novell, 3Com (network interface cards)

6. *Client-server computing:* Microsoft (Windows 3.1), Oracle, SAP, HP (UNIX servers)

7. *Wireless telephony:* Ericsson, Motorola, Texas Instruments, Nokia

8. *Home computing:* Nintendo, Microsoft (Windows 95)

9. *Campus area networks:* Cisco, Bay Networks, Cabletron

10. *Internet wide-area networks:* Cisco, Sun, Compaq

11. *Worldwide Web:* Netscape, Yahoo!, AOL, Amazon, eBay, Microsoft (IE)

12. *Intranet computing:* Netscape (server), Microsoft (Windows NT)

13. *Handheld devices:* 3Com (PalmPilot), Microsoft (Windows CE)

And there are more to come, as companies like Oracle and IBM regear themselves to dominate a reemerging *application service provider* category (what we used to call service bureaus),

Microsoft and Novell suit up to provide worldwide *network direc-tory services*, and Cisco and Lucent prepare to battle for the rapidly converging carrier market for *voice/data/video networks*. So while in high tech these massive market-shaping movements are not everyday events, they are not exactly rare either, and man-agement teams must assume that one or more is likely to occur on their watch.

In each of these waves technology created shareholder value *categorically*. That is, the new technology performed at such a marked level of differentiation from existing offerings that it cre-ated a radically new GAP just by its presence in the offer. Andy Grove calls this the "10X" factor in his book, *Only the Paranoid Survive*. And that order of magnitude—technology that offers ten times the value of the status quo—shakes markets loose from their current value chains and transfers their allegiance to the evolution of a new one.

In high tech we saw the first 10X shift occur first when main-frame computers took on their status-quo competitor—phalanxes of clerks assembling or disassembling an endless flow of docu-ments and calculations. Then minicomputers, by eliminating much of the data-center overhead of mainframes, created a sec-ond 10X advantage, opening up markets for computing in engi-neering, manufacturing, and word processing. Personal comput-ers followed, leveraging advances in microprocessor technology to create a third 10X change, this time affecting individual produc-tivity. And so it went through all the categories listed above, and so it goes on today.

The first key take-away here is that just by participating in the innovative category, an offering gains the perception of a 10X advantage, even if it is not quite there yet. Similarly, just by partic-ipating in the new technology, the company gains the perception that it is riding the next wave, and its stock rises accordingly. That is, it wasn't just IBM whose stock shot up during the mainframe era, it was also the shares of Burroughs, Univac, NCR, Control Data, and Honeywell that reaped the gains of a 10X advantage over the status quo. And similarly, it wasn't just DEC and IBM in minicomputers, but HP, Prime, Data General, Four-Phase, and Wang. It wasn't just Apple and IBM in PCs, but also Commodore,

Atari, Amiga, and Osborne. And today, it is not just Cisco, Sun, and Compaq that are riding the Internet infrastructure build-out to prominence but also Brocade, Juniper, Alteon, Foundry, and Copper Mountain.

All that these companies have done has been to raise some sails—that is, bring to market some specific product offerings—that catch the 10X wind of a new *category GAP*. That wind is the fundamental driving force behind the technology-enabled markets. It can ultimately be traced to Moore's law, named for Gordon Moore of Intel, which projects an inexorable advance of semiconductor technology to finer and finer degrees of miniaturization, allowing for a doubling in the price performance of computer chips every eighteen to twenty-four months. Three doubles make for an 8X level of change, touching the threshold for the next disruptive technology to emerge. As long as Moore's law is in effect, we can predict a continuing series of new technology waves, each holding out its promise of the next 10X competitive advantage. And so it is that all strategy in technology-enabled markets must begin with identifying which waves we will ride, which winds we shall raise our sails to catch.

The other key take-away from my list of twelve discontinuous innovations is that *none of them has yet become obsolete*! The rise in IBM's stock at the end of the 1990s is in large part due to a reappraisal of the value of its mainframe and minicomputer franchises in light of the Internet's agnosticism relative to server operating systems. These systems are now entering their fourth decade of wealth generation, no longer the hot item to be sure, but still ticking. Even technologies that have been superseded, such as Netware LAN servers giving way to more general-purpose NT servers, still retain massive installed bases with huge switching costs that will keep them loyal, and investing, for a decade or more to come. Other technologies, such as client-server computing, can be expected to adapt to the next wave, in this case Internet computing, modifying their front-end presentation services while retaining their back-end business logic, and at the same time building continuously off their underlying platforms to generate a new class of applications for the front office.

Thus not only do fundamental technology shifts create 10X

advantages—generating tall GAPs—they also have deep persistence—*creating long CAPs*. Voice telephony is still a huge value generator a hundred years into its existence, and similar points can be made about radio, television, refrigeration, microwaves, and combustion engines. These were all at one point high tech, all passing through their own adoption life cycles with their own tornadoes. Those winds have long since died down, but the value chains they created persist and contribute large revenue and earnings flows to the economy.

All mature markets at one time were technology-enabled. Bookselling seems pretty staid now, but Gutenberg was recently called out as the most important person of the millennium for his contribution to printing technology. Automobiles and steel manufacturing are now Rust Belt industries, but in their day they completely redefined the American landscape. Clothing might not seem technology-enabled to us, but three centuries ago spinning and weaving were redefined in ways that threatened the very core of the industry, as the Luddite uprising made plain.

So it is not a question of whether your company operates in a technology-enabled market so much as when technology will next raise its head with a 10X innovation. Indeed, if you are confident that won't happen anytime soon, you can probably stop reading now. For everyone else, however, class is not dismissed.

TECHNOLOGY STRATEGY AND SHAREHOLDER VALUE

The critical point about fundamental technology shifts—when entire industry sectors emerge driving trillions of dollars of expenditures over multiple decades—is that there are significant gains and losses in competitive advantage *based simply on whether your company participates in the category or not*. Thus *not participating*, or as it more frequently manifests itself, *refusing to participate*, is the one cardinal sin. IBM's failure to participate meaningfully in UNIX client/server computing resulted in a huge loss in market power and a concomitant drop in stock price from which the company is only now recovering. Similarly, Digital missing both the PC and the client/server wave, Motorola coming late to digital wireless telephony, Kodak being slow to digital photography, and

HP coming late to the Internet have all cost their shareholders dearly. In every case the executive teams saw the trend in time but were held back because organizational inertia and, in some cases, hubris would not let them make the change. Thus it is a prime goal of this book to enable future executive teams to deconstruct such inertia when called upon to do so.

Conversely, start-ups that have successfully positioned themselves in emerging 10X categories have enjoyed the opposite effect. Their lack of inertia makes it easy for them to catch the new wave, and they become the "darlings" of Wall Street—a phenomenon nowhere better illustrated at the turn of the century than in market valuations for Internet stocks. Business models that are woefully immature are garnering huge price-to-sales ratios (and astronomical P/E's in the rare instances when there are earnings) because investors perceive—rightly, I would argue—that the emergence of Internet-based institutions represents a one-time transformation of the economic landscape that will change virtually all the rules of business. Indeed, the Internet is arguably more accurately described as a *100X change*. To stake out a claim anywhere in this powerful new space, therefore, at minimum creates an investable option on a future successful business play. In such markets, investors are not so much investing in a particular company as they are investing in an emerging business model, with the company's stock acting as a proxy for that opportunity.

This must seem strange indeed to executives in mature markets whose stocks are valued primarily on their current earnings. But stocks in emergent categories have always served as vehicles for investing in the *category*, not the company. We saw it in PCs, we saw it in biotech, and we are seeing it today in the Internet. The stock market sees a huge competitive advantage in the new technology and initially allocates that advantage to all new entrants. At the same time, it begins to question the GAP and CAP of the incumbent technology in light of this new challenge and to look to the management teams of these traditional vendors for guidance on how they plan to co-opt the new forces unleashed.

And that provides the key for how established vendors should proceed. The correct strategy is never to refuse to participate. It is always to "embrace and extend" (as Microsoft likes to put it) the new category. In the best case for the company's shareholders, this phrase translates into "domesticate and neutralize," co-opting the power of the new paradigm so that it does not overthrow the established pecking order. More frequently, however, it gets translated as "accept and make do," with established players having to come down in the pecking order a few notches. This is simply a consequence of conforming to a new technology that is not their strong point, but at least they are able to retain a respectable position in the market. The result to avoid at all costs, whether through inertia or denial, is getting locked out of the new market's future altogether.

Measured against this benchmark, the current market leaders in the computer industry have done reasonably well. IBM, to its credit, showed the way initially, leaping from mainframe to minicomputer to PC, and only missing at client/server. HP leapt from laser printers to inkjet printers. Cisco started in campus networking but made the shift through routing to the Internet, leveraging that success into an extraordinary data network equipment franchise, and now it plans to make the next shift to convergent voice/video/data. And perhaps most impressive of all, Microsoft has been legendary in its ability to "fast follow" into new technologies, as witnessed by the fact that it is mentioned in association with six of the thirteen categories listed earlier.

So when high tech is played at its best, the start-ups innovate, the best incumbents co-opt the innovation, and both succeed. At its worst, on the other hand, the management teams at heretofore blue-chip corporations vacillate, research, study, plan, discuss, propose, pilot, review, analyze, consult, critique, and when all else fails, hire consultants and hold focus groups—all in preparation for just plain losing. This is not because people in large companies have gone brain dead, although that is what their competitors love to allege. It is because they are well and truly in the grip of the innovator's dilemma. That is, they have become so optimized for managing continuous innovation within established technologies that their institutions simply cannot cope with the disruptive innovation of new technologies.

To remedy this condition, executives should begin with the realization that *you don't have to be the innovator to be innovative.*

Indeed, why should public companies fund innovation at a time when start-ups can take bigger risks, get access to more and better informed capital, and recruit and motivate better talent? In this new context, it is typically a better strategy—one currently employed by Microsoft, Cisco, America Online, and Lucent, among others—to let the little guys do all the work, let all the failures happen on someone else's nickel, and then either acquire the successes or co-opt them before they can truly threaten your market power.

CATCHING UP THROUGH ACQUISITIONS

In this context, one piece of good news is that acquisition, which used to be considered the liquidity event for a failed investment, is no longer viewed as such. Now instead there is a kind of reverse "make-versus-buy" decision operating within the entrepreneurial community. Start-ups can never match the extensive distribution capabilities, the established customer support systems, or the proven supplier network of a major enterprise; yet typically these are all needed to scale rapidly to achieve the global dominance it has promised its investors. Moreover, given the pace of competition in the age of the Internet, there is no time to try to build them. So why not merge into an institution that already has them?

The logic of these mergers is so compelling for both sides that it raises the question, why don't they happen more often? The answer, in part, is a matter of stock price misinterpretation. Established companies are measured by their earnings—the market thinks of them as P/E plays on Main Street. Emerging technology companies are measured by their growth—they are thought of as P/V or P/S plays approaching or caught up in a hypergrowth market. Separately each is well understood. When you merge the two, however, the growth numbers of the start-up often get lost in the mix. They don't show because in absolute numbers they are too small. As a result, the transaction is often perceived to be dilutive, particularly by the earnings-oriented investors who own the more established company's stock. This drives these investors to sell their holdings, which causes the stock to lose value, making the acquisition less attractive and often destabilizing the deal.

This is absolutely wrong-headed, but it is the default market response *unless the CFOs and CEOs of the merging companies can successfully recruit new growth-oriented investors to take up the slack.* To escape the trap of a purely P&L view, in other words, executives must articulate the full competitive-advantage case for the merger, how each company's GAP and CAP combine to create a synergy of greater value than either would have operating alone. This is the task that Steve Case and Gerry Levin have set themselves, seeking to get their respective shareholders behind the America Online/Time-Warner merger. The argument is rooted in the grafting of a new technology onto a trunk of established business operations, or vice versa, and it makes its case by analogy, not by the numbers. Unfortunately, this is unfamiliar territory for many executives, leading them to position the deal incorrectly or shun it altogether. The result is not just that their company misses out on riding the next wave, but worse, that it is now exposed instead to the wave's destructive edge.

To be fair, part of the reluctance of management to embrace such mergers is the fear that the predicted synergy will never be realized. Such was the result in the 1980s, for example, of IBM's acquisition of Rolm, Sybase's acquisition of PowerSoft, and AT&T's acquisition of NCR, all of which led to massive losses in shareholder value. But the 1990s has seen significant management progress on this front, as exemplified by Cisco Systems' powerful use of acquisition to co-opt the emerging LAN switch market (Kalpana, Crescendo), by IBM's entry into key enterprise software markets (Lotus, Tivoli), by Lucent's transition from voice switches into data (Ascend, Stratus), and by Microsoft's move into the Worldwide Web (WebTV, FrontPage). Going forward, as more and more sectors of the economy become exposed to technology disruption, it is hard to imagine how any company can thrive without making some use of this tactic.

To close on technology-based competitive advantage, technology waves determine multiple decades' worth of wealth creation and distribution. The significance for high tech is that the larger and more diversified a high-tech enterprise, the more critical to its shareholder value that *it participate in every single one of them.* This can hardly be a "core competence" strategy—no one can predict where the next wave will come from—and thus one cannot use internal R and D investment to ensure participation. Instead, these companies often must work backward from external events to construct investments and relationships that get them back in the running. It is no accident, therefore, that the vice president of business development is becoming an increasingly visible and powerful position in high tech.

For companies outside the computer industry, who with the arrival of a "dotcom" in their market are feeling the effects of disruptive technology for the first time in a very long while, catching the Internet wave will be a bigger challenge. If you find yourself in this position, your company is likely to be deeply enmeshed in legacy systems—both in the sense of IT systems and in the sense of business processes and relationships—that are incompatible with the new paradigm, and it is going to cost a carload of consulting fees to dig your way out. The biggest asset you can bring to the table at this juncture is customer loyalty. It is critical that you connect with those in your customer base who are able and willing to help shape your transition to the new paradigm. When established corporations do this in good faith, as Charles Schwab has done in investing, for example, or as The Gap has done in retail, their customers respond with intensified loyalty and stick with them through the natural pains of any major transition. At the same time, it is also key not to align with those customers who deny the value of the new change. They will simply reinforce your own biases and, if you are not careful, lull you to sleep.

VALUE-CHAIN-BASED COMPETITIVE ADVANTAGE

To actually get onboard with the new technology, companies must understand the value chain that is forming to support it and secure for themselves a powerful position within it. Failing to do so will relegate the company to the periphery of the market where it will fight for scraps and leftovers from better-positioned competitors.

Value chains are voluntary alliances of product and service providers coming together to provide a complete offering to a given set of customers. The metaphor of the chain is a bit simplistic—

they are almost always something more akin to value webs—but anytime things get presented in more than two dimensions, I get lost. So we will stick with chains for now. In cable television, for example, members of the value chain include manufacturers of TVs, VCRs, and set-top boxes; cable head–end equipment providers and cable broadcasters; service installation, billing, and maintenance organizations; and content providers, including the major TV networks, HBO, the Discovery Channel, and the like.

In technology-enabled markets, value chains tend to develop around a characteristic set of roles, as illustrated by the following diagram:

Technology-Enabled Value Chains

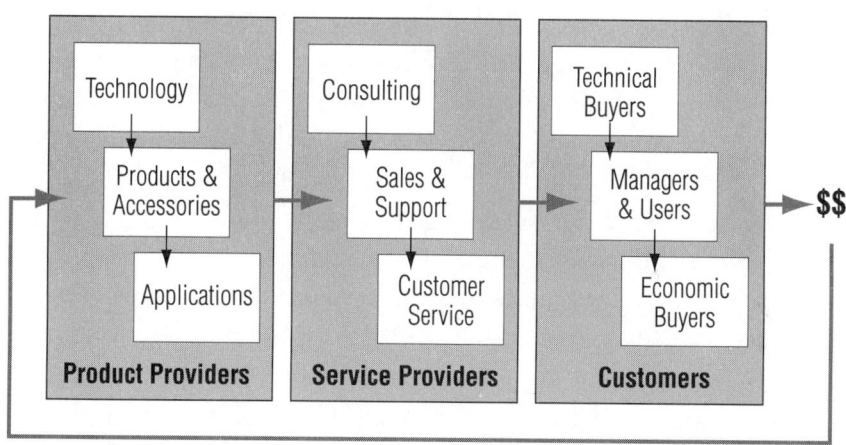

Figure 3.2

The goal of any company wanting to participate in the emerging market is to claim one or more of the product- or service-providing roles. In the computer industry, within the domain of product providers, there are three main options:

1. *Technology providers:* Be they the chip manufacturers, the software tools providers, the licensers of patents or other intellectual property, they provide the raw materials upon which everyone else builds.

2. *Products and accessories providers:* They transform the technology into all the computing devices that take up space in our offices, along with the databases, messaging systems, user interfaces, and other software that they incorporate.

3. *Application software providers:* They make technology-enabled devices useful with software that actually bridges the gap between a user's world of things and events and the computer's world of ones and zeroes.

Note the progression from raw technology to finished application. Within the domain of the service providers there is a parallel progression. In technology-enabled markets, services act as a shock absorber, evolving through three stages as technologies become more and more assimilated.

- *Consulting services:* Early in the assimilation process, when the technology is new and few customers have mastery over it, consulting provides high value, promising to integrate immature technologies and products into a useful and reliable application, often for the very first time.

- *Sales and support services:* As the technology becomes more prevalent, and users themselves take on more of the integration task, the service requirement evolves to one of sales and support, either directly from the product vendors or through an indirect channel.

- *Customer service:* Finally, when technology has been completely assimilated and there is no more technology shock to absorb, customers assign increasing value to simpler customer services such as on-line order status, vendor replenishment, broad selection of consumables, recycling, help desks, and the like.

The last segment of the diagram covers the customer domain. Note the arrow at the right pointing to the dollar signs. In technology-enabled business markets, the goal of all purchases is to make money. For that to occur, three things must transpire at the customer end of the equation:

- *Economic buyers* must agree to supply the capital necessary to purchase the products and services to the left.

- *Technical buyers* must successfully install the new system, deploy it to the appropriate users, train them, and then support the system going forward.

- *End users* must actually change their past behavior to incorporate the system into their work flow in order to gain the productivity benefits promised.

If all three roles do their piece, and if everyone else in the value chain does their part as well, then, and only then, does the customer actually make money. That money is crucial because when customers make money, they repeat the behavior that caused it, thereby making a market for the new technology. Everyone in the value chain, in other words, lives off a portion of the money that the customer makes.

Now, in consumer markets, the game is played for happiness points, not money. As such, there is less capital to put against new efforts, and thus consumer markets tend to come to the fore only after technologies have been well assimilated. Also, in consumer markets, the technology buyer, end user, and economic buyer tend to be the same person, although in families the roles can segregate depending on who the system is for and who is technologically competent. But at the end of the day the overall dynamics of the value chain are identical, with everyone in it living off money that is coming from the economic buyer's satisfaction.

Value chains, in sum, are simply internal wiring diagrams of markets, showing how each company makes a living in an overall flow of value and money. In the high-tech sector, as we discussed in Chapter 1, they were initially implemented through vertical integration and then migrated to virtual integration in the 1980s. It is worth taking some time to understand just how and why both paths came into existence. For that we need the help of an economist writing in the first half of the last century.

COASE'S THEORY OF TRANSACTION COSTS

The economist who best sheds light on this issue is R. H. Coase, who in the 1930s wrote an article entitled "The Nature of the Firm." Coase asked himself a few simple questions that are as compelling now as they were then: What exactly is a firm? Why does it grow to a given size and then level out? Why doesn't it grow larger? Why doesn't it level out sooner?

He framed his answers in the notion of *transaction costs*. Coase proposed that conducting transactions inside a company, where one can eliminate paying off the middleman, avoid sales taxes, and secure privileged access to scarce commodities, was inherently more efficient than doing so outside the company, and so over time, such transactions would migrate inside. At some point in this growth, however, he noted that the infrastructure needed to keep the internal value chains communicating efficiently and responsively would become bureaucratized to the point that it would become less responsive than the external market. At this size, increases in the company's competitive advantage from additional scale would be diluted, and other companies would be able to win and hold market share against it, causing the firm to cease to expand further. Thus a point of equilibrium would be reached that "explains" a company's given size.

This theory maps well to the history of the blue-chip companies that have made up the *Fortune* 500 for most of the past century. In the last ten years in the U.S. economy, however, as intercompany communications and commerce systems have become increasingly efficient, Coase's theory of transaction costs *has now begun to operate in reverse!* That is, the free market has become the low-cost provider of most transactions, and thus they are now migrating from *inside* to *outside* the corporation, with outsourcing, not insourcing, being the new low-cost play.

The reasons, as we already discussed in Chapter 2, are clear:

- Any task your company is doing in house to save money is one for which you must bear the *total cost*. But if another company is doing that same activity for other customers, then to do it for your business as well, that company need only bear the *marginal cost* of the effort. Marginal costs will always be lower than total costs.

- Add to this the idea that the bulk of all tasks needed to complete a whole product are not core to your company's competitive advantage. They are playing the role of hygiene factors, not differentiators, in your offer: If they are missing, your offer is unacceptable, but you do not gain any competitive advantage from doing them well. Now ask yourself, if some other company does this task for a living, so that they do gain competitive advantage for doing it well, and you do it because you have to, which organization is going to have the more efficient methods and the more progressive approach?

- Finally, realize that anyone you employ on these tasks in your company is in a dead-end job—this isn't your added value, it is just a necessary evil for you. That same person employed in a company dedicated to this type of work can be on a career path to be president. So who is going to get the best employees with the best motivation?

The conclusion from all of the above is simple: *virtual* rules! OK, let's not go off the deep end here. Virtual can only rule in economies and societies where intercompany commerce and communication is on par with or superior to intracompany processes for the same tasks. This is a relatively new state of affairs in the U.S. economy, and for much of the rest of the world it is not yet true, although one can see the changes coming.

Specifically, success with virtual value chains requires companies to significantly reengineer both culture and systems. On the culture side, they must come to terms with being both a supplier to and a customer of their direct competitors. Business values, in other words, must migrate from win/lose to win/win ideas. Thus IBM is now supplying disk drives to its archrival EMC and personal computers to its archrival Dell Computers—but only after fifteen years of struggling with its corporate values and culture to get there. And on the systems side, without all the investment in supply-chain applications and without the Internet, one could not coordinate a virtual value chain to make the "just-in-time" responses needed to win new markets and customers. That is why it is only just now, and only largely in the United States, that this new ecosystem is performing optimally, and even here it is operational only in some sectors of our economy.

But wherever these requisite conditions can be met, low-cost transactions must inevitably migrate outside the corporation. And that in turn explains why it is that small businesses, and not the traditional *Fortune* 500 companies, are generating all the new jobs in our economy. The giant corporations that built themselves up to a given size via the traditional approach to managing transaction costs will be downsizing for a long time to come. Indeed, many of them can be expected to downsize to death. They simply will not be able to make the cultural and systems adjustments needed and will instead watch helplessly as their stock price decomposes to the point where investment bankers parcel them out for absorption into more adaptive enterprises.

It is the wish and the intent of this book that this never happen to your company. If you are at risk, then the next section is written especially for you. There, by tying value-chain performance to stock price, I hope to give you the leverage you need to drive the changes that must occur.

THE GAP AND CAP OF VALUE CHAINS

In a virtualized economy, the basis of economic competition shifts from company versus company to value chain versus value chain. Pragmatic customers understand this very well. They know that as the winning value chain gains market share over its competitors, its customers are going to be better served in the long term. That is, wherever market share goes, the third parties who make up the discretionary resources in the market follow. More third parties augmenting one value chain make that chain's offerings more varied, more complete, and more cost-effective than its competitors. That fact in turn attracts more customers, which in turn attracts more partners, creating a virtuous cycle of increasing returns to the winners, and increasingly slimmer pickings for the also-rans.

Once this cycle starts, the winning value chain enjoys increasing GAP leading to increasing CAP. This condition, as we saw in the previous chapter, will always attract investment. That results in every company participating in the winning value chain getting a boost to its company GAP and CAP, and conversely, companies excluded from this chain getting discounted. This has major implications for strategy.

Consider the fate of Motorola's microprocessor business over the past two decades. In the 1980s, Motorola introduced the 68000 series to compete with Intel's 80X86 series. Virtually everyone who compared the two chips preferred the Motorola design. It is said that even Intel considered releasing a chip that was pin-compatible with it. Motorola won all the competitive design wins save one: They won at Sun, at HP, at Apollo, at Apple. The only one they lost was the IBM PC, where after all, Intel was the incumbent and all the software was Intel-only compatible. Hard to imagine a team doing any better than that.

But it was all for naught. The IBM PC dominated its rivals, and every member of its value chain—Intel, Microsoft, Lotus, and the like—rode its success to market leadership. To be sure, there were fights *within* the IBM value chain—the WordPerfect word processing software ousted MicroPro's WordStar for example—but between the chains it was a wipeout. Motorola's reward for designing the best chip of the 1980s was to be a second source for IBM's Power PC chip in the 1990s and, going forward, to get out of the microprocessor business altogether heading into the twenty-first century. At the time of this writing Motorola is trading at a market cap of around $100 billion, Intel at roughly four times that.

This is a cautionary tale. It does not suggest that you can always pick the winning value chain in advance. What it does suggest is that you cannot afford to be permanently isolated from the winning chain going forward. Thus WordPerfect and Lotus, both software market leaders in the DOS value chain, eschewed the Windows operating system in favor of OS/2. When the former value chain rose to power nonetheless, they were left out in the cold, losing their respective markets to Microsoft Word and Microsoft Excel. These were devastating losses that could have been mitigated, perhaps even prevented, by hedging bets across multiple value chains.

The key take-away from this discussion is that *choosing value-chain partners cannot be left solely to the discretion of the technical team.* All too frequently, however, that is precisely what happens. After all, what do any of the rest of us know about the internals of a database engine? But while it may be true that the Progress database is better for application development than Oracle, the fact is that QAD, the ERP vendor who committed to Progress, is fighting an uphill battle against a much more powerful value chain, and suffering the consequences. At the end of the day, it is the market-dominating solution, not the most technically elegant one, that creates the strong GAPs and long CAPs needed for sustainably high stock market valuations.

PLAYING THE VALUE-CHAIN GAME

While the term *value chain* has been in circulation for some time, the nature of value-chain dynamics in technology-enabled markets is not widely understood outside the high-tech sector. In stable, mature markets, value chains are relatively inert so that, once the power relationships are understood, they do not need a great deal more attention. In some cases, as Adrian Slywotsky and others writing on *value migration* have made clear, the primary value-creating role in the chain can migrate, say, from the product producer to the service provider. Such migrations indeed have implications for strategy that are well worth thinking through. But even that experience does not prepare one for grasping how this model plays out in an emerging, technology-based market.

In such a market, at the outset the value chain simply does not exist. It must be brought into existence for the marketplace to form. But you cannot simply plan and execute this outcome because value chains are self-organizing systems. Like flowers, you can seed and fertilize and water them but you cannot actually *make* them grow. Moreover, as they take root and grow, they mutate in form dramatically as they work their way toward their mature state.

All this makes for some intriguing dynamics that we will look at in some detail in the next chapter. Before leaving the topic here, however, I want to deal with a set of recurring questions that consistently challenge management teams making value-chain strategy decisions.

1. *When faced with a choice of supporting multiple competing value chains, how should companies determine where to allocate their resources?*

This question arises in markets where you are essentially value-chain agnostic. That is, from the point of view of your offer, it doesn't really matter which chain the customer uses so long as you are compatible with it. The critical challenge here is to minimize the cost of supporting multiple chains, for the only added value you can pass on to your customers from such investment is protecting them from ending up on the wrong value chain as well.

The primary lesson of the 1980s in this context was, *Do not bet the farm on a single choice!* That is the lesson Lotus and WordPerfect taught us at the cost of their core franchises and eventually their companies' independence. Despite the pain of supporting multiple chains, as long as the outcome is in doubt, if your core franchise is at stake, you simply must.

The primary lesson of the 1990s has been, *Don't fight Microsoft!* Actually this is not the correct conclusion to draw, although it is one that can be easily forgiven. The correct statement is: *Do not fight the market-dominating choice, even when capitulating to that choice puts you at an immediate disadvantage*. Unless you have a well-formed contrarian strategy with a manageable exit strategy, it is better to be a subordinated member of a winning value chain than a privileged member of a losing one.

Finally, however, once the winning value chain has emerged, there is much to be gained and little to be lost in consolidating into it immediately. Being loyal to losing value chains is a poor use of investor capital and frequently leads to a less competitive product on the key platform. This is how VisiCalc lost out to Lotus 1–2–3 in the initial spreadsheet wars by neglecting to optimize for the IBM PC.

2. *For companies that are the primary sponsors of value chains, how can they maximize their shareholder returns?*

The single most powerful form of value-chain advantage occurs when one company gains proprietary architectural control over the future specifications of an entire end-to-end solution and thus over all the other members in its value chain. IBM gained this level of control over the mainframe server market and its AS/400 minicomputer market. It had it but lost it in the PC market, where Microsoft and Intel eventually came out the big winners. Today Cisco has this kind of control over the core infrastructure build-out of the Internet. We call all such companies *gorillas*.

A gorilla company owns a proprietary technology that has become the de facto standard for its marketplace. No other company has the right to modify this technology going forward. As such, when new releases of its technology come out, all the other partners in the value chain must adjust their forthcoming offers to maintain compatibility. This gives the gorilla enormous power to manipulate the system to its own advantage, punishing certain companies through deliberately introducing incompatibilities to stifle their new offers, rewarding others by deliberately designing them into the new standard. Over time, every company in the value chain becomes subordinated to the gorilla, an increasing share of the profit margins from the category migrate to the gorilla, and short of seceding from the market or garnering regulatory intervention, there is nothing that anybody can do about it.

It should not be surprising, therefore, that the shareholder value of gorillas is huge. Their GAPs are tall because:

- They have no direct competition (the only market-acceptable solution is the one that is proprietary to them) so their price margins remain high.

- By manipulating the standards, they can migrate all the high-value-adding functions into their portion of the whole product and all the low-value-adding functions into one or another partner's piece, thereby further improving their margins.

At the same time, gorilla CAPs are long because:

- The market cannot find a substitute for them, and thus their competitive-advantage period ends up being equivalent to the CAP for the entire category.

- Despite resenting them, their partners actually work to ensure they stay in power because the entire value chain depends upon them being able to continue to make the market from which each member makes its living.

Thus if your company has even a slight chance of becoming a gorilla, this must be an obsessive focus of the executive team.

At the same time, however, executives must acknowledge this to be a low-probability event. There have been only a handful of gorillas in the history of high tech, and defenses against new ones emerging have never been stronger or more prevalent. To understand how one might become the next gorilla, then, one first has to appreciate what the market is doing to prevent that outcome.

3. *What can companies do to defend themselves against the emergence of a gorilla in their value chain?*

This must be a persistent focus of every company in high tech that seeks to maintain control over its fate in the marketplace. Let a gorilla in your life, and you will find yourself losing a little more GAP and CAP every year. You must seek to block this outcome.

The fundamental gorilla defense lies in open-systems standards. If the whole product specifications form around conventions and interfaces that are determined by independent standards bodies or that are already in the public domain, then no one company can gain monopolistic control over the rest of the value chain. No one, for example, controls the fax standards, modem standards, current TV standards, DVD standards, or Internet standards. As a result, while competition in these markets is fierce, no vendor has to pay tribute outside its product domain to some market maker.

Customers have become as sensitive to this issue as vendors, having discovered that they are the ultimate source of any such tribute paid—hence the effectiveness of "open systems" as a rallying cry in market competitions. This in turn has led to an "Of course, we're open" response from all vendors, even those that hold gorilla aspirations. There is simply no percentage in declaring yourself proprietary, and no one does, except through innuendo when communicating with investors.

All this leads to two key executive behaviors. The first is, if you have gorilla aspirations, you must never declare them, as nothing is surer to unite the rest of the value chain than the threat of an emergent gorilla. Instead, announce an open-systems strategy, publishing the key interfaces to your technology for all to use, and then offer some "extra value" technology that is proprietary, hoping to hook customers or partners or both. This is a known ploy, of course, but if your offer happens to enable a killer app, and thereby kicks the market into hypergrowth, such that you and only you are the hypergrowth platform, then known ploy or not, the value chain will form around you because sitting out hypergrowth is never a viable choice.

The second behavior to learn is, if you get even a whiff of a gorilla position developing around some other company in your marketplace, you must immediately ring the alarm bell loud and clear, point dramatically to the offending party, and lead a unanimous call for them to recant their offensive ways. The rest of the marketplace will join you in this outcry, for they are as concerned as you are about gorilla subordination. Thus, for example, when 3Com launched its 56KB modem with proprietary technology that was incompatible with Rockwell and AT&T's competing 56KB modem, the market, led by Microsoft, called foul, refused to embrace either one, and threatened to create its own standard instead, until the vendors finally capitulated and committed to a common platform.

As long as the alarm is raised prior to a hypergrowth market forming, this tactic will either effect the retreat you desire or isolate the company from its needed value-chain partners—in either case resulting in an end to the gorilla threat. But you must be vigilant in policing the market because gorilla rewards are so great that new gorilla threats appear constantly.

4. *What can companies with established value chains do to prevent a disruptive technology from forming a new value chain to go after their markets?*

Prior to *The Innovator's Dilemma*, the most common strategy was to stonewall. Established companies focused on creating FUD (Fear, Uncertainty, and Doubt) among prospective customers about the new entrant, pointing to the technology's incompatibilities with existing investments, the rawness of the products, the complete absence of a market track record, and the instability of the company's financials. All four of these issues send shivers up pragmatist spines, and so this technique proves generally effective—*with existing customers.*

The problem with this strategy is that the barbarians have learned not to attack the fortified hills. Instead, they now go after some marginal segment in the market where customers are not served well by the established vendors, seeking to gain momentum there and then to grow into more valued and defended market spaces. By the time they reach the spaces you care about, these attackers have developed financial credibility to complement their market momentum, have products that are no longer quite so raw, and by virtue of the new value chains they have formed elsewhere, have whole products that may actually be superior! Now, too late, you and your fellow established value-chain partners institute a fire-drill response, but the market can see who the real winners will be and responds accordingly.

The correct competitive response, instead, as we noted earlier, is for incumbent gorillas to co-opt discontinuous innovations as soon as they appear. Microsoft has done this as well as any company on the planet. Consider pen-based computing. When it first showed up in offers from GO and Momenta and the like, and industry analysts like Dick Shaffer began to build conferences around the new platform, Microsoft jumped into the mix with its own pen-based operating system offer. This diffused the sense of urgency needed to create a new value chain because, after all, if Microsoft was going to be there with something "relatively soon," why take risks with anybody else? Well, as it turned out, relatively soon never actually came about, GO and Momenta both went under, and the pen-based effort at Microsoft went on the back burner. But then along came PalmPilot, and all of a sudden there really *was* a pen-based market, and by golly, Microsoft really *was* there with a rival OS in Windows CE. Far from being a purely defensive maneuver, it has now mutated into an information appliance platform and plays a major role in Microsoft's future, integrating into the existing suite of value chains that Microsoft already dominates.

The key take-away here is that Microsoft's entry and subsequent actions in the pen-based market were directed neither by its customers nor by its direct sales force nor by its resellers. None of those constituencies wanted to see a Windows CE operating system. Indeed, as we shall see later in this book, current customers and the salespeople who serve them are two of the most conservative forces in any company's environment, and companies that allow themselves to be directed by these two constituencies will always miss the next paradigm shift. Instead, Microsoft was directed and motivated first by a competitive threat and second, as it came to process its response to that threat, by a revised strategic vision for where the market might go in the future. That's the attitude and behavior that executive teams should seek to emulate.

5. *What can sponsors of disruptive technologies do to incubate a new value chain despite the efforts of the established players to block its formation?*

To put it simply, if perhaps self-servingly, follow the strategies laid out in *Crossing the Chasm*. The key is to target a niche of customers who are under pressure to restructure their operations but are unable to do so in the context of the existing technologies. Such customers are being radically underserved by their current vendors, not because the vendors are doing a bad job, but because the world has changed in a way that was not anticipated, with the result that systems that used to work just fine are now radically out of line with the new requirements.

At The Chasm Group we have a generic name for these target customers—*department managers in charge of broken, mission-critical business processes.* Every word in this phrase has been carefully chosen.

- It is *department managers,* not line-of-business executives, and not IT executives, because when the world shifts, and the old processes fail, they do not break everywhere at once, but instead crack first in a single department, and it is these departments' managers who find themselves on the hot seat.

- The processes must be *broken,* not just bent, because nothing other than total flameout will cause a niche of customers to readily abandon its current value chain and embrace an as-yet unproven technology offer.

- They also have to be *mission-critical* processes or else the executive to whom the department reports won't have the leverage to get the funding needed to reengineer it. Discretionary funds in current departmental budgets are far too small to pay for crossing the chasm.

- It has to be a *business* market, not a consumer or public sector market, because only businesses can bear the capital burden and move fast enough to create a new value chain before the incumbents wise up to the threat and block it.

The good news for start-up companies is that established companies rarely if ever compete for these markets. The phrases *niche markets* and *vertical markets* give them the willies. From their perspective, the total market size is too small, the work too hard, and the sales cycle too challenging to take them on. From a start-up's perspective, on the other hand, the market size is bigger than whatever it has now, the work is easier (well, at least more repeatable) than the early-market projects it currently has in hand, and the sales cycle is a whole lot more predictable. So it will be motivated to focus here while the established companies won't. That's the good news.

The bad news is that it will be hard to get value-chain partners to focus with you, for all the same reasons that established companies lack interest. The difference is, however, that you are not asking them to sponsor the market development effort. That you will do. All they have to do is to follow your lead. That's a big difference, enough of one to recruit in the rest of the team, *provided* you have the market development capabilities and funding, are able to demonstrate to these partners an interesting sales pipeline within one quarter of announcing the program, and help them close some actual new sales in the following quarter.

The point of a chasm-crossing strategy is that it is *the fastest way to incubate a value chain*. Until you have an operational value chain to get your offer into the mainstream market on a reliable, ongoing basis, while you can still win customers on a one-off project basis, you cannot generate any *marketplace momentum*. That is, in an established value chain, customers get up every day and *on their own initiative* place orders with vendors for the offers they provide. In addition, every day every other partner in that value chain actively sells these same offers such that your company gets added deal flow *with virtually no additional effort*. By the same token, of course, your sales efforts create similar deal flow for your partners. It all adds up to a virtuous circle—*but only after the value chain has formed*.

So why is it so hard to get companies focused on making this happen? The answer is that most executive teams flinch in the face of demand for extreme focus. They are not thinking about value-chain incubation. They are thinking about sales prospects within established markets. In order to get a good return on those marketing investments, it is often wise to include multiple target customers, with multiple reasons to buy, leading to a whole product that is complex to configure, and a battery of partners and allies who have to be vetted before the prospect can go forward. Established markets can handle these extra burdens. Markets that lack value chains in place, however, cannot. So while it is very scary to bet on a single roll of the dice, recall that you are fighting *a time-to-value-chain-formation battle* where focus can simplify the whole product and speed the first market's formation.

This brings our discussion of competitive advantage through managing virtual value chains to a close. It represents the most radical shift in management philosophy driven by the age of the Internet. As already mentioned, while these ideas have been understood in business schools for some time, they have not migrated swiftly into the boardroom or the executive suite. But if there is one thing that sets Silicon Valley apart from other technology-oriented locales, it is that everybody here "gets" virtual value chains. As a result business development can happen at a much faster pace, and the Valley as a whole can sustain its competitive advantage and generate high valuations for its companies' stocks. For industries outside the high-tech sector, value-chain management represents the single most important focus as the market transitions to a technology-enabled structure.

MARKET-BASED COMPETITIVE ADVANTAGE

Market-based competitive advantage acts as a balancing function to value-chain competitive advantage. To the degree that a company accumulates the latter, it will be less concerned about the former, and vice versa. Here's how it plays out.

Value-chain leaders benefit from large homogeneous markets where demand is defined primarily by the *product category*. Such markets put the full power of the value chain behind the company's offers. Thus Microsoft and Intel position themselves in the PC market, Cisco and Lucent in the network equipment market,

Oracle in the database market, SAP in the enterprise application market. In every case, this positioning works well for the companies in question because they are the market leaders using product category as the defining element. All other things being equal, why wouldn't you buy from the market leader?

This approach works fine when your company wins the dominant position in its product category. But what about all the other times? Now you need to find some basis other than product category for defining your markets, else you will position yourself perpetually behind the lead dog, where the view is if nothing else obstructed. The way forward lies in redefining your market in terms of one or more specific target customers. That is, to overcome a rival company's value-chain power, you must generate market-based competitive advantage through segment-specific, customer-centric offers. Such offers trump those from market leaders whenever meeting the segment's unique needs outweighs a default preference for buying from the category leader.

Market-based strategies win by creating exceptional GAPs through specialized offers. Sometimes the specialization lies within the product, the result of extensive customization. More frequently, it is a function of the whole product, a result of orchestrating a specialized value chain to meet the unique needs of the niche market served. In this case, everyone in the chain trades off volume for status, gaining local power for being number one in the niche market by focusing the preponderance of their discretionary resources on this one set of customers. In return, the customers receiving this privileged treatment reward the niche value chain with their business and their loyalty. Thus this strategy also generates long CAPs, albeit solely within the boundaries of the niches served.

Although niche markets by definition are smaller than global markets, they have their compensating benefits, beginning with low-cost marketing communications. Consider that niche markets are, essentially, social institutions—aggregations of people who interact with each other regardless of whether your company markets to them or not. This means you need spend no money bringing together an audience for your messages; the audience is already assembled. Moreover, if you are addressing a critical need for your target niche, you may count on the fact that your potential audience is already talking to one another about the problem you intend to solve. All marketing must do in this instance is insinuate your story into the target community, letting its existing word-of-mouth communications channels transmit positive marketing messages about you.

A second benefit of niche markets is that their specialized needs are typically not addressed by the global market leaders, who find them inefficient to address, requiring too great an allocation of resources for too little return. As long as your company can overcome its own resistance to such an allocation, the field is wide open. Thus niche marketing allows companies of virtually any size to gain dominant market positions within the restricted area of the targeted segment.

It is important not to underestimate the extent of these benefits. Niche market leaders enjoy the same kind of GAP and CAP benefits in their restricted space as value-chain-based leaders do in the broader market:

- They become the local de facto standard, and all the other systems in the market must eventually conform to their interfaces regardless of what the global value-chain standard is (thereby increasing the reliability of their offer and lowering its cost of maintenance).

- Sales prospects in the market will be predisposed to select them because they will have already learned through word of mouth that they have the right solution to their specialized needs (thereby lowering the cost of marketing and sales as well as increasing the perceived value, and thus the price margin, of the offer).

- Current customers will be predisposed to remain loyal to the vendor whom they see as having made a deep commitment to their marketplace, voluntarily creating a barrier to exit while creating high barriers to entry for a competitor as well (all resulting in low cost of sales and higher forecastability of revenues).

- Partners will be predisposed to trade favors in order to get in on the winning ticket in this market (further lowering the cost of marketing and increasing the value of the offer).

- Competitors, in the face of all this, will learn to go elsewhere to sell their business (further lowering both the cost of sales and marketing, as well as reducing pressure on price margins).

In terms of competitive advantage, it doesn't get any better than this. However, these advantages come with three companion liabilities—restricted growth opportunities, complex solution requirements, and complicated sales and provisioning processes. Initially these obstacles are offset by the upside gains just enumerated, but eventually they conspire to block further valuation growth.

At this point, to increase shareholder value further, a market-based strategy must adopt a "bowling pin" approach, leveraging success in the first niche to gain entry into an adjacent niche. It has two forms of leverage from its initial segment victory to assist it in this project:

1. Strong customer references, which help gain entry into niches that have frequent contact with the "head pin" niche, and

2. Highly differentiated solutions, which are valuable for approaching niches that have a related problem set.

Via one or both of these, niche marketing can spread itself from one segment to another to another, thereby gaining scale.

Scalability is not, in other words, a function of initial segment size. Instead, it is a function of linking together a series of related niches, perpetually keeping the produce-centric value-chain leader at bay through deep niche-specific differentiation. Niche marketers, in other words, do not look to find the biggest diamond—they look to make the longest string of pearls.

Finally, in executing a bowling pin strategy it is critical to maintain the commitment to extreme customer focus. The classic mistake companies going into their second and third niches make is that they never actually replicate the customer intimacy that won them their first market niche. That is, they start acting more and more like product-centric companies despite all their rhetoric to the contrary. As a result, each subsequent market position becomes less authentic and less secure than the previous one until finally their offers become indistinguishable from those of the value-chain leader.

This is obviously a losing game. What is truly insidious about it, however, is that it takes a long time to lose. That is, customers are so starved for customer-centric attention that they will give a proven customer-centric vendor the benefit of the doubt far longer than otherwise because of their reputation from the previous niche. In fact, they may think this diluted form of attention is the real thing—how would they know differently? The problem is, sooner or later the shallowness of the offer comes through, the disillusion sets in, and the search for alternative vendors recommences. This in turn has a disastrous impact on the niche vendor, who was counting on keeping the market captive, and thus their whole marketing strategy unwinds.

So the key take-away about market-based strategies for market development is, if you talk the talk, you had better walk the walk. Easy to say, harder to do, of course, but the rewards are real.

THE GAP AND CAP OF MARKET-BASED COMPETITIVE ADVANTAGE

Once the dynamics of market-based competitive advantage are understood, the critical issue becomes, *How good are the niche markets we are in?* Here we are interested in the GAP and CAP that comes from "owning" these markets. That is, does the fact that the preponderance of our business comes from these markets and not others work to our advantage or disadvantage? Simply put, companies that own dominant positions in "good markets" get better valuations than those that lead in "bad" ones.

For example, as technology buyers the pharmaceutical industry and financial services have traditionally outspent the rest of the economy, whereas industries such as construction and real estate have underspent. In the 1970s and 1980s, aerospace and defense was a great market to have customers in; in the 1990s it has been just the opposite. Education has crying technology needs, but it is a terrible market from an investor's point of view— not only is it underfunded, but its buying processes are so time-consuming and politicized as to defeat any high-growth market-based strategy.

The GAP advantage of dominating a specific market is a function of how much more spending these customers will do compared to the global market in general. By this measure some markets are markedly cyclical. They oscillate between being flush with cash and being close to dead broke, alternately overspending and underspending, what we sometimes call the drunken sailor syndrome. The oil and gas business has this property, with a bumper sticker in Texas telling the whole story: *Lord give me one more oil boom, and I promise not to piss it away.* From an investor's point of view such a market—and we can include here the semiconductor industry as a market along with the agriculture market as well—can only lead to grief. The stocks of the companies that serve them can never settle down into a predictable earnings pattern and thus will be perpetually discounted for risk, even when times are good.

By contrast the technology sector, as a customer, has been a great market for the past decade, particularly for technology-enabled offerings. One example will suffice. Throughout the 1990s, as value chains became more visibly important, supply-chain planning became a hot new category in enterprise software. Two companies, i2 and Manugistics, were the leaders in this category. Manugistics's customer base, however, was centered in consumer packaged goods, whereas i2's was based in high tech. When the category took off, high tech adopted it much more aggressively, and thus i2's revenues skyrocketed past Manugistics's. It thus became established as the gorilla in the category, while its competitor lost its way, a victim, among other things, of market category GAP.

Market segments also confer CAP benefits as well. The CAP of owning a market has to do with its perceived durability as a good customer. Do we think that automobiles are here to stay? Then companies dominating some part of the supply chain into this industry should have strong CAPs. Conversely, however, do we think that automobile dealers are here to stay? I would argue that the Internet severely threatens the viability of such dealerships as we know them, thereby foreshortening the CAPs and undermining the valuation of those vendors who have focused on this market as their primary business. In market-based strategies, in other words, it is key not only to target niches that one *can* dominate but also to target ones *worth* dominating.

To sum up, market-based competitive advantage is a combination of targeting advantaged markets that can offer upside growth and creating defensible positions that can offer sustainably strong profit margins. The amount of commitment required to secure this type of advantage is significant, and investors would prefer in general to put their money into value-chain leaders that can dominate multiple markets with a single product. But only a very few companies are so successful in value-chain domination as to be able to build their entire strategy around it. For most companies at least some of the time, and for many companies virtually all of the time, their GAPs and CAPs would be greater, and investors would be better served, if they focused more of their efforts on the market specialization we have been outlining.

EXECUTION-BASED COMPETITIVE ADVANTAGE: THE ROLE OF VALUE DISCIPLINES

We have now reached the penultimate layer in the competitive-advantage hierarchy. Each step up has been accompanied by a diminishing set of consequences. That is, if your company missed out on a technology wave, it could be fatal. If it misses out on joining the winning value chain, it will be painful indeed, but the situation is recoverable. If it misses out on niche markets, it will still slog along, albeit suboptimally. Now we have come to the realm of *company execution*, and specifically creating competitive advantage by excelling at a single value discipline. Failing to leverage this layer is like failing to exercise properly. You won't notice any consequences in the short term, but as the market competition moves into its later rounds, don't expect to make it to the final four.

In contrast to market advantage, which is driven primarily by external factors, execution advantage is largely a matter of internal choice. Given a finite amount of resources, how should your company focus them to create differentiated offerings in the marketplace? What, in other words, is your company's strategy for *adding unique value*, and what *core competencies* are required for it to execute on that strategy?

These questions have been tackled particularly effectively in a book by Michael Treacy and Fred Wiersema called *The Value*

Disciplines of Market Leaders. Value disciplines are core competencies that add value to create differentiated offerings. The authors explore three in their book—*product leadership, customer intimacy,* and *operational excellence*—to which I have added a fourth—*discontinuous innovation*—for the specific purposes of understanding technology-enabled markets.

The Value-Disciplines Model

Figure 3.3

The particular configuration of this diagram and the relationships it implies among the various value disciplines will be discussed in Chapter 6. For now, simply consider each discipline in and of itself as a way of creating differentiated value in a potentially crowded market.

- **Discontinuous Innovation.** Companies leveraging this discipline compete by providing *a completely new category of offering.* Rather than fight incumbent competitors for market share within existing markets, they create new markets where there is no direct competition. Because this approach attacks the very foundation of the existing market, it is rarely championed by the current market leader.

Charles Schwab took this approach when it founded the first discount brokerage, Apple when it created the first personal computer, and eBay when it invented Internet auctions. In every case dramatic innovations in underlying technology made possible the creation of a new category.

- **Product (or Service) Leadership.** Companies leveraging this discipline compete by providing *feature-differentiated products or services*. They consistently field unique offerings and get them to market ahead of their competitors.

  Companies challenging established market leaders typically use this strategy. Think of Cray competing in this way against IBM, Olimar golf clubs against Callaway, or Southwest Airlines against United and American Airlines. At other times, companies use this tack to take a market by storm themselves, as PalmPilot did with its pocket-size organizer, Nokia with its long-life cell phone, or Federal Express with its guaranteed overnight delivery service.

- **Operational Excellence.** Companies leveraging this discipline compete by providing *low-cost products or services*. Their offers are differentiated on value rather than on features—they are cheaper, more reliable, and more broadly available than those of their competitors.

  This strategy is particularly prevalent in mature markets, be they commodity industries like power generation, bulk chemicals, or oil and gas; mainline manufacturers like General Electric, Motorola, or Toshiba; or discount retailers like Wal-Mart, Costco, or Crown Books.

- **Customer Intimacy.** Companies leveraging this discipline compete by providing *differentiated customer experiences*. They consistently anticipate customer preferences and exceed customer expectations, surrounding a relatively undifferentiated offer with a highly differentiated end-user experience.

  Premium-price product brands typically leverage this approach, including companies like Nike, Porsche, and Mont Blanc. The same can be said for premium-price service brands, including the Mayo Clinic, Nordstrom, Disney theme parks, and the Four Seasons Hotels.

Each of the companies cited above has succeeded in part because it has focused intensely on a single value discipline as a way to outexecute its competitors relative to a specific dimension of value. Everyone inside the company knows which discipline gets top priority, and all decisions are colored by this emphasis. The result is a highly differentiated enterprise that stands distinctly apart from its competition. For those customers who value that company's focus, the choice of vendor becomes obvious.

The lesson here is that value disciplines work best when they can stand out as differentiators. This implies singular commitment. Many people, however, interpret committing to one discipline as somehow devaluing the others. They would prefer instead to try to execute on all value disciplines equally well. But there are conflicts and trade-offs involved, and so this well-intentioned approach most often creates a mishmash of compromised efforts and a highly *undifferentiated* market position. It is far better, therefore, to privilege one discipline as *core* and treat all the others as *context*.

Indeed, value disciplines, as we shall see in the last chapter, are a key aid to identifying and communicating what is core and what is context. The prescription is to take any one of the four disciplines, privilege it as core, declare the other three context, and then reshape your company's operations in that light. Basically, the goal is to outsource everything that is not core and to put all of your time and all of your best people on assignments that directly further the chosen value discipline. In general, progress toward such a goal should be evolutionary, not revolutionary, if there is time—else you run the risk of re-creating the reengineering backlash of the previous decade. But value-discipline analysis and commitment can set a clear direction.

In sum, I am a big fan of value disciplines. That being said, however, technology-enabled markets pose a serious challenge to their underlying philosophy of focus. As we shall see in the next chapter, as these markets emerge they evolve through four different stages in rapid succession. At each stage, different value disciplines are required and rewarded, and the markets are so competitive that neglecting or ignoring the required value discipline is not an option. As a result, companies cannot rest in any one value-discipline posture until after the market has fully matured.

This creates enormous challenges for management teams, particularly those that have successfully focused on a single value discipline in the past. Specifically, their hard-earned commitment to that discipline causes them to reject the response the market is demanding. It is, in effect, the innovator's dilemma. To solve the dilemma, executive teams must first come to understand the dynamics of technology-enabled markets (the focus of Chapter 4), then unwind themselves from the internal forces that prevent them from embracing new waves of technology (the subject of Chapter 5), and finally reinvent their core culture so that going forward they can support value-discipline focus without denying marketplace requirements (the subject of Chapter 6, the final chapter).

It is a long journey, and we are but halfway there.

DIFFERENTIATED OFFERINGS

The power of differentiated offerings, and how they change over the course of the technology adoption life cycle, is a topic worthy of a book all to itself. And indeed, just such a book is being written in parallel with this one by my colleague at The Chasm Group, Paul Wiefels. Its title is *The Chasm Companion,* and it, too, will be released in 2000.

In that book Wiefels outlines a nine-point checklist for constructing differentiated offerings in technology-enabled markets, as follows:

- Identify and characterize the target customer

- Establish compelling reason to buy

- Define the whole product

- Recruit the needed partners and allies

- Field the appropriate distribution channel

- Establish an appropriate pricing strategy

- Identify the competition

- Establish a differentiated positioning

- Look ahead to the next target customer

Differentiation is not actually made explicit until the next-to-last bullet point, *positioning*. All the previous items in the list are elements of differentiation that have to be clarified in order to get the positioning right. Thus, one offer gains advantage over another by targeting a customer that the other offer neglects, by focusing on a buying motive that the other offer shortchanges, or by pulling together a more complete offer for that particular customer and buying motive. Once the offer is defined, further differentiation can come from the quality and completeness of the value-chain partners both for selling and fulfilling the offer, as well as from differences in pricing. This galaxy of six elements is then compared to comparable galaxies forming around competitive offers, out of which a differentiated positioning is created, one which positions not only your company's offer but all the competitors' offerings as well. The ninth and final element is to understand what new target customer one would go after, assuming the campaign to win this target customer is successful.

What *The Chasm Companion* makes clear is that, over the course of the technology adoption life cycle, as market dynamics shift from stage to stage, so does the nature of winning differentiated offerings. At each stage, the market privileges a different target customer with a different compelling reason to buy, leading to a different whole product, and so forth. This has enormous implications for executing market development programs, and Wiefels goes into these at length.

For the purposes of this book, it is enough that executive managers coming to grips with the challenge of the fault line know that such material exists. It is not required that we master it here. And so with that thought in mind, let us close this chapter.

SUMMARY OF KEY POINTS IN CHAPTER 3

Following up on the previous chapter's claim that shareholder value is a function of competitive advantage, this chapter has sought to give executives a model of how competitive advantage operates in technology-enabled markets. The goal is to provide strategy-setting groups with a framework of forces to consider, complementing the five-forces model of Michael Porter.

This framework consists of a hierarchy of forces in which the deeper the level, the greater its power to shape outcomes at the surface, as follows:

1. The deepest and most influential level of competitive advantage comes from *catching the technology wave*. Miss the wave, and there is no recovery. Catch it just right and it will catapult you to extraordinary heights. Come in somewhere in the middle—as most companies do—and you had best know a lot about how to work the other levels of the hierarchy.

2. The next level up is *value-chain leadership*. In its most modest form, this equates to having the largest market share in your category. This gives you de facto a major role in any value chain that requires your product or service. In its highest form, value-chain leadership transforms itself into *value-chain domination*. In this context, a company, through proprietary architectural control over a crucial piece of technology, gains "gorilla power," allowing it to orchestrate the entire value chain to its advantage on a global basis for the duration of the paradigm. If you have a shot at achieving value-chain domination, you must go for it. If you do not, you must ensure that nobody else gets it either.

3. The middle level of the hierarchy is *market-segment leadership*. Achieved through intense focus on meeting the needs of one or more specific niche markets, it results in local monopolies where enterprises that lack global power can orchestrate specialized value chains to their advantage. Niche market domination is key to creating sustainable positions in market com-

petitions where the other guy won. It is also the fastest way to incubate a new value chain.

4. The fourth level of the hierarchy is *company execution*. This is the domain of value disciplines, where companies must choose how they will focus their energies to create maximum value for their customers and their shareholders. Where the upper levels of the hierarchy create a relatively level playing field, as they do in mature markets, this level becomes the primary focus of management strategy. However, during the evolutionary stages of technology-enabled markets, an unwavering focus on a single value discipline causes failure.

5. Finally, at the surface of the hierarchy are *differentiated offerings*. We did not discuss this layer at length, leaving that to another book, *The Chasm Companion*, by Paul Wiefels.

Now that we have the various elements of the hierarchy in focus, and a sense of the relative power of each, we need to understand how they play out over time in the evolution of a technology-enabled market. That is the job of the next chapter.

4

LIVING ON THE FAULT LINE

The fault line upon which technology-enabled businesses are built is the technology adoption life cycle. It causes dramatic shifts in alignment among the various strata that make up the competitive-advantage hierarchy. As a result, competitive-advantage positions that once seemed secure are abruptly overthrown, and management teams on the verge of congratulating themselves now must scramble to recover. Here's how it plays out.

Before a disruptive technology can be assimilated into a mainstream marketplace, it must pass through multiple phases of adoption during which the market behaves in different ways specific to each phase. The end goal of all these mutations is to create and populate a sustainable value chain that can transform the new technology into reliable, deployable offerings. We call this goal Main Street, a state of business maturity in which technology-enabled businesses resemble most other sectors of the economy.

To reach Main Street, however, technology-enabled markets must pass through three prior phases. There are thus four phases of adoption in all, and each one rewards a very different market development strategy. Indeed, the competitive-advantage strategy that brings success in any one phase causes failure at the next stage. This creates extraordinary management challenges for organizations that develop momentum and inertia around any one stage.

Depending on when and how your company rose to prominence, you could have gone through your last technology adoption life cycle several years or several decades ago. That will determine to some degree your familiarity with the material covered in this chapter. Its goal is simply to lay out the market dynamics involved so that they can be readily understood by all involved in setting strategy. Then in the remainder of the book we will tackle the organizational challenge of coping with so much variability while trying to maintain a coherent business and a consistent culture.

I would like to start by reminding everyone once again that the fault line, this thing that is driving us all crazy even as it brings enormous wealth creation into the economy, is all Moore's fault! Not me, not Geoffrey Moore—*Gordon Moore*! To be specific, Moore's law, which observes that the semiconductor industry doubles the price/performance of its products roughly every eighteen months, is at the heart of the continuous eruption of disruptive technologies that has characterized the last twenty years. You can just do so much more new weird stuff nowadays than you ever could before because there is so much more horsepower to do it with. Moreover, as these disruptions build upon previous disruptions, both their frequency and their cumulative impact are increasing, so that we all feel like we are riding up a monstrous wave that shows no sign yet of cresting.

The Internet is in some sense a culmination of all this disruption and at the same time the starting point for another even bigger wave. Because it will radically shift power and wealth creation in virtually every sector of business, it is in effect a fault line running under the entire world economy. The offer it makes is at once exhilarating and terrifying—totally change what you are doing (terror) in order to achieve an order of magnitude greater effectiveness (exhilaration). This is the classic fault-line offer—discontinuous innovation enabled by disruptive technology. It has been studied at length under the heading *diffusion of innovation,* and the model that best describes its impact is the technology adoption life cycle.

THE TECHNOLOGY ADOPTION LIFE CYCLE

The technology adoption life cycle models the response of any given population to the offer of a discontinuous innovation, one that forces the abandonment of traditional infrastructure and systems for the promise of a heretofore unavailable set of benefits. It represents this response as a bell curve, separating out five sub-populations, as illustrated in the following figure:

The bell curve represents the total population of people exposed to a new technology offer. The various segments of the

The Technology Adoption Life Cycle

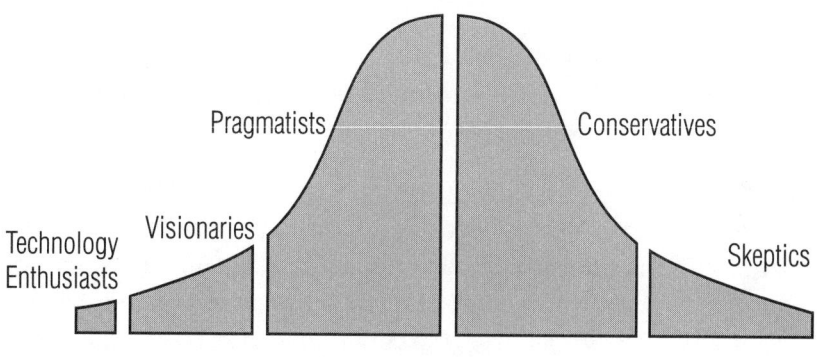

Figure 4.1

curve represent the percentage of people predicted to adopt one or another of the five different strategies for determining when and why to switch allegiance from the old to the new. The five strategies unfold sequentially as follows:

1. The *technology enthusiast* strategy is to adopt the new technology upon its first appearance, in large part just to explore its properties to determine if it is "cool." The actual benefits provided may not even be of interest to this constituency, but the mechanism by which they are provided is of great interest. If they are entertained by the mechanism, they often adopt the product just to be able to show it off.

2. The *visionary* strategy is to adopt the new technology as a means for capturing a dramatic advantage over competitors who do not adopt it. The goal here is to be first to deploy an advantaged system and use that head start to leapfrog over the competition, establishing a position so far out in front that the

sector realigns around its new leader. Visionaries are mavericks who want to break away from the herd and differentiate themselves dramatically.

3. The *pragmatist* strategy is directly opposed to the visionary. It wants to stay with the herd, adopting the new technology if and only if everyone else does as well. The goal here is to use the wisdom of the marketplace to sort out what's valuable and then to be a fast follower once the new direction has clearly emerged. Pragmatists consult each other frequently about who's adopting what in an effort to stay current but do not commit to any major change without seeing successful implementations elsewhere first.

4. The *conservative* strategy is to stick with the old technology for as long as possible (a) because it works (b) because it is familiar, and (c) because it is paid for. By putting off the transition to the new platform, conservatives conserve cash and avoid hitting the learning curve, making themselves more productive in the short run. Long term, when they do switch, the system is more completely debugged, and that works to their advantage as well. The downside of the strategy is that they grow increasingly out of touch for the period they don't adopt and can, if they wait too long, get isolated in old technology that simply will not map to the new world.

5. Finally, the *skeptic* strategy is to debunk the entire technology as a false start and refuse to adopt it at all. This is a winning tactic for those technologies that never do gain mainstream market acceptance. For those that do, however, it creates extreme versions of the isolation problems conservatives face.

Each of these strategies has validity in its own right, and a single individual is perfectly capable of choosing different strategies for different offers. But for any given technology, the market will develop in a characteristic pattern due to the aggregate effects of a population distributing its choices in the proportions outlined by the bell curve. The resulting market development model looks like this:

Technology-Enabled Market Development

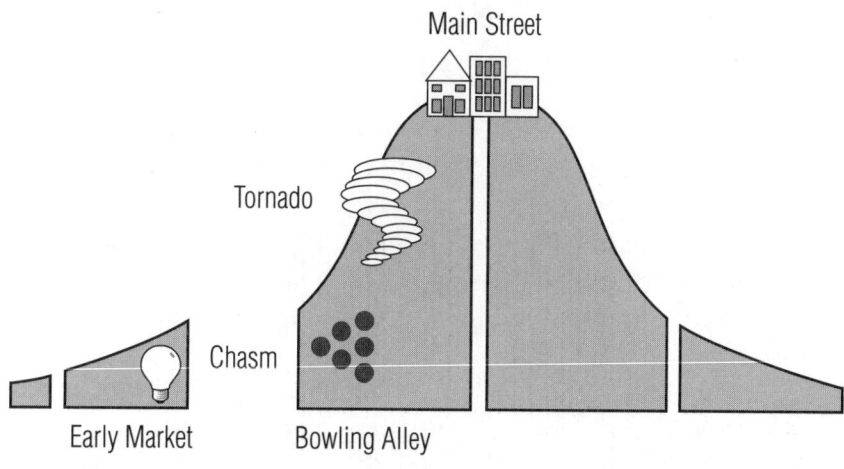

Figure 4.2

The model segments the evolution of a technology-based market as follows:

- The first phase, or *early market,* is a time when early adopters (technology enthusiasts and visionaries) take up the innovation while the pragmatic majority holds back. The market development goal at this stage is to gain a few prestigious flagship customers who help publicize the technology and celebrate its potential benefits.

- The early market is followed by a *chasm,* a period of no adoption, when the early adopters have already made their choices, but the pragmatist majority is still holding back. The barrier to further progress is that pragmatists are looking to other pragmatists to be references, but no one wants to go first. The market development goal at this stage is to target an initial beachhead segment of pragmatists who can lead the second wave of adoption.

- In the development of most technology-enabled markets, specific niches of pragmatic customers adopt the new technology before the general pragmatist population. We call this period the *bowling alley* because the market development goal is to use the first group of adopters as references to help win over the next group, and the next, and so on. Typically the "head bowling pin" is a niche of pragmatists who have a major business problem that cannot be solved with current technology but that does respond to a solution built around the new innovation. These are the *department managers in charge of a broken, mission-critical process* that we discussed in the previous chapter. Once this first group starts to move it takes much less of a motive to overcome the inertia of the next group.

- As pragmatist adoption builds in niches, one of two futures emerges. In one, adoption continues to remain localized to niche markets, creating a pattern we call "bowling alley forever." In this pattern, each niche's solution is relatively complex and differentiated from every other niche's. As a result, no mass market emerges, and the market development goal is simply to expand existing niches and create new ones as the opportunity arises.

  In the other pattern, a "killer app" emerges—a single application of the innovative technology that provides a compelling benefit that can be standardized across multiple niches. The killer app transforms niche adoption into mass adoption, creating an enormous uptick in demand for the new technology across a wide range of sectors. We call this period the *tornado* because the onrush of mass demand is so swift it creates a vortex that sucks the supply out of the market and puts the category into hypergrowth for a number of years. The market development goal here is to win as much market share as possible during a period when the entire market is choosing its supplier for the new class of technology-enabled offering.

- Once the supply side of the market finally catches up with the backlog of demand, the tornado phase subsides, and the market reaches a state we call *Main Street*. The new technology has been broadly deployed and, with the support of conservatives, now settles down to a (hopefully) long engagement as the incumbent technology. The market development goal here is to continuously improve the value of the offering, decreasing its base costs, and recouping margins by increasing the number of value-adding extensions that can supplement it. The ultimate extension in many cases is to convert the offering from a product sale to a services subscription, allowing the customer to gain the benefit of the product without having to take on the responsibility for maintaining it.

It is important to note that the end of the technology adoption life cycle does not represent the end of technology's productive market life. The category of offering can be sustained indefinitely on Main Street, coming to an end only when the next discontinuous innovation renders the prior technology obsolete. Indeed, despite all the emphasis on shortening life cycles, Main Street markets normally last for decades after complete absorption of the enabling technology—witness the car, the telephone, the television, the personal computer, and the cell phone. Importantly, however, the marketplace pecking order set by market share that emerges during the bowling alley and tornado phases tends to persist for the life of Main Street. That is, while Main Street represents the final and lasting distribution of competitive advantage, its boundaries get set prior to arrival. Thus success in every prior stage in the life cycle is key to building sustainable Main Street market success.

WHERE WE ARE HEADED

In this chapter we are going to work through the dynamics of each of these stages, focusing on three elements, as follows:

1. *What the market is trying to accomplish independent of the desires of any individual participant within it.* The framework for this discussion will be the value-chain model and how, at each stage of the market, different relationships are privileged and come to the fore. The goal here is to describe the forces at work in the market and to set the context for what any individual company can hope to accomplish at each phase.

2. *What kinds of competitive advantage are useful at each stage.* The framework here will be the competitive-advantage hierarchy

model and how, at each stage of the market, different forms of competitive advantage are privileged. The goal here is to align company ambition with market intention and to focus company management on the right critical success factors for each phase. What makes this so challenging on the execution front, where making a strong commitment to a single value discipline is the preferred tactic, is that at each stage the market rewards two of the four value disciplines and penalizes the remaining two.

3. *What impact success at each stage has on stock price.* The framework here will be the GAP/CAP valuation model and how, at each stage of the market, GAP and CAP can be expected to mutate. The goal here is to align management with shareholders, displacing the P&L statement with stock valuation as the key metric for company performance for all the market phases leading up to Main Street, where the two will finally rejoin each other to interoperate to the same end.

At the end of this review, we will have a comprehensive framework for understanding how to manage for shareholder value at each stage in the development of a technology-enabled market. We will, in other words, know the drill. The goal is to have no ambiguity on this front. That will then leave us with the extraordinary challenge of transforming our organizations to execute to this agenda, a task we will leave to the remainder of the book.

One last word of warning. The surgeon general is concerned that the remainder of this chapter may cause *market model vertigo*. There are a total of sixteen diagrams in the chapter as a whole, which vastly exceeds the recommended limit for vehicles of this size. All I can do is beg your indulgence. If I could have found a way to do this with fewer, I would have. So please, fasten your seat belts for the duration of this flight, and if need be, arm yourself with one of those little bags.

STAGE-ONE ADOPTION: THE EARLY MARKET

VALUE-CHAIN STRATEGY

The early market begins with the ambitions of two constituencies who live at opposite ends of the value chain.

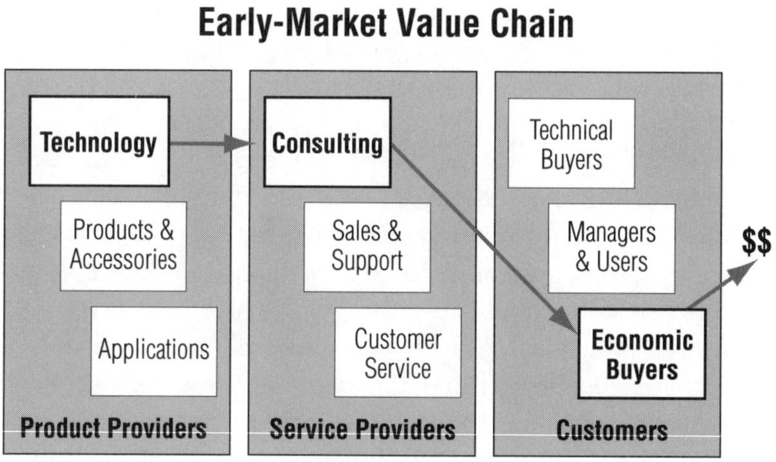

Early-Market Value Chain

Figure 4.3

On the left is the *technology provider,* the supplier of the discontinuous innovation, with ambitions of constructing an entirely new marketplace based on a new platform. On the right are one or more visionary executives, in the role of *economic buyer,* who also have ambitions of their own. They want to rearchitect the marketplaces they participate in to install their company as the new market leader—and they want to do it fast. They see in the new technology an opportunity to disrupt the established order and insert themselves into the lead.

Between these two poles, however, there is at present no existing value chain that can link their ambitions. Indeed, the existing value chain is appalled by them. There is, however, one institution in the market that can bridge the gulf between the two, can transform the technology provider's magic into the economic buyer's dream, and that is the *consulting firm*. Rather than try to incubate a value chain in the marketplace, this consultancy will instead create a temporary value chain to serve a single project's specific needs. That is, they will pull together the products, the applications, the sales and support, the customer service, and in extreme cases even substitute their own people for the customer's technical buyer (and even for the customer's end users), all to make the value chain work *in a single instance for a single customer.*

Needless to say, this is an expensive proposition. But if it pays off, if the sponsoring company really does leapfrog over its competition in a new market order, then the visionary becomes a hero, and whatever money was spent was pocket change by comparison to the appreciation in the customer company's stock price.

So much for the primary players in the early-market value chain. Every other constituency exists in some marginalized role. Thus products are not yet really productized, and applications exist primarily in presentations as opposed to in the real world. In the services sector, sales, support, and customer service are all organizations that are just ramping up. Technical buyers in corporations are leery of taking responsibility for anything this immature, and managers and end users in general think it is way too early to be reengineering their functions. Note that these constituencies are not deleted from the diagram—they are very much present during an early-market project—but they are treated more as obstacles than as allies.

What makes the early-market value chain distinctive is that the consulting services function is playing many, many roles. To do so, it must operate inefficiently in that it must take responsibility for tasks for which it has no previous experience and no currently trained resource. People who can rise to this challenge are scarce, and thus the organization must bill out its services at rates that substantially exceed those of standard contract labor. Moreover, since there is as yet no market for the new technology, once the project is done, there is not likely to be another like it in the pipeline, and thus the resources and their learning will be dispersed. Again, this drives up the costs of the project as they cannot be amortized across other efforts. Thus scarcity creates inefficiency, which in turn further exacerbates scarcity.

The end result is that neither the value chain nor the market persist past the end of the project (hence the absence of an arrow showing how money recycles to create additional business). In the early market, that is, customer sales are so few and far between that each effectively must be treated as a one-time event. Service providers can make money under this model, although it is a challenge to do so; product providers simply cannot. Although the customer is not price sensitive, and thus does not require a discount to close the sale, there simply is not enough repeatable business to make the economics of a product-focused business model work out.

COMPETITIVE-ADVANTAGE STRATEGY

In a market with no persistent value chain, what kind of competitive advantage can a sponsor of discontinuous innovation hope to leverage or achieve?

Competitive Advantage in the Early Market

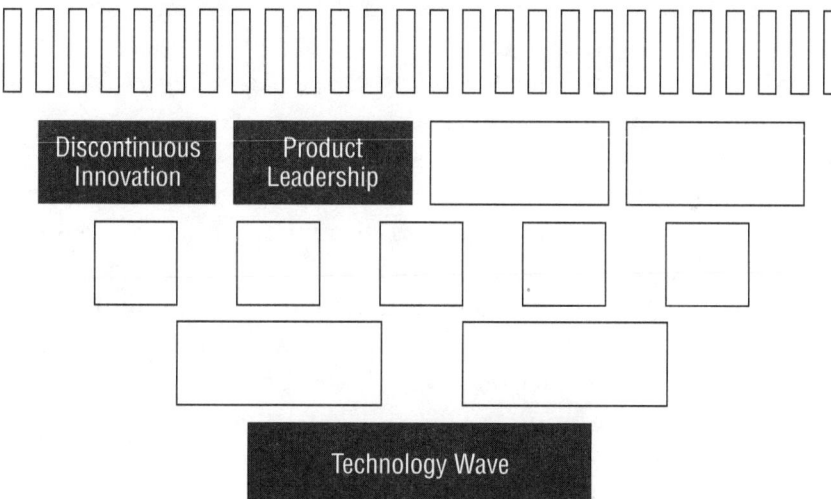

Figure 4.4

As the diagram indicates, the primary competitive-advantage strategy for the early market consists in being first to catch the new technology wave. This is often called *first-mover advantage*. Amazon.com, by catching the Web retail wave first, has created a powerful brand that its competitors cannot hope to replicate, regardless of how much they spend. By being first to introduce auctions onto the Web, eBay gained first-mover advantage also, so that even when assaulted by an alliance of extremely powerful companies—Microsoft, Dell, Lycos, Excite—it has been able to sustain market share. Four years into Web advertising, the top ten sites, with Yahoo! leading the list, garner as much as 85 percent of the total spending—largely because of first-mover advantage. The SABRE system for airline and other travel-related reservations has had a similar track record, even as Apollo and Galileo and others have entered the market. Same with United Airlines' and American Airlines' frequent-flyer systems.

In every case, first-mover advantage equates to getting the market started around your unique approach and making the others play catch-up. It is a great strategy—when it works. The risk, of course, is that the market never goes forward to adopt the paradigm. At the time when the visionaries make their moves, this is a high probability. Visionaries are always bucking the odds in that most markets, like most mutations, die out before they can reproduce themselves sufficiently to gain persistence. Indeed, market creation is very much like the origin of species in nature, with the early market equating to the emergence of at least a few vital representatives of the new order.

The key metric of competitive advantage at this stage is simply the existence of proof of having one or more such representatives. For the technology provider, the test is one or more major corporate commitments from prestigious customers who champion the new paradigm as a platform for change in their industries. For the customer, the test is whether on top of this new platform an industry-changing offer can be promulgated. Neither measure is financial. Neither measure uses market share. The goal in both cases is just to validate the category. That puts the new wave on the map, enters it in the race.

The benefit to the company sponsoring this new initiative is that it gets a lot of attention. This attracts prospective customers to it at no additional cost of marketing. It also positions it as something of a thought leader in its industry. At the same time, however, it starts a timer ticking, with the expectation that within some definable period dramatic results will appear. If they do not, then the customers lose face, and the technology providers lose their company.

To sum up, for technology providers competitive advantage comes solely from positioning for a future market and not from gaining value-chain or market-segment advantage in an immediately exploitable market. There is a key implication here for corporate strategy—at this point in the life cycle one should not invest to build either value-chain or market-segment advantage. Thus, the technology-providing organization should not at this point be ramping up sales, marketing, customer service, manufacturing, procurement, logistics, human resources, information systems, or even financial projections. The only supply-side institution that should be making such plans is the professional services organization, which, because it is not tied to any particular new technology, can amortize its investment across a portfolio of "all the new stuff." For everyone else on the supply side, however, early-market build-up of infrastructure is bad strategy.

On the customer side, the primary competitive advantage to exploit is time. First-mover advantage decays, so this is a competition that goes to the swift. Prudence is not the order of the day—the whole enterprise is by definition imprudent—and should be supplanted instead by aggressive risk taking. The goal is not to be stupid or ostentatious but rather to act boldly on the assumption that the envisioned market, which today does not exist, will emerge before the investment capital runs out. One can manage the capital to some degree, but one cannot wait and see, one must bet on the come. This is the fundamental premise of venture capital, and this approach is standard procedure in Silicon Valley. But elsewhere, with other types of capital, or operating within established corporations, this mode appears reckless in the extreme, and forces accumulate quickly to tone down its aggressiveness.

This is the pattern of events chronicled in *The Innovator's Dilemma*. Ironically, although recurrent management reviews represent an attempt to reduce risk, their effect is actually to increase it. Once one has entered into a time-based competition, the one resource that must not be wasted is time, and that is precisely what does get wasted as sponsoring institutions deflect more and more management energy into investment justification instead of market creation.

VALUE DISCIPLINES FOR THE EARLY MARKET

In order to execute on a winning agenda, management teams must understand that the early market rewards discontinuous innovation and product leadership and penalizes customer intimacy and operational excellence. Thus optimal results are gained by elevating the former and suppressing the latter, as follows:

Elevate: *Discontinuous Innovation, Product Leadership*

The early market is driven by the demands of visionaries for offerings that create dramatic competitive advantages of the sort that would allow them to leapfrog over the other players in their industry. Only discontinuous innovation offers such advantage. In order to field that innovation, however, it must be transformed into a product offering that can be put to work in the real world. Hence the need for product leadership.

Suppress: *Customer Intimacy, Operational Excellence*

When technologies are this new, there are no target markets as yet and thus customer intimacy is not practical. Moreover, discontinuous innovations demand enormous customer tolerance and sacrifice as they get debugged, again not a time for celebrating putting the customer first. At the same time, because everything is so new and so much is yet to be discovered, it is equally impractical to target operational excellence. There is just too much new product, process, and procedure to invent and then shake out before pursuing this value discipline would be reasonable. Instead, as we noted in Chapter 1, one has to make peace with the strategy "Go ugly early."

Looking at the above, it is not surprising that engineering-led organizations, who resonate with the value disciplines in favor, are much more successful at early-market initiatives than marketing-led or operations-led organizations, who lean toward the value disciplines that should be suppressed. Going forward, as we look at each subsequent phase of the life cycle, we will see that the rewarded and penalized disciplines change and so will the types of organizations that can be most successful.

STOCK PRICE IMPLICATIONS

Technology-oriented investors take great interest in early-market developments, hoping to get in on the "next big thing" before the bulk of investors catch on to it. At the same time, however, they are wary of falling prey to a lot of hype that never turns into sustainable competitive advantage. Their dilemma is reflected in the following diagram:

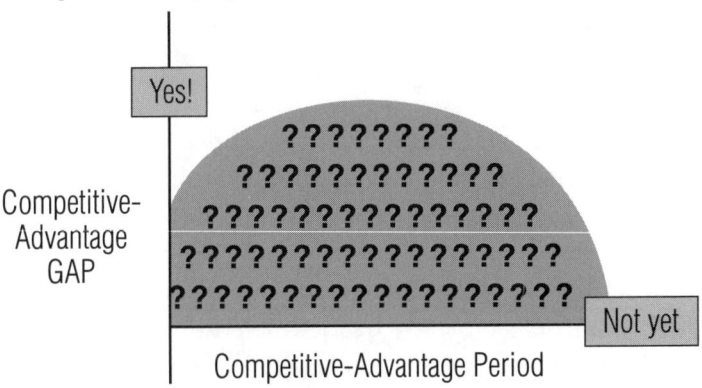

Impact of Early-Market Success on Stock Price

Figure 4.5

The chart calls attention to both the positive and negative implications of what has been accomplished—namely, that a few customers have made a major commitment to the new technology. On the positive side, this can be taken as proof of the concept that there is a true GAP. This is a big step up from theoretical GAP, and it calls into being the *shadow* of a GAP/CAP chart.

On the negative side, however, there is no proof of any CAP. There is no evidence of a sustainable marketplace as yet. That is why we have a shadow of a chart. Because there is no persistent value chain in view, it is not clear yet exactly how much ground has been captured. Hence the question marks: Is this, or is this not, the next big thing?

Nonetheless, if the company sponsoring the innovation is a venture-capital-backed start-up, the impact of early-market success is huge. Consider that its first round of funding was based on the current market value of a wing, a prayer, and the founding team's personal reputations. To get a second round at a higher valuation, it needed to garner at least one flagship customer. Now it has. Depending on how high the flag got raised and how broadly it unfurled, second-round valuations can enjoy increases of several hundred percent or more. Where has this new value come from? It has nothing to do with the actual revenues or earnings, although the bigger the deal, the better. Instead, it has everything to do with the usefulness of the new customer in communicating the value proposition of the company and demonstrating first-mover advantage. That is what captures the imagination and enthusiasm of the second-round investor. So winning a flagship deal in the early market is a very big deal for start-ups.

For large public companies, however, the issue is more problematic. Here total corporate revenues and earnings play such a dominant role in valuation that the communication of early-market wins, which typically do not show up in the numbers, must be managed carefully in order to extract shareholder value. The key audience to influence is the investment analyst community, so this communication must typically be channeled through the investor relations department. Unfortunately, that department tends over time to become "financially focused," falling prey to P&L myopia, because that is the orientation to which investment analysts default in their interrogations. To break free from this, the CEO has to be the communicator of the win, positioning it not as a financial event but rather as a market-making one, and holding up that single customer win as an icon for potential future streams of earnings.

If this approach is successful, a public company's stock will move gently upward on a halo effect. In general, however, history has shown that public companies tend to underplay early-market wins in their investor relations. This creates a relatively blank canvas upon which start-ups can paint. This used to be of no consequence because investment analysts would follow only public companies. But in the age of the Internet the transition from private to public comes so early in the life of a company that analysts must cover the start-ups if they are to have any chance of winning their IPO business. And once these analysts have gotten engaged with the idea of the next market, that begins to affect their valuation ideas about the established market. In short, it is becoming increasingly unwise for the investor relations team at established companies to neglect early-market events, both within their company and in the marketplace around them.

To wrap up this account of market development strategy for

the early market, the core focus is on winning a few flagship customers in order to demonstrate to the marketplace and to investors that the company has first-mover advantage in catching a new wave of technology. These communications are targeted to the visionaries and other forward-thinking members of the market. Pragmatists in the same marketplace overhear these communications, not without interest. This may be the next thing they adopt—but not yet. Moving the first set of those pragmatists into the adoption window is the next market development challenge.

STAGE-TWO ADOPTION: CROSSING THE CHASM INTO THE BOWLING ALLEY

For technologies to gain persistent marketplace acceptance, they must cross the chasm and take up a position on the other side. Now we are in the realm of the pragmatists. To get pragmatists to move at all, companies must rethink their marketing objective from the early market. There the goal was to win a customer, and then another, and another. To cross the chasm, however, you have to *win a herd.* Here's why:

- Pragmatists only feel comfortable moving in herds. That's why they ask for references and use word of mouth as their primary source of advice on technology purchase decisions. Selling individual pragmatists on acting ahead of the herd is possible but very painful, and the cost of sales more than eats up the margin in the sale itself.

- Pragmatists evaluate the entire value chain, not just the specific product offer, when buying into a new technology. Value chains form around herds, not individual customers. There has to be enough repeatable business in the pipeline to reward an investment in specializing in the new technology. Sporadic deals, regardless of how big they are, do not create persistent value chains.

The visible metric for crossing the chasm, therefore, is to *make a market* and *create a value chain* where there were no market and no value chain before. This is a difficult undertaking. To increase its chances for success, and to decrease the time it takes to achieve, it is best to focus the effort on creating a niche market first before trying to create a mass market. It is simply prudent to minimize the number of variables at risk.

Think of a niche market as a self-contained system of commerce with its own local set of specialized needs and wants. Isolated from the mainstream market, which does not serve these special needs, it offers a *value-chain incubator* for emerging technology-enabled markets. That is, its isolation protects the fragile new chain from direct competitive attacks from the incumbent value chain. The customer community, in effect, nurtures the fledgling enterprise because it hopes to gain great benefit from it.

VALUE-CHAIN STRATEGY

To visualize the changes in moving from the early market to the bowling alley, let us return to our value-chain diagram, this time focusing on a new set of market makers:

Bowling Alley Value Chain

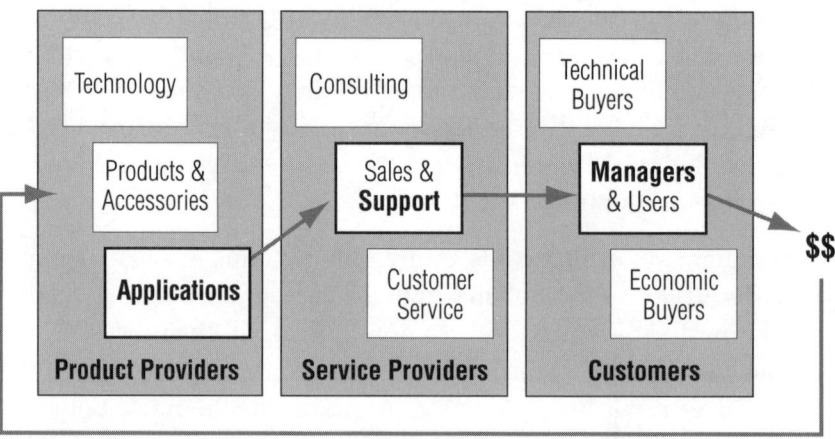

Figure 4.6

At the right-hand end of the chain, the *managers* in the customer domain represent the preassembled herd, an aggregation of relatively homogeneous demand. These are the department managers in charge of a broken, mission-critical process, all huddled in a mass. At the other end, the *application provider* in the product domain offers a relatively homogeneous solution to this herd's problem. It will bring its solution to market through a sales and support organization where it is the *support function* that really counts. That is because at the outset of a market the remaining value-chain partners are just getting recruited and cannot be relied upon to assemble the whole product correctly on their own. Later on these same partners will compete to take over the support function—and the enlightened application provider will let them, as it will greatly expand its market and its reach—but for now it is all just too new. So the application provider's support team must take the lead in working through all the glitches until a working whole product is in place, even when the problem is with someone else's part of the offering and not their own.

Note that the money-recycling arrow has now been restored to the diagram. This is the whole point of the niche-market strategy. We are now creating for the first time a self-funding persistent market where the economic gains of the customer lead to increasing and ongoing investment in the products and services that bring them about. Even if no other market ever adopts this technology, it will still be economically viable to maintain this niche. To be sure, the returns will not be all that the investors hoped for, but it will not be a total bust either. That is because niche markets have persistent competitive advantages that allow them to sustain themselves even when the marketplace in general is unsupportive of their efforts. Moreover, if the value chain extends its reach into additional niches, then it can add market growth to its already attractive price margins to produce highly attractive returns indeed.

The major beneficiary of this strategy are the application providers. It is they who harness the new wave of technology to the specific needs of the target segment, and they who rally the rest of the value chain to support this effort. Because the application provider is the company that really does "make the market," it gains a dominant market-specific competitive advantage during this market formation period. This advantage will persist indefinitely, even after the technology adoption life cycle goes forward, since once any market falls into a particular pecking order, it is loath to change.

Everyone else in the value chain—the core technology providers, the hardware and software product companies, the business consultants and the systems integrators, the customer service staff, and even the client's own technical staff—all happily take a backseat. That's because they will all be operating primarily as cost-effective generalists, making relatively minor modifications to their way of doing business, whereas the application vendor, interacting intimately with the problem-owning department managers, must operate as a value-creating specialist and invest significantly to be able to do so effectively.

COMPETITIVE-ADVANTAGE STRATEGY

The competitive-advantage strategy for this stage of technology adoption looks like this:

Competitive Advantage in the Bowling Alley

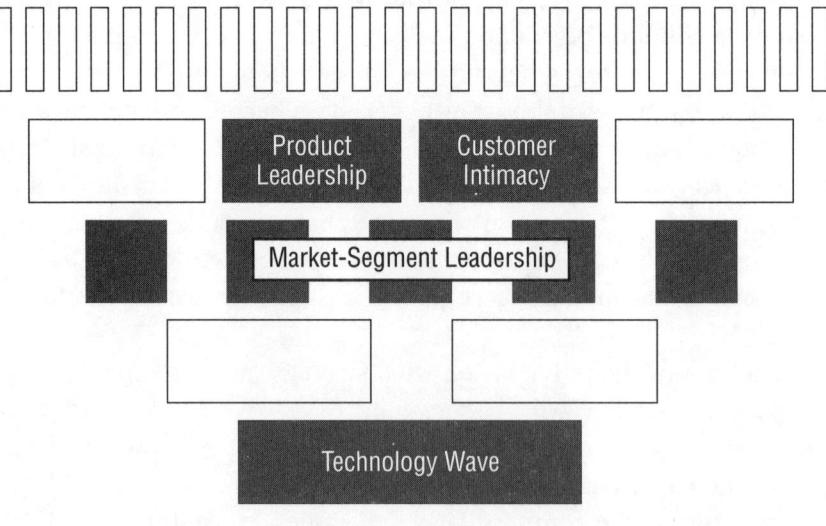

Figure 4.7

The ability to harness the technology wave to solve the critical problem of one or more specific niche markets is what creates power at this stage, and that power goes primarily to the application provider. As more and more of the pragmatist department managers in the niche see their colleagues getting out of the soup, they, too, will come forward and insist on buying this vendor's application. Thus every other company in the value chain becomes dependent on that one vendor's good graces to get into the good deals. In effect, this creates a form of value-chain domination, but it is restricted solely to the niches served, and so it has very different properties—and a very different valuation—from the kind of broad horizontal-market domination we will see develop inside the tornado.

Because they reap the bulk of the rewards, it is relatively easy for application providers to understand and adopt niche marketing, especially if the alternative is to spend another year in the chasm. It is much more problematic, however, for a platform product or a transaction services company to embrace it. Their business plans are normally predicated on either broad horizontal adoption across a multitude of business segments or a broad cross-section of consumers. They are not well positioned to go after niche markets. Vertical industry domain expertise holds little value for them, and voluntarily subordinating themselves to an application vendor just to gain entry into one little niche seems like a huge price to pay. Moreover, even if the tactic proves successful, the resulting order stream will be relatively modest, and worse, may inappropriately cause the rest of the market to misperceive the company as a niche player. For all these very good reasons, platform-products and transaction-services vendors tend to shy away from taking the niche approach to crossing the chasm. And yet it is still a mistake. Here's why.

As we shall see shortly, platform products are optimized for tornado markets, and transaction-services offers are optimized for Main Street markets. Those are the phases of the life cycle in which they will shine. So their strategy should be to accelerate technology adoption to get to "their" phase as quickly as possible. Time spent in the chasm for either strategy represents a huge opportunity cost, giving their competitors a chance to catch up to first-mover advantage while making no progress for themselves at all. This makes exiting the chasm as quickly as possible their top strategic imperative—hence their need to perform the admittedly unnatural act of niche marketing. To be sure, it is a little bit like asking a caterpillar who has a stated goal to be a butterfly to first spin itself into a cocoon and melt—the intermediate step is so disconnected from the end result that it is hard to warrant taking it. But there is now sufficient history to show that not taking the step is fatal—as demonstrated by the market development failures of ISDN networking, object-oriented databases, IBM's OS/2 operating system, pen-based PCs, infrared connectivity protocols, and artificial intelligence.

To be sure, once an initial niche market is established, the winning strategy for platform products and transaction services does indeed split off from the application providers. For the latter, the most powerful path forward is to stay in the bowling alley—this is their sweet spot—expanding niche to niche, following a bowling pin strategy. In this manner, such companies can chew their way through multiple markets with a very high probability of securing dominant positions in the majority of their niches. It is a "bowling alley forever" strategy focused on *preserving complexity* in order to create a source of profit margins for themselves and their service partners. It ends up trading off massive scale in favor of locally dominant roles and eventually makes the transition to Main Street as a leader in a set of mature vertical markets.

By contrast, for platform-product and transaction-services companies, the goal should be to get beyond niches altogether as soon as possible. Their quest instead should be for a single, general-purpose "killer app"—a word-processing program, a spreadsheet, e-mail, voice-mail, a Website, an e-commerce server—something that can be adopted by whole sectors of the economy all at once, thereby leveraging their horizontal business models' strength in being able to scale rapidly. But students of the life cycle should note that in the era prior to pervasive word processing, there were segment-specific solutions for lawyers, doctors, consultants, and governmental functions. These were a critical stepping stone toward getting to a mass market.

VALUE DISCIPLINES FOR THE BOWLING ALLEY

To execute on a niche strategy in an emerging technology-enabled market, companies must realign their value discipline orientation to meet a new set of market priorities, as follows:

Elevate: *Product Leadership, Customer Intimacy*

The bowling alley is driven by the demands of pragmatists for a whole product that will fix a broken mission-critical business process. The fact that the process will not respond to conventional treatment calls out the need for product leadership. The fact that the required whole product will have to integrate elements specific to a particular vertical segment calls out the need for customer intimacy.

Suppress: *Discontinuous Innovation, Operational Excellence*

Pragmatist department managers under pressure to fix a broken process have neither the time nor the resources to support debugging a discontinuous innovation. At the same time, their need for special attention is incompatible with the kind of standardization needed for operational excellence.

Marketing-led organizations are best at crossing the chasm, specifically those that combine strong domain expertise in the targeted market segment with a solutions orientation. Operations-led organizations struggle with the amount of customization required that cannot be amortized across other segments, all of which offends their sense of efficiency. Engineering-led organizations struggle with the lack of product symmetry resulting from heavily privileging one niche's set of issues over a whole raft of other needed enhancements.

To win with this strategy, the critical success factor is focus—specifically, focus on doing whatever it takes to get that first herd of pragmatist customers to adopt en masse the new technology.

Hedging one's bet by sponsoring forays targeted at additional herds at the same time is bad strategy. Both engineering- and operations-oriented organizations, however, are drawn to this approach because they fear that the company is putting all its eggs into one basket. Of course, that is precisely what it *is* doing. The reason it is good strategy to do so is that only by creating critical mass can one move a market and bring into existence a new value chain. Unless they can leverage tornado winds blowing in other markets, alternative initiatives subtract from the needed mass and, ironically, increase rather than decrease market risk.

STOCK PRICE IMPLICATIONS

To help management teams of public corporations support what will at first seem to be an overly focused market development effort, it helps to show them the impact bowling alley success can have on stock price. The following figure illustrates the GAP/CAP implications of winning a niche market:

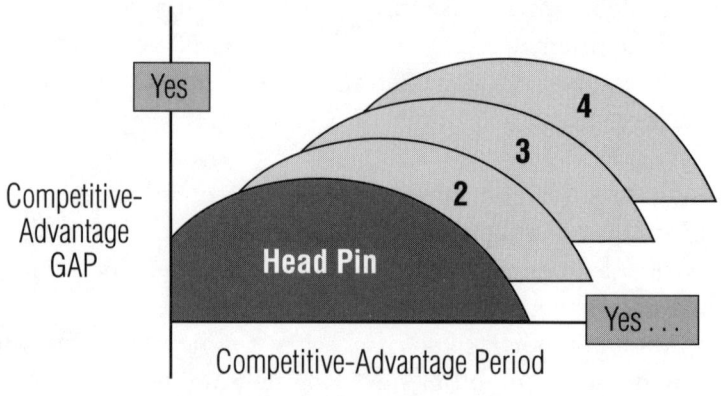

Impact of Chasm-Crossing Success on Stock Price

Figure 4.8

The size of the darkly shaded curve represents the valuation gained from winning market leadership in the first niche or head pin. It is a function of the amount of market share gained coming from sales of the new category in that niche. At The Chasm Group we use a three-tiered ranking system, as follows:

30 percent share of new sales and you can call yourself:
A leader

50 percent share of new sales and you can call yourself:
The leader

70 percent share of new sales and you can call yourself:
The dominator

For the bowling alley strategy to work properly, companies must become "the dominator" in the first niche they attack and then achieve "the leader" status in the next one or two. After that, any of the three rankings contributes to the overall market-share momentum in the sector. The rationale for these rules is that at the outset the pragmatist herd must hear a clear consensus forming around a single solution set, else they will dither in their purchase decisions and the market-capture effort will lose momentum.

So let us suppose in the head-pin niche you gain dominator status, and you have some additional niches under development: What is all that worth to investors? First, as the dominator of the first niche, it means you have a very high GAP, else others would have taken a larger percentage of the new sales. Second, it means you have secured a long CAP *for that niche* because now that the value chain has formed around your standards, there are huge barriers to entry for competitors and barriers to exit for customers and partners. So, unlike the early market, where you created *potential* shareholder value, now you have created *actual* shareholder value—hence the darker shading of the first curve.

For the first time, therefore, Wall Street can estimate with confidence the present value of future earnings at least within this one niche. For a start-up company in the application software sector, that estimate can be enough to merit a public offering. That is, a dominator position can be expected to generate high-quality earnings for a long period of time, and if these are your company's first earnings, they open up a promising future.

But if you are already a public company with a substantial earnings flow in place, then the impact on your P&L from adding the new niche may be negligible. Without a vision for how local niche dominance can be leveraged into additional niches, only modest shareholder value can be gained. You simply must go farther with the story to gain the uptick in stock price. That is why we labeled the CAP axis "Yes. . . ." To overcome lingering investment concern about future market size, it is critical to communicate the larger vision, educating the investor via the bowling alley metaphor, showing how the company will grow forward into a second, third, and fourth niche, each time securing a strong leadership position with high GAP and long CAP.

Finally, if you are a platform-product or transaction-services company, you may worry that your investors will become confused by too much emphasis on what is in essence a niche-market success. In such cases management is often tempted to downplay their market-making achievement. This is a big mistake. Crossing the chasm is a major accomplishment, and you must take credit for it. The goal is to announce mainstream market acceptance for your new offering, citing all the buzz that has formed around you in the targeted niche market, and "creatively" interpret that as a harbinger of the mass adoption just around the corner. If you do not do this yourself, you leave the door open for some other competitor coming out of some other niche to claim this achievement for itself.

To wrap up our discussion of managing for shareholder value in the bowling alley, the core focus at this stage is on value-chain creation and market-segment domination, both leading to persistent competitive advantage, particularly for application providers. For all others at this stage, crossing the chasm is a critical transition vehicle to future competitive-advantage positions. The most powerful of these are created inside the tornado.

STAGE-THREE ADOPTION: INSIDE THE TORNADO

A tornado occurs whenever pragmatists across a variety of market sectors all decide simultaneously that it is time to adopt a new paradigm—in other words, when the pragmatist herd stampedes.

This creates a dramatic spike in demand, vastly exceeding the currently available supply, calling entire categories of vendors to reconfigure their offerings to meet the needs of a new value chain.

VALUE-CHAIN STRATEGY

The overriding market force that is shaping the tornado value chain is the desire for everyone in the market, beginning with the customer but quickly passing through to all the vendors, to drive the transition to a new paradigm as quickly as possible. That calls to the fore the three constituencies that are highlighted below:

Tornado Value Chains

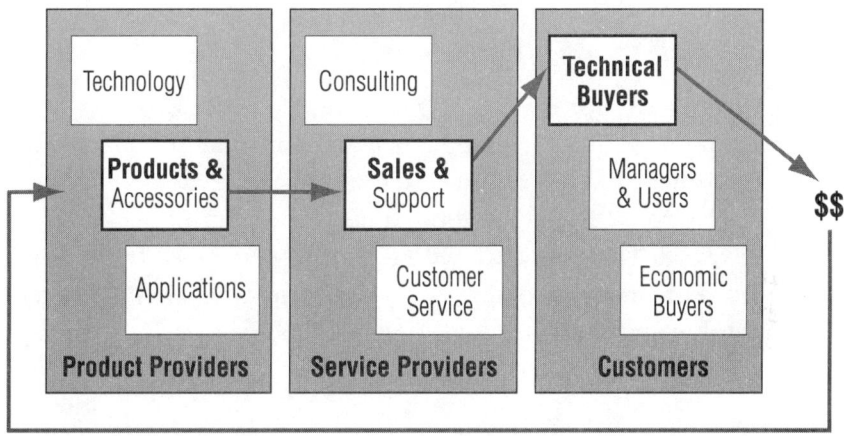

Figure 4.9

Each of these constituencies is well positioned to benefit from standardization for rapid deployment.

- In the product sphere, its is *products,* not technology and not applications, that get the privileged position. The problem with technology is that it is too malleable to be mass-produced and thus does not lend itself to rapid proliferation of common, standard infrastructure. The problem with applications is that they must be customized to sector-specific processes, and so again they do not deploy as rapidly as desired. By contrast, products, and specifically those that serve as platforms for a broad range of applications, are the ideal engine for paradigm proliferation.

Now, to be sure, there must be at least one application that warrants the purchase of the platform in the first place, but in a tornado that application must be essentially the same for every sector. Such an application is called "the killer app," and it becomes the focus for horizontal expansion across multiple sectors of the economy. *Accounting* was the killer app for mainframes, *manufacturing automation* for minicomputers, *word processing* for PCs, *computer-aided design* for workstations, and *electronic mail* for local area networks. But in every case, it was the platform product providers, not the killer app vendors, who were ultimately the big tornado winners because as other applications came on-line, they created still more demand for their platforms.

- In the services sphere, it is the sales and support function, with the emphasis on *sales*, that carries the day. The drawback with consulting is that its projects are too complex, take too long, and require resources that are too scarce to ever permit a tornado to go forward. The drawback with customer service is that it is too focused on serving existing customers at a time when the overwhelming emphasis has to be on acquiring new customers.

    Generating sales in the tornado is not a problem of winning over the customer so much as it is of beating the competition. It is critical, therefore, to field the most competitive sales force you can at this time. Because so much wealth is changing hands, and because the long-term consequences of market share are so great, tornado sales tactics are brutal, and sales aggressiveness is the core discipline. This is the time when nice guys do finish last.

    On the support side, the key issue is to get new customers up and running on a minimal system as quickly as possible and then move on to the next new customer. The more cookie-cutter the process, the faster it replicates, and the more new customers you can absorb. The push is for operational excellence, not customer intimacy. This is not a normal support profile, so once again focusing the team on the right value discipline is a critical executive responsibility.

- On the customer side of the value chain, it is the *technical buyer,* not the end-user departments and not the economic buyer, who becomes the key focus. The problem with end users is that they inevitably seek customization to meet their department-specific needs. Not only is such complexity contrary to the vendor's wishes, it also works against the host institution's imperative to roll out the new infrastructure to everyone in the company as quickly as possible. Such rapid deployment requires a one-size-fits-all approach for the initial roll-out, something that the technical buyer understands far better than the end user. It is also not the time to court senior executives in their role as economic buyers. Once the tornado is under way, they sense the need to get over to the new infrastructure and delegate the task, including the selection process, to their technical staff.

  When technical buyers become the target customer, their compelling reason to buy drives sales outcomes. High on their list is conformance to common standards, followed by market leadership status, which initially is signaled by partnerships with other market leaders, and later on confirmed by market share. The technical buyers' biggest challenge is systems integration, and this is where the support function can contribute to faster roll-outs by building standard interfaces to the most prevalent legacy systems.

The tornado, in essence, is one big land grab—a fierce struggle to capture as many new customers as possible during the pragmatist stampede to the new paradigm. Increasing shareholder value revolves entirely around maximizing market share, and to that end there are three sources of competitive-advantage leverage to exploit.

COMPETITIVE-ADVANTAGE STRATEGY

The power of the tornado comes from the simultaneous unleashing of the bottom two layers of the competitive-advantage hierarchy, as highlighted in the following diagram:

Competitive Advantage in the Tornado

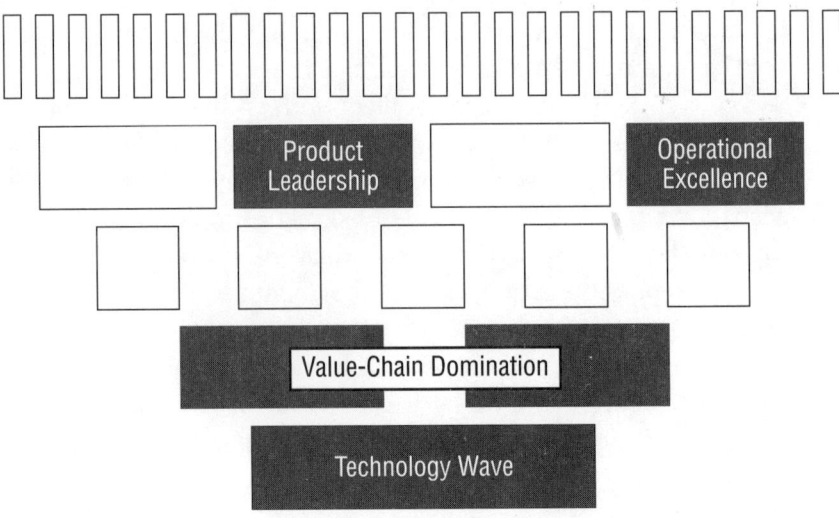

Figure 4.10

The primary source of competitive advantage is simply to be riding the new technology wave as it enters into its tornado phase. Mass-market adoption is an awesome market creation force that wreaks havoc on installed bases rooted in old technology. As the incumbents retreat under the impact of this force to protect their increasingly conservative installed bases, your company advances with the new wave of adoption to occupy their lost ground. This is *category advantage* at work, and it alone will enhance your stock price—hence the scramble of every vendor in the sector to position themselves on the bandwagon of whatever this hot new category is.

The second element of competitive advantage derives from the potential institutionalization of key market-making companies as value-chain leaders or dominators—the gorillas we referred to in the previous chapter. That is, for each element in the value chain, tornado markets seek out a single market-leading provider to set the de facto standards for that component. That role normally goes to the company that garners the most new customers early in the race. In addition, when a single company can gain power over the rest of the value chain, typically by leveraging the power to withhold its proprietary technology and thereby stymie the entire offer, the market accords even more privilege to it.

The power of market-share leadership is rooted in the pragmatist preference to make the safe buy by going with the market leader. That is, rather than rely on their own judgment, pragmatists prefer to rely on the group's. Once that judgment has been made clear, once one vendor has emerged as the favorite, then pragmatists naturally gravitate to that choice, which of course further increases that company's market share, intensifying its gravitational attraction.

This cycle of positive feedback not only spontaneously generates market leaders, but once they are generated, works to keep them in place. That is, the value-chain advantage a market leader gains over its direct competitors is that it has become the default choice for any other company in the chain to round out its offers. Thus the company gains sales that it never initiated and gets invited into deals its competitors never see. Such sales not only add to revenues but to margins, since the absence of competition removes much of the pressure to discount price. In short, winning the market-share prize is a very sweet deal, which, if it is not working for you, is working against you. Hence the need to focus all guns on market share.

Thus the essence of tornado strategy is simply to capture the maximum number of customers in the minimum amount of time and to minimize all other efforts. At each moment the winning strategy is to strike and move on, strike and move on. Anything you can do to slow down a competitor along the way is gravy. What you must not do is voluntarily slow yourself down, not even for a customer. That is, during the tornado *customer acquisition* takes temporary priority over *customer satisfaction*. The entire pragmatist herd is switching from the old to the new—not a frequent event. As customers, in other words, they are temporarily "up for grabs." Once they choose their new vendor, they will be highly reluctant to consider changing yet again. So either you win these customers now, or you risk losing them *for the life of the paradigm*.

And then there is the super grand prize bonanza of tornado market development to which we have already alluded, namely, gaining *value-chain power over the other vendors in the value chain*. As noted, this occurs when a single vendor has monopoly control of a crucial element in the value chain, the way Microsoft and Intel each do for the personal computer, the way Cisco does for the Internet, the way Qualcomm appears to do for the future of wireless telephony. In such cases, as the market tornado unfolds, the standard whole product that forms around the killer app incorporates a piece of your proprietary technology. Going forward, for the value-chain offering as a whole to evolve, it must take your technology along with it—and there is no substitute for it. This makes everyone in the chain dependent upon you, which in turn allows you to orchestrate the behavior of the rest of the chain. This can include pressuring value-chain partners to adopt or support some of your less successful products so that you gain power across a much broader portion of your product line than its actual features and benefits would normally merit.

Value Disciplines for the Tornado

Whatever position one achieves during the tornado market depends largely on your company's ability to execute a market-share land-grab strategy. To this end, the market rewards a third alignment of value disciplines, as follows:

Elevate: *Product Leadership, Operational Excellence*

The tornado is driven by the demands of infrastructure buyers for standard, reliable offerings suitable for rapid mass deployment. Here product leadership gets translated into shipping the next release with the new set of features ahead of the competition and thereby grabbing additional market share from them. Operational excellence is critical to this effort because if there is any hiccup in the process, the market can still shift to an alternative vendor, with major market-share consequences that will last for the duration of the paradigm.

Suppress: *Discontinuous Innovation, Customer Intimacy*

Any form of discontinuous innovation during a tornado creates opportunity for error, putting rapid mass deployment at risk, and is thus anathema. Customer intimacy is also suppressed for the duration of the roll-out for the same reason, sacrificed to the end of achieving reliable, consistent deployment. Once the infrastructure is set in place, then there will be time to come back and meet customer-specific requests.

Operations-led organizations tend to have the edge in a tornado, where meeting deadlines, shipping in quantity, and minimizing returns all take priority over innovation and customer delight. Marketing-led organizations, by contrast, typically flounder because they cannot bear to relinquish their commitment to customer intimacy and customer satisfaction. They need to realize that, in a tornado, just getting the new systems installed and working properly is grounds for customer satisfaction.

STOCK PRICE IMPLICATIONS

When it comes to investor returns, the tornado is the greatest wealth-creation force on the planet. It plays out to two end games depending on whether the market develops around proprietary technology or open-systems standards. In markets that develop under the influence of a proprietary technology, the roles of leader, challenger, and follower take on the following pattern:

- **Gorilla.** The market-share leader in a tornado with proprietary architectural control, this company creates massive shareholder value by gaining value-chain-domination power and forcing the rest of the market to serve its ends. Microsoft, Intel, and Cisco are all gorillas.

- **Chimp.** A direct challenger to the gorilla, this company also has proprietary technology, but it has lost the competition to establish the market's de facto standard. Once the market becomes aware of this outcome, it throws more and more of its business to the gorilla, effectively expelling the chimp from the standard value chain. Chimps have no recourse except to retreat into niche markets where they can make themselves over into "local gorillas," focusing on specialized applications where their nonstandard technology is acceptable because of the exceptional added value they supply. Apple's Macintosh, Digital's Alpha chip, and Bay Network's Wellfleet routers are all chimps.

- **Monkey.** A follower of the gorilla, this company licenses the gorilla's architecture to offer a low-cost substitute for its products that is compatible with the de facto standard. Price-sensitive customers in the market are happy to support monkeys *as a class*. They do not, however, support any particular monkey as a company, and as a result monkeys can never gain lasting market share. As soon as a cheaper, better offer comes along, the market immediately shifts its allegiance to it. Attempting to buy market share, therefore, is always a losing strategy. The correct strategy instead is to opportunistically take advantage of holes in the gorilla's product line and to move on as soon as they are filled. Hitachi with its mainframes (cloning IBM's standards) and AMD with its K-series microprocessors (cloning Intel's) are both monkeys.

In contrast to the above, when tornado markets evolve in the absence of proprietary architectural control, the competitive dynamics within the hierarchy play out very differently. Such markets are frequently termed "open-systems markets," and to understand their dynamics executives need a second set of terms, as follows:

- **King.** The market leader in an open-systems tornado, this company has outexecuted its competition early on and is now enjoying the increasing-returns effects of market-share leadership. But unlike gorillas, kings have no proprietary technology to keep customers from exiting or competitors from entering their market. As a result, they can always be replaced, and thus the valuations of kings are significantly lower than those of gorillas. In the PC market, IBM was the original king, then Compaq, and now Dell.

- **Prince.** The market challenger in an open-systems tornado, this company's long-term prospects are dramatically different from the chimp's. That's because a prince can substitute for a king, whereas a chimp cannot substitute for a gorilla. Open-systems markets embrace princes as a mechanism to keep kings responsive to the rest of the chain's needs. In the PC market, Compaq began as a prince, as did Dell. HP has always been and still is a prince.

- **Serf.** A market follower in an open-systems tornado, this company has even less power than a monkey, since princes already serve as price competition for kings. As a result, it must discount even further to get its products purchased. As a class, serfs are significant because they can drag prices down to a point where even the king's business becomes unprofitable. In the PC market, the no-name "white box" PCs that are assembled by hundreds of resellers represent the serfs—and about one-third of the total market.

Now let's see how investors value these different roles in the context of relative competitive advantage. First, for markets where proprietary architectural control is a factor:

Impact of Tornado Success on Stock Price (Proprietary Technologies)

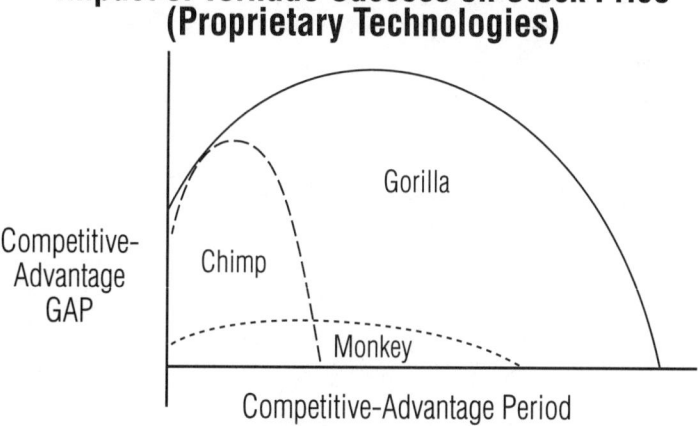

Figure 4.11a

Note first the huge market cap of the gorilla. As we have already discussed, it gains a very high GAP because it has a monopoly on a critical piece of new technology without which the tornado market cannot function. Moreover, since there is no substitute for its component, the company also has a very long CAP, essentially equivalent to the CAP of the whole market category. It is no accident that at the time of this writing, Microsoft and Cisco have the two highest market caps in the world.

Turning to the chimp, note, too, that it has a high GAP. That is because it, too, has proprietary technology for which there is no substitute. Unfortunately, however, this technology is not the de facto standard, and thus its CAP is severely limited. It can expand into niche markets where the gorilla chooses not to compete, but it has no chance in a head-to-head battle.

A monkey's prospects are just the opposite. It has a long CAP but can generate no significant GAP. That is, because its offers are compatible with the de facto standard, it can benefit from the category's persistence. However, since its presence is not required, its CAP is not as long as the gorilla's. Moreover, since it has no unique offer, it cannot generate any GAP to speak of except through price discounts. In short, monkeys do not make for good long-term investments.

In contrast to the foregoing, the following diagram reflects valuations in an open-systems competition:

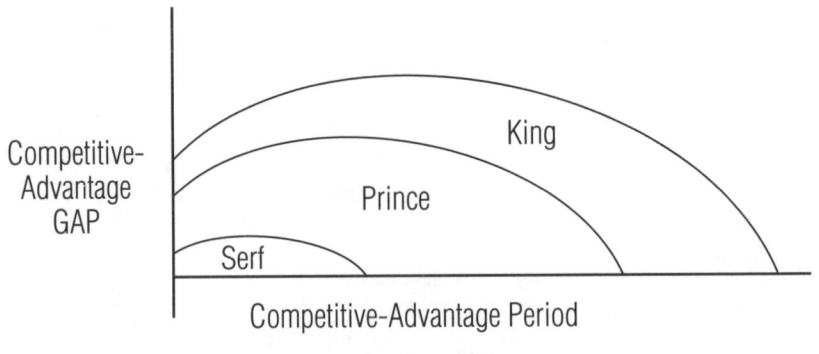

Impact of Tornado Success on Stock Price (Open Systems)

Figure 4.11b

Here the king and the prince are on more equal footing, with the serf trailing. In this type of market, brand and distribution are the critical success factors. Serfs typically have neither, hence their minuscule market caps. Princes, by contrast, can challenge market-leading kings on either front. In the PC market, in particular, exploiting new channels of distribution has led to several changes in the hierarchy, first when Compaq used its retail skills to unseat IBM, and then when Dell used its direct-selling skills to unseat Compaq. On the GAP axis, because all players must conform to a common standard, they end up competing on price to some degree, which reduces the maximum attainable GAP for any company, even the king. This has long-term consequences for every company in the market.

It is important to remember, however, that while a tornado market is in full swing, everybody gains simply by virtue of tornado demand far exceeding tornado supply. That is, the tornado creates an extended period of shortages that allow all companies to charge premium prices during this phase. Thus all stocks in the category tend to gain in valuation initially, and only after the competition sorts itself out, and the market implications of the various roles is understood, do stock prices adjust to meet these charts.

To wrap up our discussion of the tornado, the core focus is on grabbing as much market share as one can during this period of exceptional opportunity. Relatively early on in the process, these land grabs resolve themselves into one or the other of the two patterns we have just discussed, and companies end up in one of the six roles just reviewed. Once this has happened, the best strategy is to accept the role the market assigns you and execute as efficiently as possible from within that position for the duration of the tornado. Any fighting to change roles will only confuse the market and slow its adoption of your offerings. Your goal instead should be to build the biggest possible installed base as a prelude for a prolonged stint on Main Street.

STAGE-FOUR ADOPTION: ON MAIN STREET

Main Street begins as the market-share frenzy that drives tornado winds subsides. The overwhelming bulk of the pragmatists in the market have chosen their vendor, made their initial purchases, and rolled out the first phase of a multiphase deployment. Only a fraction of the total forecastable sales in the segment have actually been made at this point, but from here on out the market-share boundaries are relatively fixed. This has significant implications for the value chain.

Value-Chain Strategy

Here is the fourth and final mutation in the value chain. This one will endure for the life of the paradigm. In effect, it is the value chain we have been setting up all along:

Main Street Value Chain

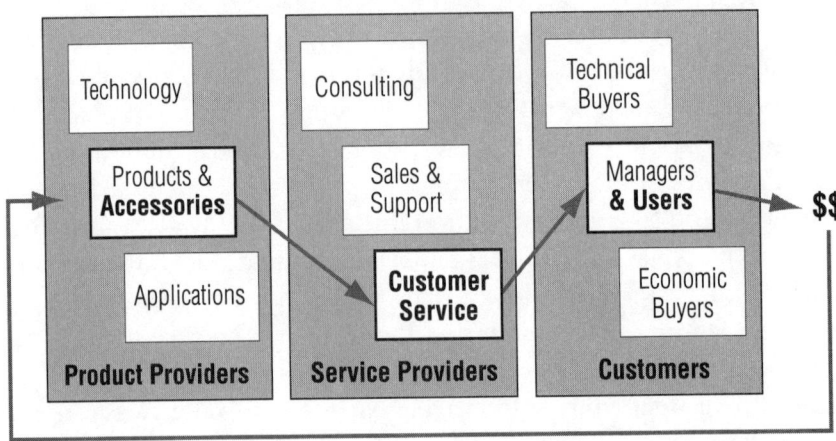

Figure 4.12

There is a key change underlying this entire value chain, which is that the technology adoption life cycle as a whole has evolved from the pragmatist to the conservative agenda, and every constituency in the value chain is affected by this change. Let's start with the customer.

When companies adopt new paradigms, conservative customers at first hang back, preferring to eke out some last bit of value from the old system. But once it is clear that the new system must supplant the old one, then they seek to put their stamp on the new vendor relationship. They remind all these new arrivals that most of the promises that were made on behalf of their products and services are as yet far from true, and they work to keep everyone focused on making incremental improvements going forward. In effect, they transform what heretofore was a discontinuous innovation into what will from now on be a system of continuous innovation.

In mature—or maturing—markets, both the economic buyer and the technical buyer recede in importance. The economic buyer is no longer looking for competitive advantage or to support a manager in fixing a broken business process; now the issue is simply staying within budget, and that can be delegated. And the technical buyer is no longer concerned about how to either manage or postpone the introduction of a disruptive technology; now the concern is simply to stay compliant with established standards, and that, too, can be delegated. Even within the user community, the managers are now taking the new system for granted, assuming that it must be doing pretty much what it was bought to do (a naive, but all too frequent point of view). Thus it is only *end users*, the people who actually interact with the system on a frequent basis, that (a) know anything about how it really works, and (b) have a stake in sponsoring improvements to it.

If these end users do not voice their desires, then the offering becomes a complete commodity, with the purchasing department driving a *supplier relationship* going forward. If they do voice their desires, however, and gain their managers' approval, then end users can drive a *vendor relationship*, a condition that allows a company to earn margins above commodity levels. We are long past the time for customers to embrace you in a *strategic partner relationship*, something that is confined to earlier phases in the life cycle.

To earn preferred margins from end-user sponsorship, focus shifts to those aspects of the value chain that end users can directly experience. On the product side, this suppresses the importance of technology, platform products, and even the core of the application. All these are still important, but they are more directly experienced by the technical buyer than the end user. By contrast, any product element that is consumable, as well as any change to the surface of the application, is highly user visible. It is here that minor enhancements for a modest increase in price can generate dramatic changes in gross profit margin, the way, for example, the cup holder has done in the automotive industry.

Lucrative as the accessories and consumables business is on Main Street, however, an even bigger opportunity lies in what we called in Chapter 1 the product-service shift. What customers used to value and buy as products becomes reconceived as service offerings—shifting the burden of system maintenance from the customer back to the vendor. Thus the move from answering machine to voice-mail, from videotapes to pay-per-view, from bar bells to health clubs. This same shift is also the basis for an economy that enables the outsourcing of context, also discussed in Chapter 1.

The primary organization tasked with masterminding this shift is *customer service*. Historically this has been a challenge because that organization was not constructed nor were its personnel recruited with the thought that it would eventually become a lead contributor to the P&L and market valuation of the company. In the age of the Internet, however, investors are now actively pursuing companies that have been founded from day one with just such an agenda in mind.

COMPETITIVE-ADVANTAGE STRATEGY

Competitive advantage on Main Street lives entirely at the top of the hierarchy, as follows:

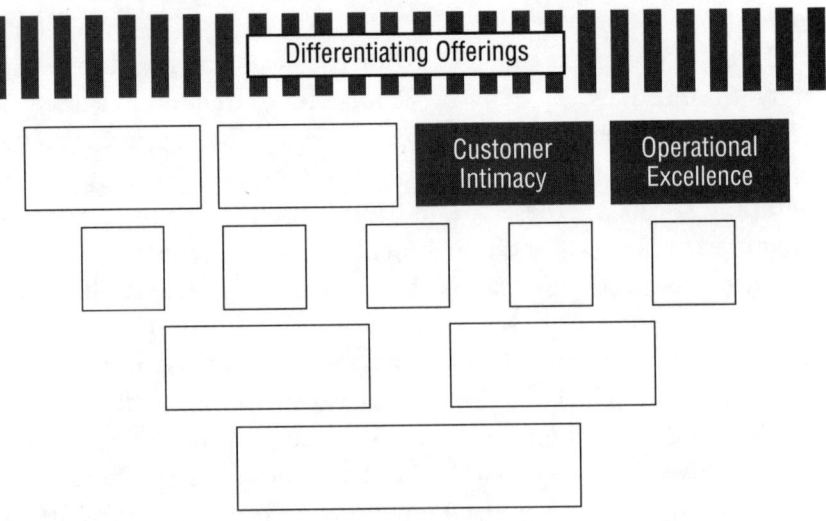

Figure 4.13

The technology wave has crested and broken and no longer provides market development leverage. The value chain is already formed, and whatever place you have in it is not going to change without massive and usually unwarranted investment. There is always the possibility of you finding an underserved market segment here or there, but the speed of market penetration now will be much slower, the impact on any local value chain much less, and thus the rewards more modest than they would have been during the bowling alley phase. And so it is that we get to the domain of company execution, to which we shall turn in a moment, and differentiated offerings.

There are classically two types of differentiation strategies that succeed on Main Street. The first is being the low-cost provider, a strategy that works best in commodity markets where it is not the end user but the purchasing manager acting as economic buyer who is the real decision maker. The other type is a customer-delight strategy, which works best in consumer markets or in business markets where the end user is permitted to behave as a consumer. The more a market matures, the more likely your company has to deliver on both of these propositions to be competitive. To do so it must gravitate toward a product or service deployment strategy called *mass customization*.

Mass customization separates any offering into a *surface* and a *substructure*. The surface is what the end user experiences. It is here that changes are made to enhance that experience. This is the *customization* portion of the offer. By contrast, the substructure is the necessary delivery vehicle for the entire performance, but it is not directly experienced by the end user. The goal here is to provide maximum reliability at the lowest possible cost, and the preferred tactic is to reduce variability and increase standardization to achieve high volume. This is the *mass* portion of the offer.

To combine the two without sacrificing the benefits of either, the customizing portion must often be done downstream in the value chain in a separate step from the mass portion. This typically leads to a need to redesign the value chain, creating new opportunities for service providers to create customization value at the point of customer contact. Think of how cell phones are provided, and you get the idea. Everything upstream from the retail outlet is totally standardized; everything downstream is customizable—the phone itself, its accessories, service options, program pricing, and the like. Prior to retail, everything is sold as a commodity; after retail, it is a value-added offering.

The implications of this restructuring of the market are far-reaching, and not just for service providers. Consumables have the same potential to deliver customized value. Consider, for example, the razor-to-razor-blade transition in Gillette's history, or Kodak's move from cameras to film, or HP's transition from inkjet printers to inkjet cartridges. In every case once Main Street is reached, it is the consumable at the surface, and not the underlying engine at the core, that becomes the basis of differentiation and the locus of high profit margins.

Alternatively, service transactions can also replace the serviced commodity as the locus of value creation. This has been the case in the automobile industry, where the bulk of the profits are made not from selling new cars but from financing the purchase, insuring the vehicle, supplying the consumables, and providing the maintenance services. In every case margins are affected by the end user's experience during these transactions. That is why companies like Lexus have been so successful with their customer-care offers. It is also why traditional car dealerships are failing with their customer-unfriendly approach to purchase and financing, driving their customers to brokers and to the Web instead.

In large part the promise of the Internet is based on it being a universal platform for value-adding customization in Main Street value chains. The systems are not yet completely in place to fulfill this proposition today, but forward-thinking executives and enlightened investors can see how with incremental improvements they will be able to generate scaleable, low-cost, high-touch offerings of the sort that create attractive profit margins on Main Street.

VALUE DISCIPLINES

To execute on this strategy of mass customization, companies as elsewhere in the life cycle must learn to elevate one pair of value disciplines and suppress the other:

Elevate: *Operational Excellence, Customer Intimacy*

Main Street markets are supported by conservative customers seeking incremental gains in value. These can be achieved either through decreasing the costs of the current set of offers—the domain of operational excellence—or by introducing a new set of offers improved through readily absorbed continuous innovations—the domain of customer intimacy.

Suppress: *Discontinuous Innovation, Product Leadership*

Discontinuous innovation runs directly contrary to the interests of Main Street customers and is simply not welcome. Even offers based on product leadership are problematic. If they require retooling the existing infrastructure, they usually just aren't worth it. What development teams must realize is that now product improvements should be focused either on keeping the core product viable, with operational excellence as a guide, or on making cosmetic changes at the surface, with customer intimacy providing the direction.

Of all the pairings, this particular set should be the most familiar to established companies in mature markets. They should see themselves as the champions of the first pair, and those wretched dotcoms assaulting their marketplace as the purveyors of the second. Note that in this pairing the established company's existing customers are very much on its side, not on the dotcoms'. That's because they, like the company itself, are ruled by conservative interests. It is instead the flock of new customers who are entering the tornado for the next big thing that are undermining this company's stock price going forward.

STOCK PRICE IMPLICATIONS

The returns from Main Street business models are based on the assumption that the market is not under a technology-enabled attack and can be forecast to last indefinitely in its present state. Within that context, investor returns are created by selling modestly profitable offerings on a repeatable basis with very low cost of sales. This is possible only when you are selling to an *existing loyal customer*. The mortal enemy of the Main Street model is churn—a continual enrollment of new customers at high cost of sales accompanied by a continual loss of existing customers, the most profitable to retain.

Companies that are able to minimize churn and maximize gains from existing customers generate one of two types of valuation depending on whether they follow a commodity or a value-added strategy:

Impact of Main Street Success on Stock Price

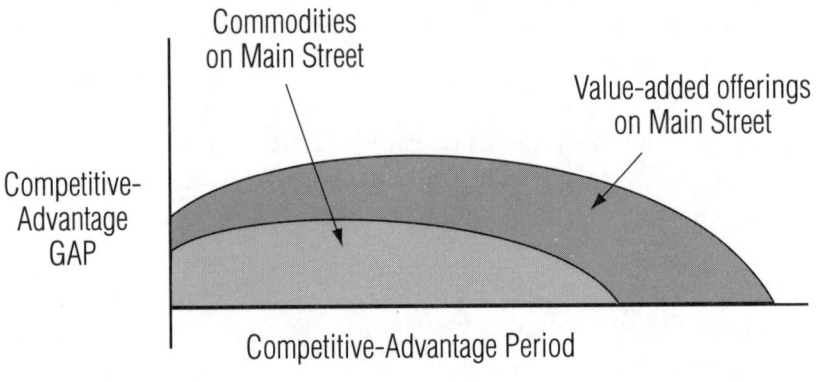

Figure 4.14

GAPs for companies in commodity businesses on Main Street are rarely high. Customer power, which is at its nadir during the tornado, reasserts itself on Main Street to create negotiating leverage. Moreover, since commodities are by definition substitutable, they have relatively low company CAPs as well. (The *category's* CAP, by contrast, is very long—we will have the salt business with us for some time to come.) Progress in such businesses is made by cost-reducing internal processes, particularly in the substructure, but even here, as competitors make the same adjustments, the savings must be passed on to the customer rather than reserved for the shareholder.

Creating value-added offerings through mass customization for end users is the preferred way to resist this erosion in margins. These offers increase GAP modestly—representing the premium end users will pay to get what they really want. They also create modest switching costs—once you get what you really want it is hard to go back—thereby increasing CAP as well. Both these effects work only up to a point of tolerance, after which competitive pricing can and will override their influence. Nonetheless, because the volume of sales on Main Street is so high, and the bulk of the business-enabling investment has already been amortized, it is here that most of the profits in any economy are made. And these do go to the shareholders.

Thus it is that blue-chip stocks are created. Decade after decade they demonstrate themselves to be earnings machines, creating modest but predictable growth in both revenues and earnings accompanied by a remarkable lack of volatility in stock price. These stocks, and the New York Stock Exchange, have been the bastion of the American economy for the greater part of the twentieth century.

All this value is put at risk, however, whenever a disruptive technology paradigm appears. The question its arrival poses for investors is, will the old category delivered by the incumbent value chain persist, or will the new category delivered by a new value chain eliminate it? If the new paradigm is seen to be winning that battle, then the following devaluation scenario comes into play:

Impact of Paradigm Threat on Main Street Stock Price

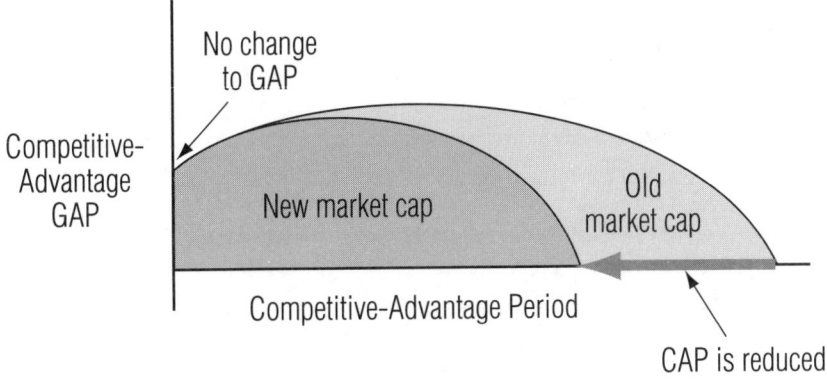

Figure 4.15

Note that GAP is unchanged. Indeed, for the immediate future there is little question that the Main Street vendors will have the more advantaged, better differentiated offers. No, instead it is *CAP* that comes under attack. The stock market's assessment of the competitive-advantage equation is that eventually the new paradigm will indeed win out. The incumbent companies are given a window to embrace the new paradigm themselves, but if they do not, then the market discounts their valuation dramatically, even if they are producing impressive P&L performances in their current quarter. That is, all the Main Street earnings beyond a given window that were forecast to go to the incumbent, based on its current market share, will now be forecast to go to one or another of the new challengers. This effectively removes those earnings from the incumbent's anticipated future earnings—hence the reduction in valuation.

In the next chapter we are going to look at the challenge that such disruptions pose to management courage and decisiveness. For now, however, it is time to stop, take a breath, and look back over all the ground we have covered in this chapter.

IMPLICATIONS OF LIVING ON THE FAULT LINE

Consider how many different value-chain permutations we have examined in the course of a technology-enabled market developing through its various stages. To summarize them, here are the four market states in a side-by-side comparison table:

	Early Market	Bowling Alley	Tornado	Main Street
Primary Competitive Advantage	Catching technology wave	Market-segment domination	Market-share leadership	Differentiated offerings
Product Focus	Technology	Applications	Platform products	Consumables

	Early Market	Bowling Alley	Tornado	Main Street
Service Focus	Consulting	Support	Sales	Customer service
Customer Focus	Economic buyer	Department manager	Technical buyer	End user
Stock Price Implications	High GAP No CAP	High GAP Long CAP (niche)	High GAP Long CAP (mass)	Low GAP Long CAP

The table maps the working out of the competitive-advantage hierarchy over the course of a technology-enabled market's development. The columns lay out the life-cycle phases these markets evolve through. The rows lay out the changes in focus that organizations must make to adapt to this evolution. The first row sets forth the layer in the competitive-advantage hierarchy that has the most impact during each phase. The next three rows highlight the value-chain elements that create the most impact during the phase because they are best suited to leveraging the type of competitive advantage available. Finally, the last row recaps the stock price result of achieving the competitive-advantage position during each phase of the life cycle.

I hope and trust by now that the logic behind these various combinations is clear. Forces in the marketplace cause them to come about regardless of whether or not the companies involved want them to. As a result, they lay out the world of "what is."

Even a cursory glance, however, shows that the changes companies have to make in order to adapt to these forces are dramatic indeed. Moreover, the time allotted to make them is painfully short. As a result, it should surprise no one that few real-world organizations are very good at actually making them. Indeed, the larger and more successful a company becomes, the less likely it is to attempt making them at all.

It is essentially a problem of inertia. Once you get a certain amount of mass moving in any given direction, the price for changing that direction begins to exceed the return on making the change. Increasingly the logic of trade-offs says let things go forward as they are. Yes, it creates problems, but not as many as trying to change course would. Over time, however, as these problems continue to be left untended, their consequences build, until eventually the cost for *not changing* does indeed exceed the price of change. But by that time things are typically so far out of control, and the time horizon for change has become so immediate, that the inertia-driven organization simply cannot make the turn and crashes into a wall instead.

The rest of this book is focused on helping you avoid that crash. We are going to take it in two chapters—"Triage" and "Building to Last." Triage is a medical term for the sort of medical care that M*A*S*H units give—real-time prioritization of who you can help and who you cannot, followed by immediate first aid given under time pressure. In the triage chapter we will assume a direct assault in your market by a dotcom and prescribe a short-term course-correction program intended to impact next year's stock price, maybe even this year's. This program is not intended as a substitute for building to last but rather as a prelude to it. The good news is, it does not undermine healthy long-term success. The bad news is, it can be painful.

In contrast to triage, building to last requires changes in culture and behavior that can take years to instill and unfold. Our final chapter, therefore, is targeted not at improving this year's stock price, perhaps not even next year's, but rather *the stock price for every year thereafter*. The chapter's premise is that organizations can indeed adjust to the demands of the technology adoption life cycle in real time provided they declare a core culture and maintain alignment with it. Indeed, it will argue that there are four proven core cultures, any one of which can support long-term competitive advantage and wealth creation for shareholders, and that the primary challenge for the board of directors and the executive team is to choose one and really develop it.

But before we go on to those chapters, let us wrap this one up first.

SUMMARY OF KEY POINTS IN CHAPTER 4

The main idea of this chapter is that technology-enabled markets evolve through four distinct stages, each of which calls for a dramatically different strategic approach. Specifically, here are the key observations:

1. Different roles in the *value chain* rise to prominence and recede from it at different points in the life cycle. The implication is that every dog has its day but that some days it's just not your turn to be the dog. The implication of that is *live with it.*

2. Different forms of *competitive advantage* are rewarded at different stages in the life cycle, as illustrated by the competitive-advantage hierarchy model.

3. Different *value disciplines* are rewarded or penalized at different stages in the life cycle, as illustrated by the value disciplines model.

4. Finally, different *stock price implications* are attached to operations that have successfully mastered the challenges of each phase in the life cycle, as illustrated by the GAP/CAP charts for each phase.

5. To ask any given organization to excel at all phases of the life cycle at all times is a good recipe for creating chaos—yet that is exactly what the high-tech marketplace demands of its leading companies.

How you should respond to those demands is the focus of the remainder of the book.

5

TRIAGE

When an earthquake strikes, social infrastructure goes into a state of shock, and the first job of the authorities is to get things back up and running. The same holds true when a blue-chip company riding a prolonged wave of competitive advantage suddenly runs smack into disruptive technology that is creating discontinuity in its traditional markets. Stock price crumbles, analysts call, partners defect, employees resign, competitors gloat, customers hedge, and investors demand action. It is a time for triage.

Triage is the discipline of first aid. It determines what can be fixed in the short term and what cannot, and it focuses all available resources on the former. The goal is to get the company back into the game as fast as possible. It is not to restore it to its former luster, it is not to re-create the past, it is to engage the unpleasant truths of the present clearly and honestly.

Management teams are generally not rewarded handsomely for doing the work of triage, but it is where they show their true character. If they act with integrity and dispatch, they build from the crisis strong relationships both inside and outside the company that will be the foundation for success in better times. Conversely, if they flinch from the challenge, there is little chance to recover later on as too many of the key resources perform their own form of triage by simply leaving.

The most useful thing to have in times of triage is an operating manual, a checklist of what to do first and how to proceed after that. This chapter seeks to fill that need.

• • •

In the opening chapter of *Anna Karenina,* Tolstoy writes, "All happy families resemble one another, but each unhappy family is unhappy in its own way." In business, I think the opposite view is more the case. Each successful company I spend time with has its own special energy and culture, but many of the struggling companies I work with have a number of traits in common. In this chapter, we are going to conduct a fictional case study of just such a company, one that is well established in a technology-enabled market, publicly traded, in the *Fortune* 500, and in all likelihood a household name, a company that in an earlier era rode a tornado market to prominence and then subsequently enjoyed a prolonged period of prosperity, a company that now finds itself up against the challenge of the age of the Internet and under the specific threat of dotcom competition.

The company's name will be *BlueChip,* and it will trade on the New York Stock Exchange. The goal of this chapter will be to expose BlueChip to a dotcom attack and explore its options going forward. We will begin by looking at how the company is organized and oriented prior to the attack. Then when the attack hits, we will look at what kind of triage must occur immediately. Finally, we will look at a fundamental change in management behavior that must occur in order for the company to regain its competitive edge. At the end of the chapter, executive teams in similar situations should have at their command a new set of management options and a vocabulary for discussing their merits relative to the challenges they face in the age of the Internet.

EXAMINING THE FOUNDATIONS

To understand BlueChip, we need to sort out what happens to a company after it goes through a tornado market and begins to settle down on Main Street. During the tornado, successful companies focus intensely on executing to a market-share-capture agenda. To do so, they organize around operating or line functions, parse out the work, suppress any distractions, and turn the crank as fast they possibly can. When the tornado market finally subsides, this team crashes into a wall, missing its top-line numbers badly, and the stock takes a big hit.

Now what happens going forward? The company has been shaken to its foundations, and a fair number of people look at their stock options now underwater, look at the next big thing in the market recruiting like mad, and leave to join up. But the rest of the company pulls itself together and begins to sort out life on Main Street. The problem is, there is not as much to do as there once was, and fairly quickly downsizing becomes the order of the day, which the company bravely takes on. In so doing, however, it does not reorganize but instead preserves the same line organization and line managers it used to run tornado operations. Without the pressure of tornado demand forcing these functions to work in harmony, however, they drift out of sync with one another, creating what some have called the stovepipe effect. Stovepipes are isolated line functions that optimize for their internal productivity and perform poorly in cross-functional tasks. This organizational structure does not penalize companies inside the tornado because assembly-line throughput is the order of the day. It does, however, penalize them on Main Street, as it is slow to respond to market changes and customer requests.

In technology-enabled markets we typically see five line functions that tend to end up as stovepipes:

- Research and development

- Operations

- Professional services

- Sales

- Finance

All five functions are core to creating value in high tech, and each has demonstrated repeatedly that it can be a breeding ground for the CEO job. We should also note that a sixth function, *marketing*, is missing from this list. In the early reviews of this manuscript, I caught no end of grief for this exclusion, but I believe it is a true one and therefore I want to take some time to explain why.

The fundamental role of marketing as a strategic function is to help the company target markets and win dominant positions in them. This is not something you hire a lot of troops to do. It is instead a consultative assignment for a trusted advisor who is expected to facilitate a team-wide discussion leading to consensus. So strategic marketing does not create a stovepipe ever.

Tactical marketing is another matter. Its job is demand creation, and it does hire troops to achieve this end. But here is the interesting thing: Even though these troops are hired during the tornado, they do not come to power or prominence until the market shifts over to Main Street. Why? Because in a tornado, there is no need for demand creation. Demand already exceeds supply. Now, there is a need to create preference for your offer over your competitors', and marketing is assigned this task, but as we saw in the discussions of the previous chapter, its efforts have little to do with the outcome. Markets in a tornado self-organize into a power structure that shapes the overall outcome regardless of tactical marketing's efforts.

Instead, during a tornado marketing becomes redefined as marketing communications and lead generation, with both functions strongly subordinated to sales. It will not be until after the sales function has dramatically failed to meet forecast—the outcome of the end of the tornado—that marketing will free itself from this form of involuntary servitude and begin to assert its power. From then on, as the Main Street market goes forward, its power will gradually increase as customer intimacy becomes the margin-creating value discipline of choice. But there is no such power and no stovepipe in marketing coming out of the tornado, hence its omission from the list.

With that off my chest, let us turn to see how the nominated stovepipe functions sort things out on Main Street. Each line function, it turns out, has a characteristic set of attitudes toward the various phases of the technology adoption life cycle. Some are more comfortable at the front end of the life cycle, others at the back, and as soon as the pressures of a tornado market subside, they tend to gravitate back to their comfort zones accordingly. This is by no means all bad. Indeed, by mixing and matching leadership responsibilities among these functions, companies can get reasonably adequate coverage for all but one life-cycle phase. Here specifically is how the various functions self-organize.

R AND D

R and D is the engineering function in high tech. In other technology-impacted markets, where companies may not employ engineers per se, think of whatever function has the charter both to optimize offerings for the current wave of technology and to catch the next wave.

Like all functions in the corporation, when R and D surveys the various market stages created by the technology adoption life cycle, it sees good times and bad times depending on which stage is active. Using icons to represent each stage, here's how this group perceives the life cycle as a whole:

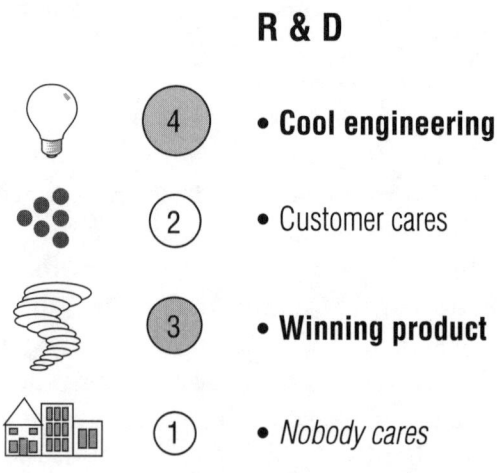

Figure 5.1

Ask most engineers where they would like to seek out their next project, and they will answer in the early market. That's where all the cool engineering gets done. Not only is such work great for the résumé, not only does it give them bragging rights around the water cooler (OK, in Silicon Valley it's more likely to be a cappuccino machine), it is just plain fun. This is what you go to engineering school for. So, by way of rating, engineers give the early market their highest score, what we'll represent as a shaded circle with a 4 inside it.

But suppose the company has no early-market projects on the

books, now what would they prefer? From among the remaining three phases, most now will pick the tornado, revealing that beneath their calm analytical exterior beats the heart of a ferocious competitor. Outexecuting the competition in a race for best product creates an adrenaline rush that can keep engineering teams running even after the caffeine wears off. So they give the tornado their second highest rating, which we'll represent by a smaller shaded circle with a 3 inside it.

When it comes to the remaining two phases, enthusiasm begins to wane, but there is still some appetite for the bowling alley. That's because at this stage of market development, although the *pure* engineering problem is subordinated to customer-specific needs, there is usually a pretty interesting *applied* engineering problem to solve. Engineers thrive on problem solving, and so they will give the bowling alley the nod as third choice, which we will indicate by an unshaded circle with a 2 in the middle.

By process of elimination, this brings us to the one phase in the life cycle that engineers, as a class, loathe—Main Street. Do you know what they call engineering on Main Street? *Maintenance!* Have you ever read a résumé from an engineer that said *seek forty-year career in maintenance?* No, nor will you. As we saw in the previous chapter, Main Street markets provide no payback for continuing to push the envelope on core system performance. Attention instead is paid to customizing the surface—an important undertaking, to be sure, but not the job for an engineer. So they give this phase of the life cycle their lowest score, which we will represent by a very small unshaded circle with just enough room to contain a lowly 1.

That's how engineers see the technology adoption life cycle as it impacts their lives. Now let's stack their view up against that of the people in operations.

OPERATIONS

Operations in this context is meant to cover a range of functions, all of which add up to doing whatever it takes to deliver our value to the market. Depending on whether the offering is made up of atoms or bits and whether it consists primarily of a product or a service, this can take on a variety of colorings. Thus in a computer business, operations is anchored in *manufacturing;* in a telecommunications services business, in *systems operations;* in a software business, in *release management;* in a distribution business, in *logistics.* In every case, however, operations acts like the drummer in a rock band, "keeping the beat" for the company, making sure it hits its marks on schedule.

Here's how operations sees the life cycle:

Operations

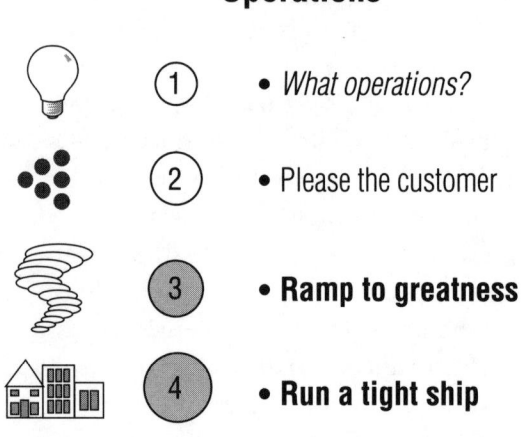

1. • *What operations?*
2. • Please the customer
3. • **Ramp to greatness**
4. • **Run a tight ship**

Figure 5.2

Ask operations people what part of the life cycle they like the best, and they will respond, *Main Street!* Why? Because that's where you can finally get things really under control. Processes are now characterized, control limits understood, continuous improvement programs in place. Our train's on track for six-sigma quality, and that's what gets us bragging rights in our part of town. With any luck we might even get a Baldrige Award for quality. Give Main Street a big 4.

If Main Street is not available, operations will then opt for the tornado. Here, though life is much more of a struggle, operations management is sorely needed. Harnessing all the conflicting demands coming into the pipeline, fusing them into deliverable goods and services, shipping them out to make room for the next batch or wave—it's the stuff of operational heroism. Think of John Henry and his hammer, and give the tornado a 3.

Of the remaining two phases, operations will give the nod to the bowling alley. The customer demands are constraining, to be sure, and there is typically not enough volume to really warrant full-on operational discipline, but there is a legitimate need for the operations discipline called flexible manufacturing, and the resulting output is highly valued. The bowling alley gets a 2.

The one phase operations wants no part of is the early market. Here in a very real sense there are no operations. Everything is still being invented. Procedures are largely nonexistent, and in the rare instances where they have been documented, they are already out of date as changing circumstances dictate reinvention. The best thing to do with an early-market project from an operations point of view is to isolate it in a skunk works and not let it corrupt the real work. So the early market garners a 1.

R and D and operations, we can see then, are almost mirror opposites. As we turn to professional services, we'll see that this line function tends to line up more with the R and D crowd.

PROFESSIONAL SERVICES

The term *professional services* is intended to refer to any consulting function in the organization that helps customers implement the company's primary offering. Its natural opposite is not "amateur services" but rather *transaction services,* the actual outsourcing of the same offering, which would be incorporated under *operations.* Professional services work as a technology shock absorber, easing early customers into the new paradigm. By contrast, transaction services work as a context outsourcer, taking a fully commoditized function off the customer's plate so they can focus their time, talent, and management attention on something more value creating.

Here's how the professional services function views the life cycle:

Professional Services

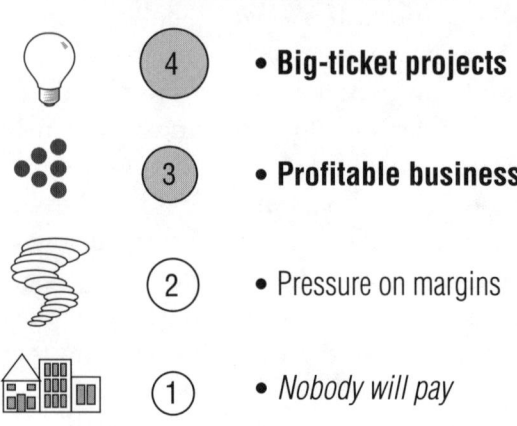

- **Big-ticket projects** (4)

- **Profitable business** (3)

- Pressure on margins (2)

- *Nobody will pay* (1)

Figure 5.3

The reason professional services tends to be the mirror opposite of operations is that it adds value precisely to the degree that operational procedures are not yet in place. Thus its greatest domain of opportunity is the early market. Here the new technology challenges everyone, vendor and customer alike, imposing extraordinary demands on systems integration, whether with computer systems, business systems, or cultural systems. Everywhere, change management is needed, and that is what professional services offers. Thus the early market gets a 4.

Interestingly, although the early market lets a professional services organization charge its highest fees, it is the bowling alley that offers it the greatest opportunity for profitability. That is because a market is forming around a vertical sector of companies all focused on solving the same problem. As a result, there is greater commonality across projects, captured learning, and thus enhanced productivity. At the same time, the problems are still challenging enough to keep margins relatively high. Ironically, however, the custom-project orientation of professional services organization often tempts them to overcustomize their offerings during this stage and thus reduce their own margins. Nevertheless, they still make out reasonably well; give the bowling alley a 3.

If the bowling alley is actually better than it looks, the tornado is the opposite. At first blush, the rush of new business opportunities appears hugely positive. But as the tornado unfolds, customers become increasingly sensitive to both cost and time to complete. Firms are asked to show up with a default solution ready to install. This works against the grain of the value-added project model at the core of professional services, and over time such operations must exit tornado markets in favor of earlier phases in some newer life cycle. Color the tornado a 2.

The same forces of commoditization that make the tornado uncomfortable for a professional services organization make Main Street uninhabitable. Markets at this stage expect solutions to be sufficiently well packaged that they do not require consulting to implement. Customers might appreciate the extra services but would not expect to have to pay much for them. Give Main Street a 1.

So if the professional services folks are aligned with the R and D people toward the front of the life cycle, and the operations people are most comfortable on Main Street, who is actually championing the tornado? Need you really ask?

SALES

For the purposes of this exercise, let us assume BlueChip is fielding a wide array of both direct and indirect sales channels, with the top executive coming from whichever channel provides the most revenues. Here is how that executive is likely to view the life cycle:

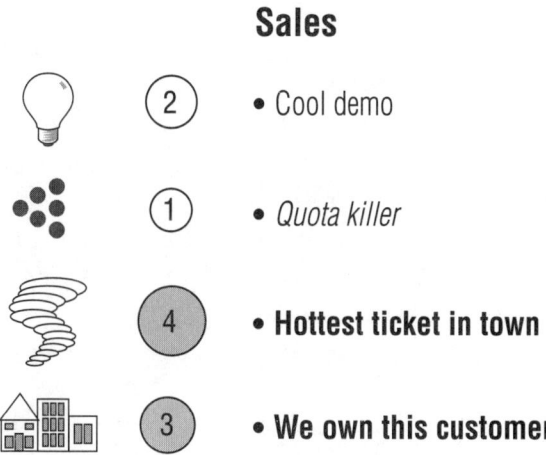

Sales

- Cool demo   (2)
- *Quota killer*   (1)
- **Hottest ticket in town**   (4)
- **We own this customer**   (3)

Figure 5.4

I have yet to encounter a sales organization that met a tornado it didn't like. It would be like a bunch of fishermen saying, "Hey, this is no fun, there are just too many fish today!" To be sure, tornadoes attract widespread market attention, so while the game is plentiful, so are the hunters. This makes for a hypercompetitive situation, but that is just the way great sales organizations like it. Winning takes aggression, smarts, and stamina—Type A behavior all the way, just the sort of energy that motivated the rest of the corporation to give these folks the sales job and get them out of the building. Give the tornado a 4.

If there are no tornadoes available, salespeople will opt for Main Street, not because it is challenging but because it is such a sweet deal. Here the customer is relatively captive, dramatically reducing the competition and increasing sales forecastability. It is a bit like fishing in a stocked pond, but the eating is good. Give Main Street a 3.

Neither of the two remaining phases are particularly attractive to salespeople, but at least the early market is likely to have a cool demo. This has two uses. Occasionally people in the direct sales force can use a cool demo to hook the stray visionary customer and land a major contract. More commonly, however, the entire sales force simply uses the demo as an excuse to have a meeting with their current customers, show them the new stuff, let the techies ooh and ahh about it, and then sit down with the conservative managers and sell them a bunch more of whatever it is they already own. For this, value-added salespeople will grant the early market a 2.

That leaves the bowling alley. Now the first time through the life cycle the bowling alley is not so bad—it is easier to make quota there than in the chasm. But once a company has passed through a tornado and made it to Main Street, the bowling alley becomes a *quota killer*. That is, compared to Main Street market dynamics, sales resistance in the bowling alley is much higher, the solution's complexity if much greater, and the sales cycle much longer. In addition, the product-leadership resources needed to succeed at this venture are long gone, either voluntarily out of boredom with Main Street or as part of a cost-reduction exercise in operational excellence. Moreover, your installed base of customers is not the right audience for this offer. They have now become conservatives and are putting pressure on your company to enhance the older stuff, not divert resources into this newfangledness. Even if the sales function were to grant the salesperson quota relief to take on this challenge, there is just too little upside gain for too much downside risk when compared to other possible ways of investing sales time.

So the bowling alley gets a 1, and the reader will not be surprised to learn that this is the phase of the life cycle that will require triage attention. Before looking into that, however, let us first see where the fifth and final function lines up.

FINANCE

In general, finance takes a view of the life cycle that aligns it with operations:

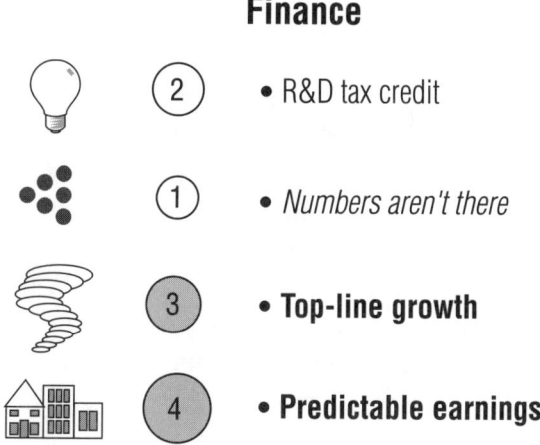

Finance

- R&D tax credit (2)
- *Numbers aren't there* (1)
- **Top-line growth** (3)
- **Predictable earnings** (4)

Figure 5.5

For finance teams, Main Street equates to normality. Markets grow at modest but relatively predictable rates. Competition is serious but comes from expected quarters. Improvements are continuous, both in offerings and in operations, all of which lead to incremental gains in productivity that, for the most part, drop to the bottom line, improving earnings per share. Stocks in any Main Street sector are measured by their P/E ratios, so this performance makes investors very happy. Main Street is a land of no surprises, and that is enough to earn it a 4 from finance.

Tornadoes come next. To be sure, by some financial metrics tornadoes might be even better than Main Street, but not when you consider that the added uncertainty and volatility take their toll. The good news is that the top line is robust and growing at eye-popping rates. The bad news is that losses can show up as often as profits, and cash flow can be a nightmare. However, with the right investors, ones who are more interested in the P/S ratio than the P/E ratio, companies can ride tornadoes to unprecedented valuation heights. Give the tornado a 3.

Interestingly, the early market also gains finance's support. Good finance people know you have to invest in the future in order to keep a going concern. They know there has to be a protected zone where the burden of profitability is withheld for an incubation period. Besides, R and D earns a tax credit. Thus the early market gets a 2.

But woe again to the bowling alley. From finance's point of view the economics of niche-market investments simply don't add up, certainly not for a company of BlueChip's size. The incubation period is over, and it is time for the new business unit to make a contribution to revenues and earnings, one that can have an impact on stock price. But a niche strategy does not generate sales large enough to make a dent in the overall revenue picture, and the investment of time and focus seems way out of proportion to the return. So finance gives the bowling alley a 1.

END RESULT: STUCK IN THE CHASM—*AGAIN*!

Now when line functions are allowed to gravitate toward their natural preferences, companies self-organize in a way that supports three of the four life-cycle phases reasonably well. Here's the overall picture:

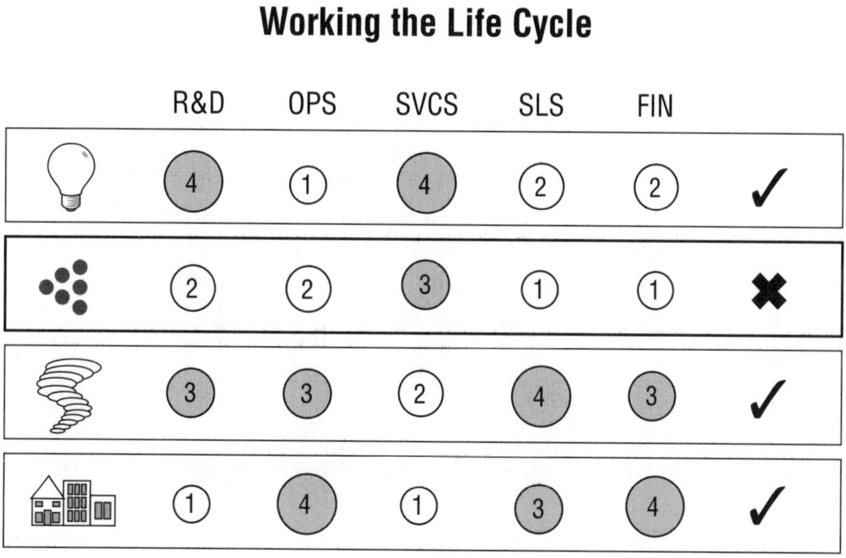

Working the Life Cycle

	R&D	OPS	SVCS	SLS	FIN	
💡	4	1	4	2	2	✓
⣿	2	2	3	1	1	✗
🌪	3	3	2	4	3	✓
🏠	1	4	1	3	4	✓

Figure 5.6

The tornado represents the highest scoring phase (15 points if you're counting). Led by sales, the other functions rally round. Indeed, except for highly customized services businesses, it is hard to image any company rejecting a tornado call. So, no need for triage here. To be sure, there are challenges, particularly when the company has been out of tornado markets for a while, but like an old warhorse, the spirit can be rekindled.

Main Street represents a close second (13 points), but here we see ranks dividing, which has sobering implications, as we shall see later. The good news, though, is that there are two strong lead functions—operations and finance—that are able to pull the organization together. The message goes out: no more Peter Pan, early-market, fly-by-the-seat-of-our-pants stuff. We're adults now, and we have to act accordingly. Thus processes are put in place and procedures followed, people slow down a bit (and organizations put on a little weight), and life goes on. Stellar Main Street performance, to be sure, does require more constructive measures, but from a triage point of view, this ain't broke, so don't fix it.

Interestingly, the early-market scores just as high as Main Street (also 13 points) because that is where the other half of the company retreated to when the operations and finance people took over. Engineers, in particular, will gravitate here regardless of what management says. And while salespeople will not actively sell the next big thing (demo it, yes—sell it, no), professional services people can be counted on to step in to help close the deal because one such sale can keep them busy for a long time. Again, stellar performance may not be in the cards, but established organizations are not directly at risk for this phase of the life cycle, so triage rules say don't focus here either.

That leaves us with the bowling alley, and specifically with the challenge of crossing the chasm—making the transition from the early market into the bowling alley. Over and over again, it emerges as the truly broken process in virtually all established organizations. To be precise, the problem is actually *recrossing the chasm* because organizations like BlueChip have made it across at least once before. That's how they got into a tornado in the first place and then later on graduated to Main Street. Now that it is time to reenact this feat, however, *there is no function willing to champion the next crossing.* The people that accomplished this feat last time are long gone, and thus the "institutional memory" can no longer be relied upon.

The implications of this realization are chilling. If no one will champion the effort, no innovative R and D can cross the chasm. That means all R and D investment in breakthrough technologies is essentially futile. Future discontinuous innovations will occur, to be sure, but they will lead to tornadoes for other companies, and BlueChip will be playing catch-up to those market-making efforts, not spearheading its own. In the best circumstances, this means that BlueChip technology can come late to an open-systems market with some chance of becoming a prince and perhaps in the future overthrowing the king. Worst case is it will come late to a gorilla game with a chimp technology and be crushed by the market's rejection of any standard other than the gorilla's. Neither scenario has much upside.

Combine this observation with the fact that the installed base of customers has become conservative, urging the company to stick to its old knitting, and one that generates an environment in which managers learn it is not wise to take technology risks.

Indeed, over time they learn not to take any risks at all. This is the beginning of the end.

In such an environment, good people move on, and with nothing to recruit new good people to join, the team in aggregate gets weaker and weaker, losing its leadership and its savvy. For a while it may appear that all is well because the current set of customers is truly loyal and the offers made to them truly valuable. Sure, one might rationalize, some new customers on the margin are going to the new technology, but that business is not really profitable anyway, and there is still plenty of demand for our established offerings. But sooner or later the next wave of technology does arrive, and with its advent all the frailty of the current position is exposed. This is where triage is well and truly needed.

To state the triage problem succinctly, *the internal line functions of companies on Main Street actively repel adoption of any future disruptive technologies.* As Pogo once observed long ago, "We have met the enemy and he is *us!*" At BlueChip we might imagine it playing out as follows:

1. In line with their predilection for Main Street markets, operations and finance have taken control of the company and instituted management by the numbers. The P&L has become the basis for judging success, and return on assets the key metric when weighing alternative investment decisions. ROA, in turn, is judged primarily on forecastable sales. This has led to investment decisions that have a high sensitivity to GAP and low to no sensitivity to CAP. Thus CAP has been routinely and often unknowingly sacrificed to GAP. BlueChip has indeed hit its earnings metrics, but in part because it has not been investing sufficiently to catch the next big technology wave.

2. When challenged on this point, however, operations and finance deny its validity, pointing instead to the large amount allocated to R and D funding. R and D corroborates this argument. We have sixteen different products in the pipeline, it testifies, and over 40 percent of current sales come from products that were invented in the last three years. We are a healthy and vibrant institution. Moore's criticisms do not apply to us.

3. Marketing, however, intercedes on Moore's behalf (an all too often career-limiting move). The new products, it observes, are continuous innovations extending the old paradigm. They do not answer the need to get on the new wave. And speaking of that new wave, the problem is not a lack of new offerings—to R and D's credit they *are* being created—but rather our company's inability to cross the chasm with them. It is additional *market development* investment that is required, not more R and D. All the other line functions, however, interpret marketing's testimony as a thinly veiled attempt to garner more departmental budget, and marketing is asked to sit down.

4. Sales is called to testify. It confidently takes the floor to assure everyone that Moore is indeed off base. Look at the numbers. Revenues are at record levels, and profit margins, although squeezed a bit, are still good. We need to stay on course. (What sales does not say is that this includes supporting a sales compensation plan that continues to pay commissions appropriate for winning market-share battles in the tornado but significantly overgenerous for selling into a captive installed base on Main Street.)

5. Professional services is called to testify. It reluctantly points out that indeed customers are not taking up the new technology as fast as one would like, but it goes on to report that its own backlog has never been higher, albeit largely from helping integrate other people's technology into the company's legacy systems. R and D and sales both take this occasion to complain that professional services is not helping to promote the new stuff. Services replies, however, that it must maintain a degree of neutrality in order to keep the trust of the customer and that, after all, selling *is* sales' job. A round of recriminations follows, brought to a close by the lead executive, who moves the meeting to the next agenda item.

Meanwhile, as this executive staff meeting winds its way through another familiar if long morning, another set of meetings is happening on Wall Street, and these do not bode well for BlueChip.

EARTHQUAKE

While BlueChip's stovepipe functions debate among themselves, its investment bankers, with their financial analysts, are meeting with some start-up championing the next big wave. Both sides of the table are hoping to get together to make an initial public offering, garnering the investment bank a 7 percent commission for so doing, and the start-up founders and venture-capital backers a big slug of capital gains. In the course of these briefings the financial analysts begin to see from the start-up's business plan just how exposed the current market leaders are. This causes them to make a note to raise the issue at BlueChip's next quarterly conference call.

BlueChip management, not privy to the start-ups' briefings, comes to the next conference call prepared to discuss the current quarter's numbers. When the question of market threat from a new quarter is raised, the team is simply not able to respond crisply. Let us get back to you on that, says the CFO. The analysts actually are somewhat tolerant the first time this happens, and so they acquiesce, and the issue is deferred to the following quarter. But after two or three such quarters with no definitive response from BlueChip, one or another of these same analysts breaks ranks and converts the company's coveted STRONG BUY rating to a lukewarm BUY or to an even chillier ACCUMULATE or to a truly frosty HOLD—and the stock price tanks. Even if no analyst breaks ranks, the first time BlueChip misses any of its numbers, it is devalued some horrific percentage, serving as a kind of catch-up in accounting for competitive-advantage deterioration.

When the stock market correction strikes, BlueChip management is appalled. How in the world can the market give credence to these start-ups who have no earnings and precious few revenues and be so harsh on us who have plenty of both? The question is rhetorical, of course, for the management team is in complete denial relative to the true answer. What should be clear to readers of this book by now, however, is that the market is simply tracking to competitive advantage. Specifically, it is looking at the deteriorating CAP of the older technology and the increasing GAP of the emerging technology and forecasting a point at which the lines cross. Beyond that point it is crediting the challenger with the advantage going forward and discounting the incumbent's stock to make up the difference.

There is no way out of this box. Accounting for competitive advantage is as relentless and remorseless as traditional financial accounting. The market may be a little slow in balancing its books, but that only results in more violent adjustments when the correction comes. In short, the fault line has shifted, the earthquake has hit, and the company has been dramatically devalued. Now the question is, how can BlueChip respond?

Going forward let us assume the best. The management team is chastened and resolved. It absolutely commits itself to do whatever it takes to restore shareholder value. Now what?

TRIAGE IN THE LINE FUNCTIONS

In the short term, there is no time to change course or correct strategy. What matters instead is how quickly BlueChip can shift resources to support its core value-adding functions in the marketplace. Bringing up the troops and driving them to fill in the value gap is the short-term answer to the emergency. This translates into a fast-paced, hard-edged exercise in determining *core* versus *context*. The question is stark: We must gain traction through increased focus, so what do we save and what do we jettison?

To answer this question, each line function management team must take a snapshot of its current resource allocations and then determine where to reallocate them going forward. Here's how it plays out.

R and D Triage

True to its own interests, and those of the shareholders, R and D has kept a major effort going in early-market research. Because of the inability of BlueChip to support crossing the chasm, however, none of these efforts have successfully made it into the mainstream market, and so to earn its keep R and D has split the remainder of its resources between supporting the previous generation of technology, now on Main Street, and doing its best to catch up to other companies' tornado technologies by cloning them as best it can. As a consequence, BlueChip has not been first to market with any new wave in so long that it has lost much of the market clout it once had. For some time, it has not been able to get in on the best deals nor enjoy the premium margins it once did. As a result, the company's position is more vulnerable to a disruptive innovation than that of a more vital market leader in its category.

From a triage point of view, now that the disruption has arrived, the company has two choices. On the one hand, it can decide it is too late for any last-minute chasm crossing and write down all its in-process R and D as scrap. In the short term, it will then shift all these early-market resources to the pending tornado based on the new technology, playing catch-up once again. The results will not be first class—this is not BlueChip's forte by any means—but they will blunt the impact of the immediate assault and reassure customers and partners that the company "gets it." Longer term there should be play for a respectable position in the emerging market.

Alternatively, BlueChip can elevate the status of one of its own early-market projects in progress and bet a large chunk of the company's future on creating its own version of the next big thing. Following this course, it will take people off the tornado work on other people's technologies and put them instead on its own discontinuous innovation. This is a riskier gambit, to be sure, but if it works, the rewards are much higher. From an objective point of view, however, jumping from worst to first is normally a low-probability bet, and the executive team must be careful not to take this course simply as a move to soothe wounded pride.

Neither of the choices offered is particularly attractive, but that is the price for many prior years of denial. For the purposes of working through the remaining triage scenarios for the other line functions, we will assume that BlueChip has chosen the first option. After we are done, we will then go back and show how it can execute a recrossing-the-chasm strategy with the second.

In either case, however, to support the triage shift in resources, ongoing R and D on Main Street technology must be cut back sharply. In general, this work must be redefined as context and outsourced with all possible speed. Until management gets it out of the corporation entirely, its inertial weight will inevitably retard all efforts to change course or speed. As part of the transition, BlueChip should support initiatives led by marketing and customer service, focused on altering the surface of the offering, and restrict the outsourced R and D efforts solely to cost-reducing the existing substructure and maintaining its reliability.

R and D Triage Checklist

- Shoot or promote current early-market initiatives.

- Chase the tornado or race across the chasm.

- Outsource Main Street maintenance work *now*!

Operations Triage

The major triage task in operations is to extract the rest of the company from the myriad of context operations into which it has lackadaisically allowed itself to become entangled. The goal is to free up as many resources as possible to focus on core. The tack to take is aggressive, immediate outsourcing.

It is critical to note at this juncture that the triage challenge cannot be solved either by downsizing or reorganizing. Recall that the scarce resources in the age of the Internet are *time, talent,* and *management attention.* Downsizing or reorganizing do not reduce the demands on any of these elements—indeed, in every case they increase them. So the classic response of a round of layoffs, while providing some immediate running room for cash flow, does nothing to solve the basic problem. Only outsourcing can provide the needed relief.

In looking at BlueChip, there will be two major sources of context operations to outsource. The first consists of operations that have always been context. Why, one might ask, did BlueChip ever bring them in house in the first place? Actually the company acquired these resources during the last tornado when the emphasis was on capturing market share as fast as possible. In support of that goal, it wanted to ensure that high throughput in the line functions would not be disrupted, and so rather than rely on an external supplier, it brought the function in house, albeit at the cost of some inefficiency. Given the pressures of tornado-market competitions, this may well have been correct strategy at the time. Now that the tornado is over, however, there is no rationale for persisting on this course, and these same resources need to be shed.

But operations has an even greater challenge in store for it than this. Most of the people in operations, after all, were recruited to perform core tasks. What should we do with them? The sad truth is that over time these very same tasks, which used to be core, have gradually become context. As we noted in Chapter 1, as the technology adoption life cycle marches forward, tasks that at one time represent differentiated capabilities become gradually transformed into hygiene factors. BlueChip still has to provide them, but it no longer gets stock market credit for so doing. But try telling that to the people who have given their all to get the company where it is today. Nonetheless, if it is going to successfully compete for capital going forward, the company must find a way to shed itself of these context responsibilities so it can focus the bulk of its time, talent, and management attention back onto core.

Note that freeing up of resources—and not cost reduction—is the primary goal of a triage outsourcing effort. To be sure, going forward an outsourcing relationship must provide for the systematic cost reduction of context functions. Those cost reductions will be key to maintaining margins in the older technology, thereby contributing working capital to the next generation of market development. But in the short term, it is more important that outsourcing simply happen quickly and reliably. With so many changes in the wind, the last thing management wants to worry about is the wheels coming off a hygiene operation.

To manage this process, operations needs to find external service providers who are willing to take some or all of these monkeys off BlueChip's back. As discussed in Chapter 1, one creative response here is to put the in-house team itself into an outsourcing business, offering it a committed contract for some amount of time to ease the transition. The key here is to make sure that when the team does transition, it takes the monkey with it. Enduring the disruption of outsourcing and then having to recommit time, talent, or management attention to managing the outsourcer is the worst possible outcome in this situation.

While all this outsourcing of context is under way, top management will be focused on what it believes will be the new core. In so doing, it is likely to conclude that the company lacks many of the skills needed to compete in the new category. Its initial response will be to seek these skills outside the company—in effect, to outsource core rather than context (or even in addition to it). This is a mistake. Core must be kept inside the company. If the skills simply cannot be found, then they must be acquired, or the company must let itself get acquired. In the very short term, it is possible to second-source gap-filling products and services, but this is a short-term fix only. The real fix is to challenge your own people to step up to a completely new mark. My experience is that you will be pleasantly surprised. All those people you thought did not have it in them, in fact do have it in them, if you have the skills to pull it out.

Operations Checklist

- Drive a core versus context exercise across the corporation.

- Manage the outsourcing of context for everything except R and D.

- Focus first on transferring responsibility safely, not cost reduction.

- Do *not* outsource core, regardless of how little in-house expertise you have.

Professional Services Triage

As the consulting arm of BlueChip, professional services finds itself in a peculiar position. There is actually heavy tornado-market demand for its services, but that demand is based on integrating some other company's hot new technology into BlueChip's installed base of legacy systems. Because the company is under attack, management may be so grateful for the revenues that it misses a key point: None of this work does anything to improve the company's stock price. Stock price is a function of securing sustainable competitive advantage—GAP and CAP. That can be achieved only when professional services helps further technology and product offerings coming from BlueChip itself.

The triage problem the services group faces is that BlueChip's own offerings are either too early in the life cycle—stuck on the other side of the chasm—or too late in it—stuck out on Main Street—for the organization to make its most valuable contribution. The systemic correction needed here is better recrossing-the-chasm behavior, a topic we shall turn to later in the chapter. In the short term, however, professional services needs to put its wood behind BlueChip arrows, wherever they may be.

Thus if the company is playing catch-up inside the tornado, then this group needs to provide discounted services as a way of creating a temporary GAP for a set of product offerings that cannot yet compete effectively on their own. If the company has instead decided to bet on the next big thing from R and D, then the group has to put all its weight behind the chasm-crossing effort needed to make that technology a success. In neither case should the group view maximizing its own revenues and earnings as the appropriate goal or correct metric.

Professional services, in other words, should treat itself as a fungible resource that can be configured to support virtually any competitive-advantage strategy the company undertakes. Its critical metric in this light is to make sure it puts its resources to work on core work and not on context. To put this as clearly as possible, *nonbillable work on core will create more shareholder value than billable work on context.*

In particular, what professional services must guard against is being co-opted by a sales organization under intense pressure to make quota and unable to do so with the current lineup of BlueChip products. In such a situation, sales teams will often resort to offering "random acts of service," selling early-market projects in support of some other company's discontinuous innovations. This is bad business. It is almost never profitable for the services organization, it does not contribute to the company's competitive-advantage position, and it may well enhance the position of a potential future competitor. Of course, such projects are flattering to the services folks, and the revenue numbers will be hungrily eyed by the finance department, but the truth is, this is toxic revenue and must be shunned.

Professional Services Organization Triage Checklist

- Identify the top corporate market initiatives and focus all resources there.

- Reset performance metrics based solely on the success of these initiatives.

- Do not get lured into pursuing revenues or margins as a primary goal.

Sales Triage

When the earthquake hits, of all the functions sales is typically the one most in need of realignment and yet most resistant to change. Its misalignment is that it has the bulk of its resources dedicated to Main Street, but BlueChip needs it to reallocate them to more competitive customer-acquisition efforts earlier in the life cycle. The resistance is a function of an organizational structure and a sales compensation program that has not kept pace with value migration. Here's what has transpired.

When technology-enabled markets move to Main Street, shareholder value is created by working with existing customers to extend their investments in current systems. These are not typically competitive sales situations. Rather they are a matter of ratcheting an already committed investment stream upward a few notches. Customer service relationships are key here because they create the kind of customer intimacy needed to make useful recommendations going forward. They also help remove the biggest obstacle to increased investment, which is typically customer dissatisfaction with the shortcomings of current offerings. In sum, consistent account presence is the critical element to gaining the credibility and trust needed to upsell this customer. Tornado-oriented sales organizations, however, are staffed with people who thrive on beating the competition and who are very transaction oriented. As soon as a deal is done, their instinct is to go off and find another deal. They do not like to stay around and work through all the inconsistencies. Thus, when the market goes to Main Street, there is an inherent mismatch between task and capability.

So why doesn't this get fixed? In large part it is due to a problem in compensation. Sales organizations are typically compensated by commissions or revenues. To spur competitive behavior, commission rates are set high during the tornado. These high commissions are more than offset by the value to the company of gaining a new customer to whom it can sell for years to come. When the market moves to Main Street, however, more and more sales come from existing customers. These sales are neither as challenging to make nor as valuable to the company as tornado sales. But commissions are not immediately reset to a lower rate—in part because the transition is never obvious at any one point in time. This in turn creates a temporary condition of overcompensation.

Now whenever people are overcompensated, their natural reaction is not to rock the boat. Instead they hunker down to protect their franchise. The resultant behavior is that the salespeople in place lock onto the customer-facing responsibility and block any attempts at customer contact that do not go through them. In effect, they hold the customer hostage. In so doing, they screen out any offer or program that would threaten their ability to control the account and the sales process. This behavior occurs both in direct sales forces at the high end of the market and in resellers at the low end, and in both cases the only sales that succeed in passing through the filter are upgrades and enhancements to the existing infrastructure, and for these BlueChip must pay an increasingly exorbitant commission. In addition, in direct sales channels there is increasing political pressure not to disintermediate any channel partner, leading in some instances to paying multiple commissions on the same sale.

Sooner or later the company has to call an end to this game. The triage fix is to migrate mature offerings from a higher cost channel to a lower cost one and correspondingly to migrate top-talent sales teams from the task of customer retention to that of new customer acquisition. Depending on the scope, severity, and urgency of the need to change, sales management chooses from the following escalating series of interventions:[1]

---

[1] I am indebted to Mike Meisenheimer and Jim Triandiflou, executives at Ockham Technologies Inc., a sales management software company in Atlanta, Georgia, both for this escalation model and for their general framework for managing sales organizations through the various stages of the technology adoption life cycle.

1. *Tell.* For minor changes, just tell people what the desired new behavior is and then monitor their performance for compliance to the new directive.

2. *Measure.* For more significant offers, where the consequences are important, but the scope of the change does not merit a new channel or a revision in compensation, measure the current channel's sales success against the desired new behavior. Use public reporting against measures as the prime motive to drive the new behavior.

3. *Compensate.* For still more significant offers, but where a channel change is still more work than it is worth, change the compensation program to reward the new behaviors and penalize persisting in the old ones.

4. *Redefine the job.* This is effectively what happens in a channel change. The existing team members can keep their current jobs and change products or keep their current products and change jobs. What they cannot keep is the status quo.

5. *Replace the person.* This is what happens when a member of the sales team simply cannot handle the previous choice.

Conducting this escalation is the job of sales management. One reason it is so challenging is that the sales executives in charge typically owe a lot of their personal success to the people they are managing. It can easily happen that they have too many "relationship debts" outstanding for them to be able to hold strictly to this line. When that's the case, it is critical that BlueChip executive management step in and change the team at the top.

Again, this is nothing personal—it is simply a matter of stock price. Don't change the team, and the existing channel will block access to the customer and withhold support from any new offers. Other companies not hobbled by such a channel will get in behind the BlueChip team, build up a new market around the new paradigm, and stick the company with a legacy customer base and an aging product line. In the long run nothing is gained and nobody is served.

Sales Triage Checklist

- Redefine Main Street metrics and compensation and match staff accordingly.

- Charter a new team to tackle the new-customer-acquisition challenges.

- Where needed, change the channel of distribution to drive change.

- Where needed, change the people doing the job to gain traction.

Finance Triage

The triage crisis for finance actually begins outside the operations of the company, in the domain of investor relations. The company's stock has been devalued, and the shareholders are angry. Moreover, since the executive team and many of the managers at BlueChip are compensated in stock options, they are mad too. Add to them BlueChip's value-chain partners who are now concerned about the company's competitiveness in the market, and key customers who call to make sure the company is still viable, and finance has a whole list of people to call back. The good news is they all want the same thing—a simple explanation. The bad news is that is precisely what is not available.

The actual "cause" of the stock devaluation was not anything BlueChip did but rather the emergence of a market challenge posed by a disruptive innovation. The company's stock got hit in its CAP, in other words, not in its GAP. As a result, there is nothing on the P&L to explain the stock movement, only market momentum moving on to the next technology wave. Thus finance must communicate a new model of the marketplace that repositions the company in light of these new developments. To get such a model in play, however, requires galvanizing the entire executive team to construct a new competitive agenda.

Thus the core triage activity of finance is to help BlueChip realign its goals and metrics by changing the tools and feedback it gives to executives to help them manage for shareholder value. A prolonged stint on Main Street has institutionalized a P&L orientation, but in addressing the new triage challenge, that viewpoint is counterproductive. Instead finance must help the executive team focus on the competitive-advantage crisis, in large part by communicating Wall Street's interpretation of the change in the category. GAP and CAP charts, and indeed the entire discussion of finance in Chapter 2, are intended to provide a foundation for this discussion. Finance must not let the team yield to the temptation to mock the dotcoms for their lack of revenue and earnings but instead explain why, in spite of their absence, investors still value these competitors highly—indeed, on a P/S ratio basis, far more highly than BlueChip. This will almost certainly lead to a series of heated and defensive discussions, but the team must work through these issues if it is to get back into the game.

The evidence for having achieved a true course correction is a revised positioning of BlueChip based on (1) acknowledging the changes in the marketplace, and (2) explaining how BlueChip is redeploying its assets to achieve greater competitive advantage. Part of this story must show how BlueChip is catching the new wave. Dismissing the wave as either wrong-headed or premature will only cause investors to believe the company is in denial. Even if the long-term strategy is to start or ride some other wave, in the short term there needs to be some accommodation of the current one in the company's immediate repositioning to investors.

Finally, all the while this is going on, another group within the finance department should be working internally with those parts of the business that will stay on Main Street. This group must retain an emphasis on standard P&L metrics for several reasons. First of all, the better the quarterly bottom line, the more forgiving the investors will be of BlueChip having fallen temporarily behind in the new competition. Second, the more that Main Street operations can contribute to working capital, the better, since at the moment investor enthusiasm for providing that same capital is waffling. And third, by holding Main Street operations' feet to the fire, finance will actually help accelerate the outsourcing of context that is so key to their role in getting the company on track to recross the chasm. One final note: The finance team must support the outsourcing of context first to shed inertia and second to reduce costs. That is, despite all temptation to the contrary, it must not force a cost-reduction agenda too soon.

Finance Triage Checklist

- Reset the internal orientation from P&L to GAP/CAP.

- Relax financial controls on change initiatives.

- Tighten financial controls on Main Street operations.

- Don't force immediate cost-reduction goals on context outsourcing.

At the end of the day, however, despite its immediate criticality, triage within the line functions solves no long-term problems. All it can do is take the company out of range of crisis and buy it some time to regroup and redirect its efforts. In technology-enabled markets, this means BlueChip must sooner or later sponsor its own discontinuous innovations and get them across the chasm to compete for mainstream market share.

RECROSSING THE CHASM

The triage manual for realigning BlueChip so that it can recross the chasm is organized around four cornerstone behaviors the company must adopt:

1. Get the board of directors focused on the real challenge.

2. Construct a dedicated chasm-crossing team focused on appropriate goals and metrics.

3. Deconstruct lingering resistance.

4. Don't stop with the first pin.

The remainder of this chapter is dedicated to describing these behaviors in more detail.

GET THE BOARD OF DIRECTORS FOCUSED ON THE REAL CHALLENGE

Ninety percent of success in triage lies in prioritizing the right problems to address. Well, we just did that. We've flat-out said, *It's recrossing the chasm, stupid!* Surely that is enough to get everyone focused? Fat chance.

The inertial forces behind business as usual are huge. They routinely overpower even the most well-articulated management insights, independent of manager rank. So even if you're the CEO, and you're up there turning the wheel and setting the new course, what makes you think that wheel is attached to anything? The easier it is to spin, the more you may be sure that it is affecting no real gears. *Fortune* 500 companies are simply too big for any one person to turn.

So now what?

The first job is to get the board of directors engaged. This begins with a reminder: If anyone is the steward of stock price, it is the board. Discontinuous innovations—when they cross the chasm—have dramatic impact on every company's stock price in the sector. Therefore, the current status of such innovations, be they ours or someone else's, is a board-level issue that deserves board-level attention annually at minimum, and in rapidly changing markets more like twice a year.

In this review, the entire domain of discontinuous technologies should be laid out—the company's internal bets, the bets of competing companies, and the status of each relative to the chasm. Management must lead here in terms of which bets are best to make, but the board must lead in ensuring that alternative bets are not ignored and that contingency plans are in place in case the other guys' bets win instead of ours. In particular, if we are unable to get our technology across the chasm in time, what is our fallback position if we have to adopt their technology? The fates of Wang, Lotus, WordPerfect, and Digital Equipment Corporation—all of whom bet their companies on some competitor's technology not succeeding and then lost their companies when in fact it did succeed—should keep boards alert during this session.

Please note that the focus here is not on technologies in the early market but rather on technologies crossing the chasm. Therefore, instead of getting reports from R and D on the latest cutting-edge projects, which is how boards typically engage this issue today, they need to get reports from marketing on market development. Specifically, they need to get a *technology adoption report.*

The key questions the board must see answered in this report are as follows:

1. *Have any of our new technologies proven themselves in the early market?*

   The answer to this question is yes when one can point to a handful of visionary customers who have deployed the technology successfully and are referenceable. And if the company's own professional services organization has helped in the process, that is a big plus, for it is likely to have captured key lessons that will help in crossing the chasm.

2. *Is it time to cross the chasm?*

   The answer to this question is yes if management believes, with the help of partners, the company could field a replicable solution to a thorny problem that a niche of customers is clamoring to see solved. By contrast, if early-market deployments have revealed that such a solution is not currently feasible or that the benefits envisioned for it simply are not sufficiently compelling, then the candidate technology gets scratched from the list.

3. *What is the target beachhead segment?*

   Assuming it is time to cross the chasm, the answer to this question must call out a single vertical market segment, defined in terms of geography, industry, and the department or profession of the system's end user. It should further be delineated by a list of target customer companies that represent all the significant players in the segment. Absent a single definitive list, segmentation-based programs cannot be held properly accountable.

4. What are the metrics of success?

The primary success metric is the number of sales of the new technology to companies on the target list. This is measured against sales by any other company of any competing discontinuous innovation into the same prospect base. The market share of established technologies is not the issue, as that represents the legacy, not the future. Sales outside the target segment are also not a relevant metric, as they do not help generate adoption momentum to cross the chasm.

5. What is the goal to which compensation rewards are tied?

The goal is to dominate sales of the new technology to the target segment. Recall the rule of thumb that if a company wins 30 percent of these sales, it is *a leader,* 50 percent and it is *the leader,* 70 percent or more and it is *the dominator.* In crossing the chasm the goal is to dominate the first segment, be the leader in the next one or two, and then be a leader from there on out. Executive compensation programs should be reshaped to reflect the top board-level priority given to these goals.

6. What is the status of the chasm-crossing program today?

Once a chasm-crossing program is initiated, members of the board should inquire into its status every occasion they have to speak with management. After a while even the most resistant manager capitulates under this single-minded treatment. There is simply nothing more motivating than knowing the question you are going to be asked and knowing that if you do not have a good answer, you're going to look like an idiot.

Most important of all, however, the board needs to hold executive management accountable *as a team.* This forces them to work as a united force to directly engage the inertial forces of business as usual. Anything less than that simply will not turn the boat.

To ensure this behavior, the entire team's compensation and recognition should depend upon chasm-crossing success. That is, no individual member of the team should be allowed to win big if the chasm is not crossed—not the VP of Sales, even if the sales organization beats quota; not the VP of Professional Services, even though it turns in record revenues; not the head of R and D, despite the fact the company won several product awards; not the VP of Operations, who achieved six-sigma quality; not the CFO, whose accounting folks lowered Days Sales Outstanding by fifteen days. Why? Because every one of those achievements ignores a triage crisis in the making.

Finally, to put all this in perspective, chasm-crossing assaults might occur once or twice a decade. They are not the stuff of every year's plan. Moreover, when they do arise, there are only a small number of people who are actually assigned to make them happen. Everyone else is simply expected to help out, if only by not resisting. The entire action is expected to be brought to a conclusion within a year or two. Indeed, if it is not, the risk increases dramatically that it will never be accomplished at all. So we are not asking for a major revolution in board oversight, management compensation, or even business as usual. All we are asking for is the simple recognition that *the entire company's stock price is at stake, and all its members should act accordingly.*

Construct a Dedicated Chasm-Crossing Team

Because, as we have seen, there is no natural leadership emerging from the line functions for recrossing the chasm, it must be artificially constructed in the form of a cross-functional chasm-crossing team. The team should be led by a *senior executive sponsor.* This person is not an active agent in the process but rather a highly placed connection who can power through any resistance from lower-level line functions to the niche-market initiative.

Without this kind of sponsor engaged it is all too easy for the business-as-usual coalition on Main Street to prevail. Indeed, that is also why it is so important to get the board of directors focused on the problem and to tie the entire senior executive team's compensation to chasm-crossing success. Visibility and consequences at the very top of the organization are key to ensuring that this initiative never gets lost in the shuffle.

The chasm-crossing team itself must be cross-functional because the effort requires coordination across all of the line functions. The team should be led by an *industry marketing manager* who has strong domain expertise in the target customer's vertical market. Because there is no time to do market research, this person has to know the customer requirements from the outset. He or she leads the rest of the company by identifying and characterizing the problem to be solved, helping the marketing communications organization target the right audiences with the right messages, and holding the rest of the company accountable for delivering the whole product, either from internal work or from partner contributions.

There are three key team members who must work closely with this leader. The first of these is a *sales manager* in charge of a dedicated sales team focused exclusively on sales into the target niche. The goal here is to create not a separate sales organization but rather a separate sales territory that reports in parallel to the other, typically geographically organized, territories. People on this team must get a deep orientation to the target vertical, its general industry dynamics, the specific dynamics of the broken mission-critical process, and the likely job description for the department manager who is the target customer. Until the company reaches dominator status in the vertical niche, this sales manager will spend all his or her time either teaching or conducting consultative sales sessions within the target domain. Once dominator status has been reached and the company's market position is solidly in place, then sales responsibility will be migrated to an indirect channel that has more strength in demand fulfillment than in demand creation, and the direct sales resources can be refocused on the next niche market in the bowling alley.

The second key team member is a product marketing manager responsible for delivery and quality of the whole product. At The Chasm Group we like to call this person the *whole product manager* to make sure that everyone understands that the job does not stop with what your company makes and delivers but rather extends to managing every other component of the solution as well, regardless of whether it comes from a partner or even from the customer. End-to-end integrity of the value chain is this person's fundamental focus, and he or she is the point of control for solution accountability. Once market momentum is achieved, the whole product becomes self-correcting as more and more players compete to improve its quality. At this point the job reverts to a more traditional form of product marketing, with the whole product management task migrating to some other individual responsible for building the solution for the next niche market.

The third and final core team member is a *professional services manager* whose sole assignment is to support sales and to provision project teams focused on bringing the whole product into existence in the target segment customer's environment. At the outset this person's role leans more to the sales side as the early customers seek reassurance that their needs will get met. Once market momentum is established, the focus shifts to the delivery side of the equation, emphasizing knowledge capture, whole product component reuse, interface simplification between solution components and the partners who provide them, and training of newly deployed teams on lessons already learned. Over time, much of this function can migrate out of professional services into field sales support, at which time the resources can be released to support penetrating additional niche markets.

The remainder of the crossing-the-chasm team consists of liaisons to the line functions of R and D, operations, and finance. In each case the goal is to regulate interaction with the function so as to minimize disruption to business as usual and to restrict the impact of Main Street inertia on the chasm-crossing effort. The key principles here are as follows:

- With R and D the team needs to isolate market requirements for vertically specific functionality. The trade-off is whether to build workarounds outside the product, either through a partner or professional services, or to engage with R and D to modify the product to incorporate them. The latter does more to secure power within the niche, but it opens up the program to Main Street inertia, putting the request in the hopper with every other enhancement request. The ideal solution here is for R and D to split off a vertical release team to build vertically specific modules that plug into a standard architecture.

- With operations, the team needs to isolate and bundle niche-specific exception requirements from the standard operating procedures and to work through their resolution in an organized fashion. It is important to involve the other solution partners in this process (a) because they can explain the particulars of the exceptions they require, and (b) because they may be able to provide alternatives that can relieve the stress on inside operations. If the conflicts are found to be inherent and deep, outsourcing chasm-crossing operations is a legitimate alternative. This decision can stimulate Main Street resistance, however, hence the need for executive sponsorship as a backup.

- With finance, the team needs to build an accountability model as a cost center meeting time-sensitive market development objectives, not as a profit center contributing to the P&L. This will seem odd, to say the least, because the group will in fact generate revenue with attractive margins, albeit with modest volumes. But the company must stay focused on the key competitive-advantage issue, which is that breaking through into the mainstream marketplace will create future revenue opportunities far greater than those of the initial target niche market. Therefore, the company wants to optimize this effort for time, not for money, and must provide financing, metrics, and oversight to support that end.

DECONSTRUCT LINGERING RESISTANCE

Regardless of how important top management determines recrossing the chasm to be, there will be large segments of middle management in threatened context positions who will resist the effort. The notion that a company could somehow clean house all at once, once and for all, is neither practical nor desirable. Such reengineering would shock the culture to its very core and typically would be fatal to the organism.

Instead, the winning behavior is simply for management to act like a snowplow and clear the path. That is, it must make it unmistakably clear that in any conflict between a chasm-crossing effort and an established Main Street institution, the latter will lose. As in all such things, the breakthrough communication does not happen until the favored side wins an argument it really had no right to win. That is, until everyone can see that the contest is blatantly rigged, some players will continue to try to resist. So the best executive behavior is to demonstrate favoritism early and often.

Once this favoritism is made clear, the organization actually rebounds in the other direction, and many individuals inside the company compete to join the vertically focused chasm-crossing efforts, while others in horizontally oriented organizations complain that their teams need more vertical focus. When this happens, you know you are well on your way. The only danger in it is that, as these other organizations adopt the protective coloration of vertically focused chasm-crossing efforts, management will actually take them at face value and think it has multiple target markets under development. Almost certainly this is not the case. Instead, we have set up the dynamics for a final state of jeopardy—stopping bowling alley strategy after knocking down only one pin.

Don't Stop with the First Pin

As we have just noted, niche-market domination, once it gets going, is self-reinforcing. The results get better and better within the niche, and the organization as a whole gains enormous confidence about its market development acumen. But then a funny thing happens. It comes time to transition from the head pin to the next couple of bowling pins in the market development sequence, and all of a sudden every lesson that was learned seems to fly out the window. The organization announces its next two target niches, each of which is not a niche at all but a wholly separate bowling alley. Then, when it goes after these new markets, it forgets all about broken mission-critical processes, or even bent ones, and reverts to product-centric selling. In short, even as the company is congratulating itself on its terrific grasp of vertical niche marketing, what it is actually doing is shedding the behavior as fast as it possibly can.

What is going on? What has happened is that, as the Main Street organization saw the privileges granted to the chasm-crossing group's vertical niche approach, it took on the lingo and dressed up its other offerings in similar clothes. Management took these representations to be the fully developed constructs created in the first niche and planned for their success accordingly. But in fact they were nothing of the sort.

The consequence of this behavior is that the wheels start to come off. The first niche is fine, but none of the other efforts deliver. The managers complain that they aren't getting the support the first niche got, but the executive team doesn't see it that way, preferring instead to blame the team. In the marketplace, meanwhile, the company starts to get a single-niche reputation. This causes both partners and people inside the company to polarize, either wanting to join the winning niche team or to move on to something completely different. Now executive management is faced with two unattractive choices—become a single-niche player forever or transition back to being a purely horizontal competitor from a position of weakness.

The correct path instead is to leverage one's initial niche victory by seeking out one or two more pins *within the first bowling alley*. These will be niche markets from the same vertical sector but with different applications. Because of the credibility gained in the first niche, the numeric target for new sales wins in these follow-on pins can be lowered from 70 percent domination to 50 percent leadership. At the same time, one can target a second bowling alley if it has a 70 percent dominatable head pin. But that's the limit, regardless of how big or global your company is. It is just too easy to forgo niche ways in a publicly owned, successful corporation.

However, once you have multiple pins falling in one bowling alley, and the head pin knocked over in a second one, you can seriously undertake a broad horizontal attack on the market. The key here will be, have you discovered a killer app? That is, is there some use of the new technology that has broad common-denominator appeal and is sufficiently compelling to cause the pragmatists here en masse to stampede. If so, then you will change strategy once again, moving to take a tornado approach, and leave behind this bowling phase, albeit continuing to enjoy a special status in the niches you have already won. If not, you will continue with a bowling-alley-forever strategy.

SUMMARY OF KEY POINTS IN CHAPTER 5

This brings to a close our discussion of that form of managing for shareholder value called triage. Its premise has been that, by virtue of the natural inclinations of the powerful line functions in a technology company, three of the four phases of the technology adoption life cycle can be adequately handled following business as usual, but the fourth, what we termed recrossing the chasm, cannot. Instead, these same powerful line functions, left to their own devices, block any discontinuous offering from entering the mainstream market, even when it comes from their own labs.

To overcome this obstacle, we prescribed acts of triage within each of the line functions, as follows:

- *R and D* must either get its own technology across the chasm or put itself in service to some other company's tornado technology—now.

- *Operations* must lead the effort to outsource context activities throughout the company, thereby freeing up time, talent, and management attention to devote to the next wave of core differentiation.

- *Professional services* must eschew the revenue-generation opportunity of serving other companies' tornado demands and focus its talents instead on serving the shareholder-value-creation opportunity of getting its own company's technologies across the chasm.

- *Sales* must forgo the comfort of business as usual and force each sales channel to either redirect its value-adding skills to offers earlier in the technology adoption life cycle or take a significant cut in pay.

- *Finance* must substitute shareholder-value metrics for P&L metrics in order to focus the company on the need to reconstruct its competitive-advantage position, all the while maintaining P&L discipline in its Main Street operations.

All the while this triage effort is under way, the company must also launch its next chasm-crossing effort on a successful trajectory. The critical success factors here are:

1. Get the board of directors focused on the real problem. Shareholder value is not renewed through early-market R and D unless and until it has crossed the chasm.

2. Construct a dedicated chasm-crossing team. Here customer industry-focused marketing must lead with the help of professional services and sales, with the other line functions subordinating their interests to the effort.

3. Deconstruct lingering resistance. Executive management must make clear that there is no winning outcome in obstructing this effort.

4. Don't stop with the first pin. Niche-market development must return a series of niche victories before it pays off in the kind of sustainable competitive advantage that appeals to shareholders.

Taken altogether, these prescriptions constitute a direct remedy for the innovator's dilemma. That is, while in and of themselves they cannot make for a great company, they can and will keep a new technology from causing a great company to fail.

It now remains to see what it would take to build a great and lasting company. That is the subject of our final chapter.

6

BUILDING TO LAST

To live on the fault line—to embrace the challenges of the technology adoption life cycle and manage for shareholder value in the age of the Internet—one must, in the words of Jim Collins and Jerry Porras, build to last. What we have learned from the study of earthquakes is that buildings with rigid structures (with bricks-and-mortar construction, interestingly enough, topping the list) fare the worst when the ground underneath them shifts. By contrast, buildings engineered to sway with the wave of force are able to restore themselves to balance safely. There is a similar need in corporations to find points of balance that can absorb and survive the shocking changes in market dynamics involved when discontinuous innovations disrupt established markt positions. This chapter, the last chapter in the book, argues that that balance is to be found in culture.

At a high level, a business culture provides unifying values and practices that equate to "how we like to get things done around here." Like the stars to ancient travelers, these function as an orientation aid to navigation. They do not purport to get you across town, but they do propose to get you across large bodies of water. Culture in this sense is a global proposition.

Below this level, on the other hand, culture is deliberately unspecific. That is, instead of specifying procedures, it prescribes a style of action—a set of basic questions to use in sizing up a new circumstance, a set of preferred strategies and tactics from which to craft an appropriate response, and a core set of values for judging outcomes. Rather than being a set of rules, a culture is a rule-making framework that enables its members to cope with unpredicted and unprecedented circumstances.

Businesses benefit from this sort of capability at all times but particularly so in the current era, when deep changes in market dynamics are occurring with such disturbing frequency. This is not an era for the one-minute manager. These are not problems that can be solved by the twenty-two immutable laws of anything. We are all being asked instead to reach deep into ourselves to come to grips with new business models and find ways to align ourselves and our organizations with them. How we do this individually is largely a matter of personality. How we do it collectively is largely a matter of culture.

In this chapter we are going to examine four different styles of business culture, each of which takes a significantly different approach to the challenge of managing change. All four have proven their ability to support sustained excellence in business, and thus no one of them is to be preferred to any other. Nonetheless, because they are fundamentally differentiated from one another, it is important to pick one if people in your company are going to be clear about "how we like to get things done around here." Without this choice and the commitment it implies, everyone in the corporation will be fundamentally in doubt about which way is north.

This poses a huge challenge for executive management, and frankly, most teams duck it. Each of the four cultures described has characteristic virtues that make it attractive to incorporate, so ruling out any one of them is hard, and ruling out three of the four virtually impossible. Indeed, coming to the challenge with the mental framework of *ruling out* makes it highly unlikely one will get anywhere. Instead, the right thought is *place above*. The key question to ask throughout this entire chapter is, when the pressure is really on, and the cultures give very different feedback on how to proceed, which one of the cultures will you and your team encourage everyone in the company to place above the other three?

In the interests of maintaining diversity, you should understand that all companies have multiple cultures operating within them all the time. That is, because companies are organized at multiple levels, the corporation as a whole can have one culture while particular departments, line functions, or business units can operate under others. Indeed, as we shall see, there is a way to exploit this property of culture and organizations to help meet the varying demands of an evolving technology market. So we do not want to exterminate such diversity within the corporation.

But cultural flexibility can be carried too far. When different cultures interact, there is a kind of "import/export tax" upon any form of interculture commerce as each group translates the issues and values of the other into its own frame of reference. In relatively benign times, this tax is worth paying just to gain the flexibility of capabilities it enables. But in crisis, this same tax causes bottlenecks in execution that result in lost competitions wherever speed of response is required. By contrast, companies that can automatically resolve such conflicts by falling in line with a preestablished, unifying global culture have a huge advantage in execution.

As we have seen, living on the fault line repeatedly calls for executing rapid cross-functional changes in market development strategy. There is simply no time to negotiate a sequence of intercultural exchanges while putting these changes in place. The company has to be prewired to fly in formation. That is what making an abiding commitment to any one of the business cultures described in this chapter delivers.

FOUR BASIC CULTURES

To support executive teams in selecting their culture of choice, there is an extremely useful model, described by Bill Schneider in *The Reengineering Alternative: A Plan for Making Your Current Culture Work,* which divides the cultural landscape into four differentiated choices:[1]

---

[1] *The Reengineering Alternative: A Plan for Making Your Current Culture Work,* William E. Schneider, McGraw-Hill (New York, 1994). I have taken some liberties with the book's diagrams, so while Bill should be credited with the value they provide, he should not be blamed for any errors I insert. I am also indebted to Brad Spencer of Spencer Shenk Capers, an organizational development consulting firm, for drawing my attention to Schneider's work and for pointing out the parallels to Treacy and Wiersema's *The Value Disciplines of Market Leaders* that I discuss later in this chapter.

Four Cultures Model

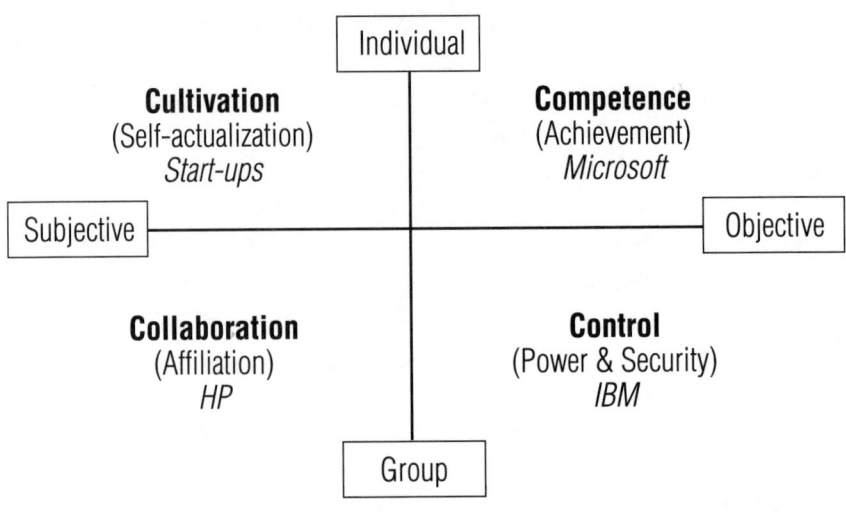

Figure 6.1

We are going to look into each of these four cultures in detail, but first we need to orient ourselves to the set as a whole. Each of these cultures is rooted in a fundamental human motivation that drives people in business as well as in the rest of their lives. That characterizing motivation is where the core energy that drives and unites each culture comes from. Schneider references the work of D. C. McClelland for three of these motives and Abraham Maslow for the fourth:

- The desire for *power* (to which I have added a complementary desire for *security*), which motivates *control culture.*

- The need for *affiliation,* which motivates *collaboration culture.*

- The drive for *achievement,* which motivates *competence culture.*

- The pursuit of *self-actualization,* which motivates *cultivation culture.*

The separations within the model derive from two sets of paired dipoles that have characterized Western culture from its onset. The first of these asks us to weigh our allegiance to the individual versus our allegiance to the group. In competence and cultivation cultures, the balance comes down on the side of the individual; in collaboration and control cultures, on the side of the group. But we need to be clear here. No culture is denying the value of the opposing dipole; each is simply stating a bias toward one of the two sides. It is this bias that helps organizations expedite working through thorny questions that otherwise would take prolonged negotiation to resolve.

The other dipole in operation here is what C. P. Snow once called the two cultures—the humanities and the sciences—which divide their interests along a subject/object distinction that contemporary culture has tagged right brain, left brain. The issue at stake is, on what basis will the organization make its tough decisions? Along this axis competence and control cultures come down on the side of objective data, tying their key decisions wherever possible to quantifiable changes in observable metrics that can be externally verified. By contrast, cultivation and collaboration cultures gravitate toward subjective insights, looking to representative examples and anecdotes to capture the essence of the situation and putting their trust in qualitative perceptions and judgments that are internally validated. Again, no culture denies the validity of the opposite dipole; each simply states a bias toward one side or the other. The purpose of this bias is to foster consistency across multiple decisions and decision makers operating simultaneously and independently of each other—to allow, if you will, the corporation to fly in formation.

The four culture choices that emerge from pairing these elements in different combinations are all sufficiently rich and flexible to support a global business culture that scales. But each proposes a different way to prioritize the essence of business success, raising a different flag in its call to battle, as follows:

Competence culture:	"Show them you can!"
Control culture:	"Stick with the plan!"
Collaboration culture:	"Trust the team!"
Cultivation culture:	"Trust the dream!"

Even if all the cultures were aiming at the same goal, these are four very different paths toward achieving that end. To which flag do you want your troops to rally? If you do not make this clear prior to the crisis, people will rally to the flag of their individual choice during the crisis, dividing the corporation into four camps, preventing it from reacting as a unified and coordinated whole. Thus to get maximum traction on building shareholder value, corporations are best served by declaring one culture as preeminent over the other three.

Lest this all seem too one-dimensional, recall that different line functions tend to generate local cultures optimized for the types of tasks they specialize in. In a global control culture, for example, the customer service group might well have a local collaboration culture whereas the sales team might have a local competence culture, and the finance team a control culture. Local cultures are normal to groups and are neither a detriment to global culture nor a substitute for it. They simply mean that within the group, as within a family, there can be operating rules that do not apply in the larger context, and vice versa.

The value of both the local and the global culture lies in their stability over time. When people have history with a culture and can internalize its norms, they can unite smoothly and spontaneously when swift changes in direction are required. Thus customer service reps can "know" what to do based on the norms of their group. They can also "know" how the corporation as a whole is going to respond. This kind of knowing is what permits swift, unified action in times of rapid change.

WHERE DO YOU STAND?

Electing a culture is a highly personal decision. Different members of the executive team will want to make different choices. Eventually someone has to yield in the interests of the greater good. That someone may be you. Therefore, before we go into our discussion of each culture in detail, let's find out where you stand. To test your personal orientation toward this model, simply ask yourself these two basic questions:

1. When shareholder value hangs in the balance, do you think it is better to put key decisions in the hands of an *individual* or in the hands of the *group*?

2. Again, with shareholder value hanging in the balance, is it better to base key decisions on *objective data* or on *subjective insight*?

If you are like most people, neither of these two choices is obviously superior to the other, and in most real-world cases you would work hard to incorporate all the alternatives. But the purpose of the exercise is to identify for yourself the one quadrant in which you "play better" than in any of the others. So as a final check on your answer, ask yourself that question: Not excluding the other choices, but simply putting one of them above the other three, where do I feel most comfortable? Treat that quadrant as your "home quadrant," and anticipate that throughout the rest of this discussion you may have a bias toward its orientation.

And with that thought in mind, let us turn to a closer look at the first of our four cultures.

Competence Culture

Competence culture celebrates individual accomplishment as verified by objective data. Its essence and spirit are to harness the *achievement* motive, creating great work products out of the desire in individuals and teams to excel. Implicit in excelling is the notion of beating the competition, and outperforming competitors is a prime motivator of competence cultures, not always to their benefit. At their best, however, these organizations are marvelously adaptive in their strategies and awesome at execution.

Competence cultures begin with the question, *How?* That's because competence itself is all about knowing how. People in this culture want to know *the best way*. They instinctively seek out the most efficient means to get anything done, even something as simple as the shortest route between two points, and will debate that issue strenuously. They love data, specifically quantifiable, observable metrics, as a means for calibrating and corroborating such discussions.

Leadership in a competence culture is a function of demonstrable expertise and a proven ability to execute, and authority must be constantly renewed on this basis. Leaders, that is, must communicate their proposals clearly and persuasively, and anyone is permitted to challenge them as long as it is on the merits of the argument. Expertise is the currency of legitimacy, not job title or entitlement.

The resulting organization is typically a work-centric meritocracy where people are organized around projects—a client engagement, a product launch, or a case load—and promoted based on their ability to execute the tasks assigned to them. The element of consistency in the system is the work itself, with people being shifted from one group to another as work demands. Its key to success lies in hiring the best people and then holding them to a high standard going forward. Standards are set deliberately high, but not unattainably so, and are often reinforced via internal competition. Performance management typically incorporates forced ranking of people, with exceptional rewards going to the top performers and pink slips to those at the bottom. This can raise hackles when interacting with cultivation and collaboration cultures, both of which reject such behavior as destructive to the fabric of the group.

When it comes to reacting to shifts in market dynamics, competence cultures rely on individuals to detect the change, analyze it, propose a modified course of action, and provide metrics by which both the change and the response to the change can be tracked. The strength of a competence culture is the competitive intensity its members bring to this task, which translates into an unmatchable ability to act quickly and decisively. Its weakness is a tendency to burn out its people, particularly by forcing sustained intensity when the market's dynamics don't require it. Competence cultures tend to know one speed only.

Microsoft and Intel are notable examples of companies with global competence cultures. At Microsoft, prospective employees are put through a grueling interview process during which the company makes no effort to sell the virtues of the company but instead focuses exclusively on testing the competence of the candidate. People who don't like this process are typically not a good fit for the culture. On the other hand, people who have a high achievement motive actually thrive on this stuff, making them a good match not only for the test but the company as well.

Within corporations, the line functions of engineering and sales tend to have local competence cultures. In both disciplines there is fundamental emphasis on concrete and tangible results that measure and validate superior performance. Managers from these organizations love the clarity that such measures create and tend to look down on the fuzzier disciplines of human resources and marketing, in part because they lack any such definitive metrics for excellence.

CONTROL CULTURE

Control culture celebrates achieving a plan as verified by objective data. Its essence and spirit are to harness the dual motives of *power and security,* using the discipline of planning to gain mastery over a changeable world. Here leader and follower alike live by the same credo: *Plan the work—work the plan.* Accountability to the plan of record is the fundamental mechanism for achieving success in this culture. It is a marvelously reliable system, and more than any other, it has a proven capability to create large-scale operations that endure. At the same time, more than any other culture, the weaknesses of control culture are being brought to light by the challenges of the new economy. Specifically, the fault line's recurrent demand for rapid changes in strategy and execution even within a given planning period violates the fundamental discipline and rhythm it relies upon. Thus, to contemporary eyes, control culture is the most problematic of the four.

Control cultures begin with the question, *What?* Its members are expected to seek clarity and find security in well-articulated missions, goals, objectives, assignments, job descriptions, and task definitions. Data is highly valued, less as a metric and more as a means for classifying things properly. At its best, this clarity around classification is what allows these organizations to scale so effectively. At its worst, it can degenerate into a nightmare of red tape.

Leadership in control cultures is a function of authority, and decision making is tied closely to title and role in the organization. Leaders call the shots, with the rest of the organization chartered to supply them with the data and the issues. This creates the single greatest point of weakness in the culture, since underlings can manipulate decisions, and thus the entire culture, by slanting or withholding their inputs.

The resulting organization is typically a hierarchy of command organized around distributing work across a system of line functions. The element of consistency in this system is the organizational hierarchy, into which first people and then work are fit. The organization is galvanized into action by a commitment to achieve the metrics in the annual plan. Standards derive from the plan, which creates another potential weakness, as they can be set artificially low to ensure "success." Such behavior alienates members of cultivation or competence cultures, both of whom want much more from life than such artificial power and security. Worse, if the market as a whole outperforms the metrics in the plan, companies can beat their plan and still fall behind. Nonetheless, control culture is virtually unstoppable when it comes to executing its plans—and as long as the world does not change on it in the meantime, this creates dominant advantage.

Staffing in a control culture is based on finding people who have demonstrated success in meeting previous plans and who present well to upper management. Hiring and promotion, therefore, are at risk of becoming politicized, resulting in too much energy diverted into the internal politics of "looking good" and too little on doing whatever it takes to create success in the outside world. Risk taking and personal commitment are frequent casualties in this process.

When it comes to managing changes in marketplace dynamics, control cultures rely on the system to detect the change and to plan and execute an appropriate response to it. The strength of a control culture is its ability to execute such plans efficiently and with high quality over a large-scale operation. Its weakness is its inability to cope with phenomena that change faster than the planning cycle, or worse, that require changes in the planning process before they can be addressed at all. Control cultures, like the *Queen Mary*, find it hard to turn sharply.

IBM, General Electric, and Motorola are all examples of highly respected global control cultures. In each of them the planning process is the cornerstone of management activity. As long as this process can maintain an external focus, as Jack Welch has been able to achieve at GE, it is powerful indeed. When it becomes internally focused, however, when planners worry more about cannibalizing or being cannibalized, when managers worry more about their place in the hierarchy than about getting things done—as happened at IBM during the late 1980s and early 1990s—then things become grim indeed.

Within technology-oriented companies, the line functions of manufacturing, logistics, and accounting all tend to have local control cultures. That's because their disciplines readily translate into procedural systems that run best when exposed to a minimum of creative disruption. Such systems drive people from cultivation and competence cultures to distraction as they need to push against the norm, not reaffirm it.

COLLABORATION CULTURE

Collaboration culture celebrates the power of teamwork as verified by subjective insight. Its essence and spirit are to harness the *affiliation* motive, accomplishing great outcomes through many working together as one. Unlike competence and control cultures, collaboration culture puts people and relationships ahead of the work per se, trusting that by nurturing the former the latter will take care of itself. It is particularly good at incorporating diverse talents and points of view, including reaching outside the company to involve suppliers, partners, and customers. More than any other culture, collaboration culture excels both at serving others and allowing others to serve it. In this sense it provides the best platform for a *virtual organization.*

Collaboration cultures begin with the question, *Who?* People in this culture make an effort to get to know the others around them, spending what looks to advocates of other cultures like an inordinate amount of meeting time on introductions and icebreakers. Data is nowhere near as interesting to this culture as are stories and anecdotes, for these better capture subjective insights into personality and relationships. At its best, this culture engenders the kind of trust that makes great deeds possible. At other times, it can degenerate into a complacent and uncompetitive social club.

Leadership in a collaboration culture is role-based, not person- or title-based, and authority is situational. That is, the role of team leader is central and constant, but who that leader will be is allowed to shift with the situation. Stability comes from process, and decisions are reached through working the process until consensus is achieved. The goal is to allow the natural expertise of individuals to come to the fore in those situations for which they are best suited to lead. Used immoderately, however, consensus decision-making creates analysis paralysis and a culture in which everyone believes they are entitled to participate in every decision. Thus collaboration cultures need to master delegation if they are to be competitive.

The natural organization of a collaboration culture is cross-functional teams aligned to go after specific market opportunities. Consistency is achieved by keeping teams intact even as work assignments come and go—essentially the dead opposite of a competence culture. Standards and metrics are calibrated to the outcomes of the team, not the individual. This can create a "dumbing down" effect that drives members of cultivation and competence cultures crazy, both of which thrive on individual accountability. Team culture, however, is impressively powerful whenever there is call to build a new value chain to penetrate a new market. There the marketplace power gained from forming new linkages outweighs the gains achievable from superior performance within any one link. On the downside, collaboration culture tends to become inefficient whenever market dynamics reward performance within line functions more than cross-functional coordination.

Staff in a collaboration culture is recruited based on people's ability to get along with others. The goal is to maximize synergy across functions, getting superior results through teaming behaviors. Team players, therefore, are highly valued and get promoted. Conversely, the organization is leery of prima donnas and superstars who in turn are better suited to competence and cultivation cultures.

When it comes to managing changes in market dynamics, collaboration cultures rely on the team to detect the change and work out an appropriate course of action. The strength of the collaboration culture is its ability to adapt to change by leveraging diversity. This makes it exceptionally good at accommodating the interests of others into its own internal plans. At its worst, however, collaboration culture fails to weed out its mediocre performers and thereby loses its ability to compete effectively.

HP is the most prominent example of a collaboration culture in the technology sector. In particular, HP's culture—the HP Way—has often been called out both for its virtues, which were widely hailed in the early and middle 1990s, and its weaknesses, which have been the focus of more recent attention. There is a wonderful story from the early days of Bill Hewlett taking a fire ax to a locked supply cabinet one weekend when employees were in working and could not replenish their supplies—very much the sort of "people first" kind of anecdote that collaborative culture thrives on. More recently the culture has been overwhelmed by size and bureaucracy—effectively, too many resources devoted to context rather than core—something that collaboration cultures struggle with as they wish to honor everyone's contributions.

Within the corporation, marketing and customer support tend to be local collaboration cultures. In both cases there is a conscious attempt to embrace and reconcile multiple points of view, a task for which members of competence and control cultures have little appetite. It is no accident that neither engineers nor salespeople tend to have much time for marketing.

CULTIVATION CULTURE

Cultivation culture celebrates the creative expression of the human spirit as verified by subjective insight. Its essence is to harness the desire for *self-actualization*, the complete fulfillment of one's human potential, enabling individuals to unleash capabilities they did not know they had. It does so by articulating a compelling vision of a possible future and then calling on its members to turn that vision into reality.

Like a collaboration culture, cultivation culture puts people first, but as individuals rather than as teams. Teams, in its view, are too likely to compromise and accept the actual instead of stubbornly pursuing the ideal. Cultivation culture is inherently icono-clastic and attracts maverick individuals with high creativity and a low tolerance for external control. More than any other culture, it succeeds at producing breakthrough innovations that simply could not come from planned, measured, or collaborative approaches.

Cultivation cultures begin with the question, *Why?* This serves as a two-edged sword, both as an outward-facing challenge to existing orthodoxy and as an inward-facing challenge to oneself to drive to a deeper level of understanding. As with collaboration cultures, anecdotes take priority over data in this realm, but here they are valued not for their personal touch but rather their ability to capture and transmit insights, as in the example of Zen Koans or parables.

Leadership in a cultivation culture comes in two forms—highly visible charismatic leaders who attract willing troops or absolutely invisible administrators who create sanctuaries for mis-fits. In both cases, the leaders are motivated by a deep and abiding vision that they recognize cannot be achieved by ordinary means. As a result, they eschew objective measurement and supervisory control and substitute for them loyalty and devotion to a common goal. Power gravitates to people in the spotlight who perform bril-liantly. At its best, this creates hugely refreshing novelty—at its worst, unmatched arrogance and increasingly tedious egotism.

The natural organization of a cultivation culture is antiorgani-zational. That is, the culture seeks to celebrate the individual and resists structurally subordinating any member to any other mem-ber. Titleless organizations are therefore commonplace. Work worth doing is perceived as a self-organizing system that will recruit and deploy talent spontaneously, without the need for externally applied infrastructure. Standards are often set impossi-bly high, not with the thought that they will be achieved but rather to provide a target to aspire to, very much along the lines of Browning's "A man's reach should exceed his grasp, / Or what's a heaven for." This can cause problems, however, when interacting with competence and control cultures, both of which define clo-sure as hitting targets, not simply aiming at them.

Staffing with only the best and the brightest is the key to suc-cess in a cultivation culture. The good news is that these best and

brightest are attracted by the privilege of working in such an atyp-
ical environment, and they are hard to recruit away for the same
reason. Promotion should never be an issue, as there is nowhere
to promote anyone to. Compensation is also a second-tier concern. The only form of discipline is based on controlling access to
the resources needed to do one's work. Weaker members of the
culture are eliminated when their funding runs out and they are
not invited into the next round of projects.

When it comes to managing changes in market dynamics, cultivation cultures rely on individual insight both to detect the
change and to capitalize upon it. The strength of a cultivation culture is that it can anticipate and react to changes long before any
of the other cultures even detect them. That is because the insight
of brilliant individuals activates well in advance of any substantive
corroborated evidence. This capability, however, also underlies the
culture's most serious weaknesses, a tendency to chase phantasms
and defend the practice with self-indulgence, righteousness, and
insularity.

The premier example of a cultivation culture is the Silicon
Valley start-up, founded by a pair of twenty-somethings, glorying
in brilliance and unconventional behavior. The original prototype
for this was the Apple Computer of the early 1980s during Steve
Jobs's first period of tenure. Steve, in particular, is a superb example of both the strengths and weaknesses of a cultivation culture
leader. He is phenomenally charismatic and can motivate people
during even the most trying times armed with the most improba-
ble of value propositions. At the same time, he drives people oriented toward control or collaboration cultures to distraction, continually overruling decisions that have been made by the person or
the process in authority, and thereby makes it virtually impossible
to scale an organization beyond his personal boundaries.

Internal to a corporation, skunk works R and D groups are the
most prominent localized manifestation of cultivation culture.
These typically form around genius designers and architects who
are able to recruit and retain others like them, with everybody else
just tiptoeing around the outside for fear of disturbing genius at
work. In general, however, as corporations scale, they become
increasing hostile to cultivation culture, as it actively defies the

norms by which the other cultures negotiate—accountability to the plan of record, subordination of the individual to the team, measurement relative to specific quantifiable objectives. Thus it is no accident that breakthrough innovation tends to happen at the periphery of established institutions, not at their cores.

To wrap up and summarize the preceding, consider the following table. Like all things human, cultures do not really lend themselves to being pigeon-holed, but the various comparisons and contrasts should help executive teams navigate where their own culture fits.

	Competence	Control	Collaboration	Cultivation
Cherishes	Achievement	Power and security	Affiliation	Self-realization
Celebrates	Superior individual	Meeting the plan	Power of teamwork	Creative expression
Prioritizes	The work	The system	The people	The idea
Asks	How?	What?	Who?	Why?
Leads by	Expertise	Authority	Role	Charisma
Organizes as	Work projects	Hierarchy	Persistent teams	As little as possible
Recruits for	Competitiveness	Reliability	Cooperativeness	Brilliance

CULTURES ON THE FAULT LINE

If the preceding sections have done their job correctly, each of the four cultures should seem sufficiently attractive in its own right that a corporation would be foolish to reject any of them. At the same time, however, it is critical to prioritize one culture above the other three if companies are to react swiftly to the shifts in market dynamics that characterize living on the fault line. So let us size up each of the four cultures in light of the models we have been developing throughout this book. Specifically, we want to look at the relationship of each to value disciplines, stages in the technology adoption life cycle, competitive advantage, and shareholder value.

CULTURE AND VALUE DISCIPLINES

The link between culture and *value disciplines* can be represented as follows:

The Four Cultures & The Value Disciplines

Figure 6.2

The series of one-to-one mappings work out as follows:

- *Cultivation culture* attracts and retains the mavericks needed to think outside the box and create *discontinuous innovation*. As we have already noted, all three other cultures create obstacles to this end—competence by its insistence on measurable performance criteria, control by its demand for accountability to a plan of record, and collaboration by its need to bring the whole team along together. All three recoil from what economist Joseph Schumpeter called the "creative destruction" inherent in such disruptive technology. Cultivation culture, by contrast, maintains total allegiance to the creative individual, whatever the consequences.

- *Competence culture* ensures superior competitive performance against virtually all measurable outcomes. This makes it a natural for achieving *product* (or *service*) *leadership*, a title that by definition must be earned competitively. All three other cultures, by contrast, are demonstrably less competitive, cultivation culture being unwilling to subordinate its focus on higher goals, control culture being unwilling to make resource sacrifices outside the plan, and collaboration culture being unwilling to make human sacrifices that injure the team. Competence culture, by contrast, can willingly embrace a win-at-any-cost agenda.

- *Control culture* imposes a planning discipline that allows operations to become increasingly more precise and reliable with each iteration of the plan. It thus has a natural correlation with *operational excellence*. By contrast, all three other cultures bridle at the discipline of standardization needed to achieve this outcome—cultivation culture seeing it as offensive to the human spirit, competence culture as a dumbing down of the challenge of work, and collaboration culture as undermining of diversity. Control culture, by contrast, values the power and security gained from achieving planned outcomes.

- *Collaboration culture* embraces win-win exchanges among diverse constituencies, creating the necessary framework for successful cooperation with others. It creates a natural platform for *customer intimacy*. All three other cultures, by contrast, are more self-centered in their motives, cultivation culture being caught up in its need to be brilliant, competence culture in its need to be best, and control culture in its need to be right. Collaboration culture, by contrast, takes gratification from being in touch and in tune.

These mappings help explain why the prescription to focus on a single value discipline is so attractive. Value disciplines become subsumed by the cultures that foster them. Thus, by concentrating on a single value discipline, a company can in effect create or reinforce a core culture and gain all the benefits for so doing. It can have huge positive effects.

The obverse of this is also true. When a company declares it will change its focus from one value discipline to another, it is serving notice on its old culture. If in fact it does not modify its culture, then sooner or later the change initiative must falter. As an alternative, one can call on local cultures to champion new value disciplines, provided the behavioral changes required can be confined to that group. What must be avoided at all costs is hyped global changes that never come about. These teach everyone involved that the corporation has no leadership, only inertia.

CULTURE AND THE TECHNOLOGY ADOPTION LIFE CYCLE

We have already seen that the technology adoption life cycle favors different value disciplines at different points in the evolution of a technology-enabled market. It should come as no surprise, then, that the same is true of cultures. The relationships can be diagrammed as follows:

The Four Cultures & The Technology Adoption Life Cycle

Figure 6.3

The implications for cultures operating in technology-enabled markets are as follows:

- *Cultivation cultures are useful only in the early market.* As soon as technologies cross the chasm, cultivation cultures are simply too mercurial to perform effectively. Historically, corporations have tried to cope with this challenge by isolating and insulating such cultures in skunk works. With the emergence of Silicon Valley, however, along with other similarly venture-funded enclaves of entrepreneurship around the world, the new winning model is to leave the cultivation cultures where they lie. That is, let the mavericks found start-ups and foster discontinuous innovations on the venture capitalists' nickel, and then, if and when the innovations cross the chasm, let them be acquired and brought into a more scaleable culture. As these maturing ventures become assimilated into other cultures, the mavericks that spawned them spin out and return to the early market to repeat the performance. Thus while individual companies do not scale as cultivation cultures, Silicon Valley as a whole has.

- *Competence cultures are unique in that they are useful in three of the four life-cycle states.* In the early market, they thrive on helping cultivation cultures translate possibilities into actualities. In the bowling alley, they team with collaboration cultures to forge superior solutions to challenging customer problems. In the tornado, they team well with control cultures to win market-share battles, driving to beat the competition to market with the next product or service release. The reason competence cultures are so versatile is that they put power in the hands of individuals, which makes them more adaptable to the rapidly changing early phases of the market, while at the same time they navigate by objective metrics, which keeps them on track and executing during a tornado.

  Only on Main Street do competence cultures become a liability. Here their ferocious competitiveness finds no outlet, since the bulk of the business comes from existing customers who are already predisposed to buy from their incumbent vendor. Moreover, their drive to excel in their core work runs head-on into an installed base that is no longer as interested in pushing price/performance envelopes as in getting a better customer service experience. Competence cultures not only burn their own people out, in other words, they burn out their customers.

- *Control cultures thrive inside the tornado and on Main Street.* Once the market achieves sufficient stability and mass for operational excellence to become a critical success factor, a planning-based culture becomes a competitive advantage. By contrast, control cultures are painfully challenged by the early phases of the life cycle, so it is no wonder that the innovator's dilemma resonates so roundly with *Fortune* 500 management teams.

  Specifically, in the era just prior to the age of the Internet, where each new wave of product technology started a whole new life cycle and cast old plans to the winds, control cultures simply had no chance of keeping up. When instead they reacted defensively against the innovation, the market punished them severely, and business pundits prophesied the death of control culture. Today, however, as more and more innovation comes in the form of new transaction services deployed over the same underlying Internet protocols, the need for operational excellence in maintaining the underlying fabric of computing and communications is reasserting itself. Traditional carriers and new entrants competing for the business of building, maintaining, and collecting toll on the information highway should foster a resurgence of next-generation control cultures, about which we will have more to say later in the chapter.

- *Collaboration cultures are the wild card.* Collaboration culture takes its power from being able to embrace the issues of others and shape them into win-win scenarios. This is key to success both in the bowling alley, where the focus is on teaming with the various constituencies into an emerging value chain, and on Main Street, where it is on identifying and serving a variety of different customer needs within a single installed base. But between the bowling alley and Main Street intervenes the tornado, a time in which collaboration gets suppressed in the win-lose competition for new customer acquisition. Because collaboration cultures recoil from win-lose scenarios, they rarely win the market-share battles that shape tornado market outcomes. Instead, they tend to thrive by securing high-margin niche-market leadership positions in the bowling alley, which they later carry over onto Main Street.

For complex technologies that do not lend themselves to mass-market deployment and thus foster markets that will never tornado, this is clearly the winning strategy. But for broad technology changes it is not—not, that is, until the age of the Internet. Now things may be about to change. Internet-enabled markets are demonstrating themselves to be self-organizing communities. They are, in effect, spontaneously collaborative, as witnessed by such varied phenomena as the rise of customer support chat groups, the emergence of investor advice exchanges, and the whole open-source movement that led to the creation of Linux, the Internet's favorite operating system to oppose the proprietary offerings from Sun and Microsoft. We do not yet know what all the implications are of this behavior, but one would imagine that a collaborative culture should have the inside track for capitalizing on them early.

The overall take-away from looking at culture through the lens of the life cycle is that whatever culture you choose, there will be some times when you will be delighted you did and others when you wish you hadn't. Again the interplay between global and local culture is needed to help keep the ship on course. When the life cycle rewards your global culture, the preferred tactic is to play offense and lead with your "home" value discipline. Elsewhere, the tactic is to play defense and give support to any group within the corporation whose local culture is a better match for the current market phase.

CULTURE, COMPETITIVE ADVANTAGE, AND SHAREHOLDER VALUE

The reason we care about the technology adoption life cycle is that it creates different competitive environments at each stage, each of which rewards different forms of competitive advantage. Competitive advantage, in turn, is the basis of stock price. Thus we are building a chain that puts culture at one end and stock price at the other. Each culture has a characteristic approach to generating wealth, and it is imperative that management teams embrace that approach thoroughly if they are going to commit to that culture globally.

- *Cultivation cultures create shareholder value through creating or catching very early technology waves that engender new markets.* They generate tall GAPs and long CAPs, in other words, by being the first to market with a new category. At the turn of the millennium, cultivation cultures are creating an enormous amount of new wealth. The public markets are willing to value them on their own terms as new market creators, and that has allowed larger institutions to acquire them at exceptional premiums without diluting their own valuations.

In the traditional sense, cultivation culture does not scale because its vitality depends so heavily on subjective communication among a small core of brilliant contributors. For a long time, therefore, this culture was treated as aberrant when it came to wealth creation, and indeed its proponents often implied that they did not really care about wealth much in the first place. For better or worse, however, the age of the Internet has changed this perception permanently.

The truth is that cultivation cultures do scale—and broadly—through viral infection and replication. That is, a person imbued with the culture's spirit leaves the initial cell and either starts or takes over a new one. We call these people "serial entrepreneurs." Think about how much wealth a Jim Clark, or Steve Jobs, or Bill Joy, or Mitch Kapor has helped create. How much wealth, for that matter, have the handful of venture capitalists that populate Sand Hill Road created? Their key to scaleable wealth creation is not to tie themselves down to expanding a single corporation's culture but rather to infect a whole series of companies with their vision, enthusiasm, and intelligence.

Infectious charisma, then, is the essence of cultivation culture's approach to building to last. Instead of through genes it reproduces itself through memes—ideas that are sufficiently compelling to attract people to embrace them, act them out, and recruit others to do the same. Historically this mechanism has been more associated with religion, the arts, and education, and thought of as not for profit. The age of the Internet is proving it may become the most profitable of all.

- *Competence cultures create shareholder value by winning time-to-market battles during tornado markets.* They end up capturing dominant market shares that translate into long CAPs with variable GAPs, depending on whether they gain proprietary architectural control or not.

  For a product-oriented company with a competence culture, scalability is key. Unlike control cultures, however, it is the product, not the company, that has to scale. Software companies in particular, because they require neither a physical plant nor logistics, have been able to generate extraordinary shareholder value through remarkable revenues per employee, and even more remarkable return on invested capital. Moreover, the remaining drag on their capital—the need to build up either a direct sales force or an extended indirect distribution network—promises to be removed by an increasingly full-service Internet channel.

  Competence cultures take a similar approach to wealth creation in Internet-based transaction services businesses. Here they are best focused on contests that are characterized by increasing returns and winner-take-all outcomes. Winning the lead position early and defending it at all costs are the keys to victory and things competence cultures excel at. This required ferocity was first displayed by America Online, which single-handedly defeated not only Prodigy and CompuServe but Microsoft and Netscape as well in making itself the overwhelming market-share leader for consumers. Now we are seeing that same competitiveness in business-to-business market competitions to create the digital marketplaces and brokered exchanges that will supplant older, less efficient modes of commerce. In all these efforts competence cultures should create the preponderance of shareholder value.

Fierce competitiveness is the essence of competence culture's approach to building to last. By capturing markets early it secures future streams of privileged earnings. Its biggest challenge is middle age. Like Alexander the Great, it weeps when there are no more worlds to conquer. But until that point, watch out.

- *Control cultures create shareholder value through continuous innovation in Main Street markets.* They excel particularly when they focus on cost reduction through operational excellence—six-sigma quality, as several corporations have come to call it—with the gains applied to increasing market share, improving earnings, or both. In either case they seek to consistently ratchet up GAPs from a market position that has a stable CAP.

  Control cultures are the natural heirs to competence cultures. The competence culture creates the market position that the control culture then exploits. Neither is well suited to the other's job, so the relationship works perfectly for both sides. Classically this would consist of a global control culture with local competence cultures in sales and engineering, with the latter, taken in the broad sense, applicable to anything that is core—anything, that is, that could be better engineered for competitive advantage.

  The challenge to this hybrid comes after a period of prolonged stability. Over time, the global culture's focus on standardization minimizes diversity in the name of efficiency. This pretty much ensures that the next discontinuous innovation will not come from within. At the same time, it also creates an increasingly less satisfying ambiance for achievement-motivated individuals who make up the competence subculture. While they may not leave, they lose the enthusiasm needed to recruit top candidates to form the next generation. Thus, when the next wave hits, the company is literally not competent enough to meet its challenges. The way out of this dilemma, as we discussed at length in Chapter 1, is to focus the global control culture on aggressively outsourcing context operations while continuing to focus the competitive subcultures on enhancing core functions.

  Relentless improvement is the basis for control culture's

approach to building to last. While it will remain vulnerable to massively discontinuous innovations, anything short of that is not likely to knock it off its mark. In essence, this has been the driving force behind the century-long success of blue-chip stocks.

- *Collaboration cultures create shareholder value through superior alignment with external market forces.* In the bowling alley they align better with other value-chain members, creating a higher probability that a value chain will form and that their offers will garner a privileged position within it. This generates strong CAPs. On Main Street they align better with customer preferences, creating more attractive offers that earn higher margins. This generates strong GAPs.

  In contrast to all the other cultures, collaboration cultures are best at *doing the right thing*. By contrast, competence and control cultures focus more on doing things right, and cultivation culture on doing its own thing. Doing the right thing creates competitive advantage by focusing core operations more accurately on the desires of the marketplace. Its better-targeted offers simply win more support both from customers and partners.

  Although collaboration cultures are at a disadvantage in win-lose tornado-market competitions, they can still succeed against competence and control cultures when the latter persist in missing the target. This happens whenever the internal self-interests of these cultures conflict with the market's desires. Thus, for example, Charles Schwab was able to pass Merrill Lynch in the age of the Internet because it did the right thing—reducing price on all of its trades to Internet prices—at a time when common sense said to retain a two-tiered price scheme as long as possible. HP also did the right thing in the 1980s when it made its superior printing technology compatible with the IBM PC instead of taking Apple's approach and making it work only with its own computers.

  To make sure it is doing the right thing, collaborative culture must locate its best resources in direct contact with the marketplace, where it can capture new learnings for the group to fashion into win-win offerings. Organizationally, in other words, it needs a high surface-to-volume ratio, where most people in the company have some regular contact with outside constituencies. Large centralized organizations, which have low surface-to-volume ratios, are anathema to this culture and must be continually broken apart into smaller divisions. In sum, collaboration cultures can scale using the model of a bunch of grapes, but not using the model of a watermelon.

Perceptive adaptation is the basis for collaboration culture's approach to building to last. It permanently commits itself to staying in touch with changes in the outside world and to bending itself to meet emerging needs. Its number one enemy is the unchecked growth of context operations that will divert more and more of its attention inward. Collaborations cultures, more than any other, must be outwardly focused on the marketplace to succeed.

DECLARING A CULTURE

By now I trust that the benefits of each of the four cultures have been sufficiently described that you as an executive would like your team to have them. Well, they don't come for free. You have to commit to a culture and live it for some time before your company can profit from it. This section is about making and living that commitment.

The first step is to identify the culture best suited to your company's mission, its markets, its history, and its current leadership. There is no right answer here, but there has to be *an* answer before anything else can proceed. If you take this decision seriously, it may be that the very approach you take will itself reveal your cultural preference. In any event, one way or another, with consulting help or without, you have to make the choice.

Once a culture is selected, it must be *declared*. Declaration is what activates a culture. It is not a matter of *saying* anything, although it does not hurt to provide a word or two of explanation. Rather it is a matter of focusing the corporation on the core activity that defines the culture. For each of the cultures, the core focus is as follows:

Cultivation culture	Shared vision (communicated with infectious charisma)
Competence culture	Measurement and compensation (targeted at winning fierce competitions)
Control culture	Business planning (focused on relentless improvement)
Collaboration culture	Customer focus (emphasizing perceptive adaptations)

All companies can benefit from all four activities. Declaring the culture means prioritizing one of these four above the other three. Management communicates the declaration by consistently and continually making this particular emphasis a part of all core activities. It takes every occasion to bring it up, talk it up, relate present circumstances to it, and explain success or failure in its terms. It does not suppress any of the other three; it simply obsesses on the fourth.

This is most easily seen in the management of local cultures. Most sales cultures are competence cultures. How do we know? Because most sales managers are always talking about quota and compensation. Most financial cultures are control cultures—they are always referring to the business plan and variances from it. Similar observations can be made about marketing cultures and their emphasis on customer focus or about R and D lab cultures and their interest in sharing vision.

By taking declaration up to a global level, the executive team gives the corporation a distinctive personality, one that employees, customers, partners, and investors can all rally around. People are absolutely clear about "how we like to do business around here." They *know* that General Electric is a control culture. They can count on that. If they want serious attention, they know they have to relate their issue to the business plan. Similarly, people at Charles Schwab *know* it has a collaboration culture. If they want serious attention, they know they have to relate their issue to a burning customer concern. These are hugely useful frames of reference.

Conversely, when companies shift cultures, particularly when they do so without declaration, then they create queasiness in their constituencies. A lot of the queasiness today, for example, surrounding Silicon Valley start-ups can be traced to an undeclared shift from cultivation culture to competence culture. Writers and pundits bemoan the loss of idealism when in fact the new crop of entrepreneurs never signed up for those values and are instead driven by a competitive spirit to win a big market battle. Founders of start-ups who do seek to establish cultivation cultures often end up at loggerheads with venture capitalists when a similar undeclared shift ends up displacing their visionary leadership with a newly recruited, compensation-driven CEO. More generally, many Americans raised on the old Silicon Valley mystique feel the same disillusion when what they thought was supposed to be all about an idealistic vision turns out to be all about striking it rich. But that is what competence cultures are all about, and for many of the current generation there is no such queasiness because they had no other expectation.

The critical point to note here is not that one culture is preferable to another but rather that undeclared shifts in culture create damage. More generally, refusing to declare a culture at all puts any enterprise at risk. There are simply too many expectations that are developing in undirected, uncontrolled ways. This must inevitably lead to miscommunication and disappointment, at minimum resulting in a withdrawal of support, at worst spurring active resentment and counterattack.

DEVELOPING A CULTURE: INTEGRATING, BALANCING, AND COMPLETING

Once a culture is identified and declared, it needs to be systematically developed. In *The Reengineering Alternative*, Schneider lays out three steps to this end, the first of which is *integration*. Here one revisits all of the corporate systems to ensure they conform to the value and style of the selected culture. The following is a representative but not exhaustive list:

- Organization
- Information systems

- Planning

- Compensation

- Human resource management

- Public relations

- Legal

- Facilities

- Security

Every element of the business takes on different coloration depending on the culture, even something as seemingly mundane as facilities or security. That is because all acts have symbolic overtones, and it is the job of executive management to orchestrate those overtones to communicate a common cultural theme. What would it say about a cultivation culture if everyone had to wear badges? What would it say about a control culture if executives did not? How about a collaboration culture where all the line functions are housed in separate buildings? How about a competence culture where everyone has to punch a time clock and merit raises are limited to 3 percent? Nothing is nonsymbolic. Everything communicates. Integrating a culture is a major effort to initiate and requires ongoing vigilant maintenance.

The value of integration is that it reinforces the style and strength of the culture, all of which is rewarded by stronger competitive advantage in the market—when the culture is in phase with the technology adoption life cycle. The challenge comes when the market and the culture go out of phase. How can a company respond when the market wants to reward the culture that is the diagonal opposite of the one it selected? It is here that one must learn the second discipline of culture management, what Schneider calls *balance*.

The key to balance is to achieve the effect of the opposing culture without abandoning one's own. Thus, for a collaboration culture, it must achieve the effect of a competence culture—say, intense competitive behavior in an all-out winner-take-all battle—without forsaking its collaborative roots. The way it does this is that it collaborates to become competent. That is, it competes as a team, not as a set of individuals. It seeks, indeed, to co-opt the referee, to use its own strengths to change the field of battle. It does everything but become a competence culture.

Similarly, a competence culture that is called to collaborate must not try to adopt some touchy-feely approach to "getting closer" to the other party, giving up one's competitiveness for the greater good. That is an unnatural act in a competence culture. Instead, it must leverage the competitiveness of its people to see who can score highest on the latest set of customer satisfaction metrics. In other words, it must use its competence to mimic collaboration and achieve its ends. It's a bit like Amazon.com. Their customer service software isn't *really* customer intimate, but it manages to make you feel that way.

This brings us to Schneider's final step in cultural development, the move to *completeness*. Up to this point our discussion of culture has been focused exclusively on company culture as a monolithic whole. But as we have already noted several times, subcultures exist at every level of organization. That is, each division, each line function, indeed each department or work group is sufficiently local and self-organized to sustain an internal culture independent of the corporate culture, if it so chooses.

This creates an environment within which a global culture can learn to embrace the behavioral capabilities of its two *adjacent cultures*. It is accomplished not by any systemic change but rather by simply drawing attention to the accomplishments of one or another of the local cultures. The tactic is to celebrate some accomplishment in that organization that is "countercultural" and yet has clearly contributed to the health and well-being of the company. The goal is to keep the company from becoming "Johnny One Note," to stretch beyond playing every song in the key of C.

Stepping up to this last growth objective is key to getting consistent sustainable performance across the entire technology adoption life cycle. The world is just too varied to be "solved" by any one equation. But in seeking out these complements, it is important not to call into question the commitment to the global culture. That is why local cultures are the appropriate place to celebrate these virtues.

The basis for this step is that alternative cultures are likely to be found in those functions within your company that reward the value disciplines most natural to the alternative culture. This can vary by company, but I propose there are general alignment tendencies, as follows.

Culture	Value Discipline	Aligned Functions
Competence	Product/service leadership	Sales, development, support
Control	Operational excellence	Manufacturing, logistics, finance
Collaboration	Customer intimacy	Marketing, customer service, consulting
Cultivation	Discontinuous innovation	Research, visionary senior executives

The idea here is that a sales team is likely to be highly competitive regardless of what the company's core culture is. That's because competitiveness is an attribute that Darwinian evolution selects for in successful salespeople. Now outside its local competence culture, the group has to learn to tone this tendency down a bit (privately grumbling about the political correctness of so doing) because that is part of *alignment* and *integration*. But every so often it is good not only for the group but for the culture as a whole to cut these folks loose and let them have at it. And should the company come under a heavy attack, one might temporarily let them run the government, the way Britain turned to Churchill during World War II, even though both before and after the war his style of leadership was incompatible with the popular culture.

Overall, however, the goal of a completeness program is not really to *do* anything. It is simply to *listen better* to ideas and values that are normally suppressed in the global culture. This does not fix any specific problem. Instead, it makes people aware of creative possibilities that otherwise might fall in their blind spot.

To sum up, developing an integrated, balanced, complete culture is a journey, not a destination. It is the nature of our Darwinian world that any level of accomplishment sooner or later is challenged to reinvent itself. That being said, in the age of the Internet, with its emphasis on growth through acquisition, this need for reinvention tends to come sooner than expected.

MERGERS AND ACQUISITIONS: WHEN CULTURES COLLIDE

In our review of the technology adoption life cycle, we saw that natural forces operating within successful established companies make it increasingly unlikely that the next discontinuous innovation can be sponsored from within. Thus, the most successful corporations in high tech in recent years have turned to merger and acquisitions to keep themselves current with the market. Despite all the work done by M&A advisers, however, not to mention the high premiums paid in recent years to acquire companies, the sad truth is that most mergers and acquisitions simply do not work out very well. That is, given a couple of years to shake out, one discovers that the shareholder value of the new entity has gone down, not up. What is going wrong?

Typically, most mergers fail when the cultures of the two companies conflict and the executive team does not resolve the conflict swiftly. The correct response is simply to reset the culture counter to zero, assemble the decision-making body, and replay the sequence of identifying, declaring, and developing a global culture for the new combined entity.

Perhaps, the simplest way of doing this is to simply assert the current global culture of the acquiring entity. This is the way Computer Associates successfully managed a whole series of acquisitions in the 1980s and early 1990s. It had a control culture, and it made no bones about it. The acquired company was stripped bare to only its products and a core of supporting engineers, which were then assimilated into the corporation. Everyone else was sent packing. Draconian, to be sure, but effective and, I would argue, fair.

Cisco Systems is the current champion in successful acquisitions. It operates as a competence culture. It plans to retain the R and D and product marketing of its acquisitions—indeed it must if it is to continue to compete across an increasingly broad line of network equipment technologies. So it does not try to assimilate those teams but instead encourages them to remain autonomous. At the same time, it immediately works to assimilate all the other functions—sales, support, manufacturing, logistics, finance, and human resources, all of which are expected to conform to the Cisco culture.

Consider, by way of contrast, several acquisitions that have backfired. In the 1980s, IBM, a control culture, acquired Rolm, a cultivation culture. For a while it vowed to let the Rolm folks do it their way, but undeclared cultural shifts led to miscommunication and mistrust, and soon the IBM folks came in to reassert their control culture. This led to mass defection by the key Rolm engineers and ended ultimately with IBM exiting the business.

A similar saga played out when HP, a collaboration culture, acquired Apollo, a competence culture. HP was confident its adaptive style would win over the Apollo engineers, but in fact the latter perceived the company as dumbed down by a consensus culture they wanted no part of. As a result, the alliance that was supposed to overthrow Sun did nothing of the sort, and HP ended up refocusing its UNIX business on commercial servers instead.

The point of these tales is not to assign blame but to point out how culture is a force that must—and fortunately can—be managed. In every M&A go-forward plan there simply has to be an assigned task to identify and declare the new culture. To ignore this work is to put the combined organization at risk to no purpose. Even if it is known going in that the plan is to assert the acquiring company's culture, that assertion will play out differently depending on the culture of the acquired company. Talking through the issues and building the right transition can save millions of dollars, perhaps even billions of dollars, in shareholder value.

This brings to a close our discussion of culture *going forward*. There is one final way to engage the topic, however, and that is culture *looking backward*. Successful cultures have a tendency over time to become self-involved and to lose their vitality. They begin to fall in love with their past instead of creating their future. They retreat from the demanding world of core into the cocoon of context. This does not bode well for shareholders.

AGING CULTURES: WHEN CONTEXT OVERTAKES CORE

In any culture, when the mass of activities that we have termed *context* begins to meet or exceed the mass of activities that we have termed *core*, the culture ceases to contribute vital energy and becomes instead *confining ritual*. This happens more easily than one might think.

When context tasks are dressed up in the global culture's trappings, they fool the company's immune system into thinking they are friends when in fact they are foes. For every such task extracts its daily dose of the three most scarce and precious resources of the corporation—time, talent, and management attention. But in return it gives nothing back in the way of shareholder value, makes no contribution to competitive advantage. Now we have already agreed that these context tasks need to be done. But we also agreed that they represent *hygiene*, not differentiation, and should be done not at the expense of scarce resources but rather of plentiful ones—capital, packaged software, and outsourced service providers. To permit them to masquerade as core is a serious management offense.

Whenever a culture loses it core resources to context tasks, it becomes a parody of its best self. The results are ludicrously obvious to outsiders but are virtually invisible to long-time members of the culture. So it helps to know what to look out for. By way of helping executive teams stay on their toes, we'll close this chapter with a review of what each culture looks like when it becomes *at risk*.

CULTIVATION CULTURE AT RISK

When context overcomes core in a cultivation culture, the result is a *cult*. You can see the trappings anywhere. What used to be inspired bits of whimsy—say, a Ping-Pong table in the lunchroom or a fireman's pole to slide down between floors—start to become fetishes. People *require* the right to bring dogs to work, the right to dress sloppily even though a customer is coming that day, the right to send a flaming e-mail if they think it is warranted. Now in a vibrant cultivation culture hard at work on its core mission, any one of these behaviors could, and probably should, be overlooked. But when they become the very stuff of work, then the culture is in deep trouble. It happened in spades at Apple. It is at risk of happening at the research labs of IBM, Lucent, HP, and Xerox. And of course, high tech has no monopoly on this sort of thing: It is clearly happening routinely at any number of advertising agencies, investment banks, and Hollywood agencies.

The disease these companies fall prey to is *unbridled extension of the ego*. Because their culture eschews metrics—metrics being artifacts of an obsolete world view that they have long ago transcended—its leaders fall prey to the vice of denial. No event or result can cause them to self-correct their entrepreneurial willfulness because they can simply choose to ignore it. Boards of directors in such cases are often intimidated by these charismatic leaders and typically lack the will, although not the inclination, to replace them. It is a death spiral that has one attribute unique to it—it tends to end with a bang, not a whimper.

Cultivation cultures gone awry cannot be reformed. They have to be abandoned and then reconstructed elsewhere. Once the magic is lost, "reconstructing" it is like trying to reconstruct a romance—it is just not in the cards. What makes Silicon Valley such a great breeding ground for cultivation culture is that it is so easy to abandon failure, to simply walk away from it and start over. There is a dark side to this, something that might be approximated by a twist on Jack Nicholson's great one-liner from the movie *As Good As It Gets:* "When I want to imagine a charismatic entrepreneur, I just think of a man and then take away reason and accountability." In the end, however, Silicon Valley actually does enforce accountability by denying future access to capital—hence the ongoing vitality of its ecosystem.

COMPETENCE CULTURE AT RISK

When competence culture gets caught up in context rather than core, it devolves into a *caste system* ruled over by an aloof and increasingly cynical elite. All the trappings of a meritocracy remain, but the competition for rewards becomes inwardly focused, with less and less impact on the outside world. The culture continues to subject its members to innumerable tests and measurements, but at the end of the day they do not correlate to creating value. They do, however, correlate to promotion within the culture, and so they are pursued vigorously. The end result is a tightly controlled guild—law, medicine, and accounting all come to mind—training its members to master reams of data and procedures while failing to prepare them for the changes that really matter. Why does this happen?

In a competence culture, the metric acts as proxy for the goal—it ceases to be questioned and is simply made the focus of achievement. Get the new product into the market in time for the Christmas season. Ratchet up the megahertz on the next microprocessor. Reach the next lower price point with the new printer. As long as these goals are in line with what the marketplace values, all is well. But when context overtakes core—when the marketplace no longer values the behavior—the culture has no mechanism for detecting it. It thereby falls prey to missing the next new thing, persisting instead at becoming *ever more efficient* at a performance that has *ceased to be effective*. The external marketplace has, in effect, transformed core into context, and the culture just misses it.

At the time of this writing, the Internet threatens to do this both to Microsoft and Intel. The former is the greatest software product company in history, but the Internet is rewarding a migration from product to service, and selling services on the Internet is not where Microsoft is excelling today. Meanwhile, Intel has created the greatest microprocessor of all time, optimizing for the PC, the most proliferated computer of all time. But the Internet threatens to marginalize the PC in favor of a network of servers and services behind it, and an array of cell phones and PDAs and embedded devices outside it, none of which need rely on the next Intel chip. To their credit, both companies have been aware of this problem for some time, but neither has yet succeeded in adapting its culture sufficiently to even be sure that they are setting the right goals.

Control Culture at Risk

If we look at a control culture, its parody takes on a familiar form: *bureaucracy*. Indeed, this condition is so familiar to us we tend to treat it like dandruff, but it is much more like heart disease—slow acting but ever deteriorating to quality of life, and ultimately fatal.

Bureaucracy is the application of the processes and procedures of control culture to context tasks that are unworthy of them. These control processes are industrial-strength phenomena requiring enormous expenditures of time, talent, and management attention to deploy. When they are directed toward context instead of core, they divert the bulk of an organization's resources into inconsequential projects, sapping the energy so desperately needed for creating real value. Thus a large part of business's frustration with government is not that its agenda is wrong, not that its intentions are ignoble, not that the targets of its programs are unworthy, but simply that there is so much bureaucracy mandated by law that too few resources ever get applied to the problem at hand.

But before business takes government to task, it behooves it to look considerably more closely at its own operations. Bureaucracy built up around context tasks is the number one cause of failure to recross the chasm. The new innovation is not only starved for resources because the bureaucrats have sopped them up, it is also called upon to waste additional resources by sending representatives to an endless stream of meetings, not one of which has any hope or intent of improving stock price. And should the new group refuse to comply, it will be ostracized and denied the political allies it needs to win its next battle for resources. Thus any initiative that might actually change shareholder value is quickly tamed and it is taught that context, not core, is the way we really do business around here.

As we noted in Chapter 1, this depressing outcome has been brilliantly parodied by the cartoon *Dilbert*, which chronicles life in a world that is all context and no core. Indeed, the number of Dilbert cartoons posted on the outside of cubicles is a thermometer for taking the "context temperature" of an organization. If they are rampant, you are in trouble. Or, as the kids say when they want to mock a loser, if you see a lot of Dilbert cartoons around your workplace, "Paste the big *L*, baby."

As we have already noted, neither downsizing nor reengineering solves this problem. Both only add to the tax on time, talent, and management attention. The only way forward is to do an aggressive core-versus-context housecleaning with major outsourcing of context functions. Every day you put this off allows the bureaucracy to siphon a little more vitality from your corporation.

COLLABORATION CULTURE AT RISK

Collaboration cultures find it easy to succumb to context because just by assembling a team to do any task—core or context—it fulfills its primary motive of affiliation. Thus a collaboration culture can feel great about itself for an extended period of time, all the while making no contribution to shareholder value. But when the stock price finally reflects this performance, then the culture goes into a funk, realizing belatedly that it has let one of its prime constituencies down.

A collaboration culture overrun by context becomes a *club*. Each member is allowed a say even when (a) it is not their business, and (b) the thing isn't worth talking about in the first place. That's because the culture so honors the individual and their place in the community that it hesitates to call out—or cull out—inappropriate or mediocre performances. The result is that all action becomes subject to a paralyzing web of review. At the time of this writing, HP has fallen prey to this problem and is learning painfully it is not the sort of thing one can fix quickly. Digital Equipment Corporation fell prey to it in a prior decade and lost its independence altogether.

To reform a collaboration culture, the directive must come from the top, but the performance must come from the middle. That is, in this culture middle managers collectively have more power than top executives because the culture "happens" in meetings, and middle managers attend a lot more of them. To get out of the context trap, top management must personally reorient and even retrain the middle to be more selective in its use of meetings, to be proactive in disciplining members who are abusing this privilege, and to weed out members who are holding back performance. This task cannot be delegated—else it becomes just another piece of context—hence the true enormity of the task, considering who has to do it and what other tasks are also calling for their attention.

CLOSING ON CULTURE

For as long as I have been engaged with business, culture has been relegated to that class of things that are both terribly important and hopelessly unmanageable. (You know the class, it's where you also put rekindling the romance with your spouse, keeping up with the music that your teenager is involved with, and getting the 49ers into the Super Bowl.) The occasional inspired CEO manages to create great effects, but for the most part culture has been more talked about than taken care of.

The problem with such a strategy of benign neglect is that, in the age of the Internet, it simply won't work. Two emerging trends have brought the issue to a head:

- The need to respond swiftly and globally to the shifting dynamics of technology-enabled markets.

- The need to supplement organic growth with mergers and acquisitions.

Neither of these needs can be met successfully without actively managing culture. The goal of this chapter has been to offer a framework and vocabulary within which executive teams can approach this task. The ultimate deliverable is to identify and declare a culture that enables your corporation to compete successfully given its heritage, its core competence, its position in the marketplace, and the talents and aspirations of its executive team.

The discussion leading up to this decision needs to be initiated at the board level. Here the board should act in an advisory capacity to the executive team, letting it explore various possibilities, providing it with advice and counsel but not direction. Then once the go-forward culture has been identified, all hands, board and executives alike, must join as one to declare the culture via sustained emphasis on that culture's defining activity.

There is nothing in this call to action that is radical *except the insistence that it no longer be ignored.* I am making the claim that declaring a culture is a direct determinant of shareholder value and that it is the fiduciary responsibility of the board and the executive team to see that this declaration is managed appropriately. Them's fightin' words, so either dispute the claim or get on with the activity. It's your call.

SUMMARY OF KEY POINTS IN CHAPTER 6

The main claim of this chapter is that to keep up with the rapid shifts in market dynamics brought on by the technology adoption life cycle, corporations must unify themselves through a common commitment to a global culture. Specifically, executive teams need to understand the following:

1. There are four proven cultures that can sustain long-term competitive-advantage strategies: cultivation culture, competence culture, control culture, and collaboration culture.

2. Each culture aligns with a different value discipline, as follows:

Cultivation culture	Discontinuous innovation
Competence culture	Product leadership
Control culture	Operational excellence
Collaboration culture	Customer intimacy

3. Each culture shines at different points in the technology adoption life cycle:

Cultivation culture	Early market
Competency culture	Early market, bowling alley, tornado
Control culture	Tornado, Main Street
Collaboration culture	Bowling alley, Main Street

4. Each culture creates shareholder value in its own distinctive way:

Cultivation culture	Infectious charisma
Competency culture	Fierce competitiveness
Control culture	Relentless improvement
Collaboration culture	Perceptive adaptation

5. Each culture declares itself through a characteristic global focus:

Cultivation culture	Shared vision
Competency culture	Measurement and compensation
Control culture	Business planning
Collaboration culture	Customer focus

6. When companies merge or acquire each other, managing the transition to a new declared culture is a critical task for preserving shareholder value.

7. When cultures age, they fall prey to context overtaking core and degenerate into the following parodies of their true selves:

Cultivation culture	Cult
Competency culture	Caste system
Control culture	Bureaucracy
Collaboration culture	Club

Finally, since culture represents a major force in creating shareholder value, this chapter concludes with a call to action that executive teams and boards of directors use its framework and vocabulary to explicitly identify and declare a culture for their corporation.

Epilogue

SHEDDING CONTEXT, EMBRACING CORE

Now I believe we have come full circle, where as T. S. Eliot put it, "the end of all our exploring / [is] to arrive where we started / and know the place for the first time." In our case, where we started was with a notion that, to manage for shareholder value in the age of the Internet, organizations must shed context in order to embrace core.

From that vantage we said *core* was any activity that could raise stock price, a claim that drove us into the second chapter, a discourse of shareholder value, the main point of which was that stock price is an indirect measure of competitive advantage. To raise stock price, we realized, meant one had to increase competitive advantage. That claim in turn caused us to review the very nature of competitive advantage in technology-enabled markets (Chapter 3) and how it evolves through four different stages over the course of the technology adoption life cycle (Chapter 4). What we learned is that competitive-advantage strategy has to change much more frequently and dramatically than most organizations are prepared to support. When organizations do not rise to this challenge, the result is a series of default behaviors that culminate in the innovator's dilemma. We explored these behaviors briefly in Chapter 5 and then proceeded to outline a program of triage for correcting them. At the end of the day, however, triage is only a temporary expedient, and so in Chapter 6 we set out to describe a platform of four cultures, any one of which, if properly declared, can support the kind of ongoing adaptations required.

It remains for us to validate this last claim by exposing it to the test set forth in Chapter 1—how would each of these cultures meet the challenge of shedding context and embracing core? By now we know the short answer—*differently*! But by way of bringing this book to a close, I would like to at least sketch out the four paths forward, leaving it to you and your team to pick the one most to your liking.

Cultivation cultures have the easiest time shedding context— they simply walk away from it. Often this behavior is described as absent-minded, but I assure you it is nothing of the sort. It is instead the same atavistic mechanism by which teenagers everywhere evade cleaning up their rooms, an innate response that keeps them true to their messy cores despite every parental encouragement to the contrary. The end result in cultivation cultures is a kind of spontaneous outsourcing in which a supporting cast, managed by one or more invisible administrators, simply takes up the discarded work so that the geniuses can attend to whatever it is that genius attends to, or the work simply does not get done at all.

This mechanism works perfectly well, provided it is monitored at some level by a genius. Because it is so blatantly subject to abuse, it must continually be vetted by someone who can discriminate between the real stuff and a fraudulent imitation. Think of this individual as an artistic director, someone whose taste instinctively discriminates between what is truly fresh and new and what has become stale or derivative. It is a role that Steve Jobs has played quite visibly at Apple and that venture capitalist board members play on many a board—the person who keeps the organization climbing up the down escalator, always moving it out of its comfort zone to the edge of innovation. People not climbing fast enough or high enough are goaded to go higher and faster or to withdraw from the field (or have their funding withdrawn from them). It is a brutally Darwinian mechanism that must be fully exercised if cultivation culture is to keep itself relevant to the world.

Competence cultures can also keep themselves on track through constant testing and proving of themselves, but instead of letting their core be defined by the subjective insights of an artistic director, they must objectify it in observable, measurable outcomes. Context can overtake core in these cultures in two ways. In the first, the overall goal itself becomes context. This occurs whenever competing institutions have already reached the goal so that it no longer provides competitive differentiation.

In such instances competence cultures can shed context simply by raising the bar. But in so doing they must actively manage the growing accumulation of context work by systematically outsourcing it. If they do not, they will increase the burden on their talent pool beyond the point of tolerance, burning people out with work they really should not be doing. One tactic here has been to assign context work to temporary employees and contractors, but social and governmental resistance has now blocked this path. The only sustainable response is to reconstruct the workload into an outsourced/insourced workflow and proceed accordingly. Because competence cultures are so proficient with observable metrics, they are able to design highly effective service-level agreements with outsourcers and thus are well positioned to succeed in this effort.

The more insidious threat to competence cultures occurs when the metrics it has targeted no longer reflect true progress toward the end goal. Metrics, after all, are simply representative outcomes intended to signal change relative to a larger scheme. When they instead become enshrined as goals in themselves, competitive individuals find short cuts to achieving them that meet the letter of the challenge but violate its spirit. Alternatively, management setting the objectives can fall into the trap of simply replaying the old metrics blindly instead of rethinking goals anew and constructing new metrics in light of changed conditions. It is the signature characteristic of competence cultures that you get what you pay for. Thus management must vigilantly assure itself each year that it is indeed paying for the right things.

Competence cultures keep themselves in touch with what is truly core through a healthy paranoia. They navigate, in other words, by keeping a safe distance between themselves and their competitors. If they exhaust the current set, they must take on a more ambitious one or in the absence of a suitable external opponent find ways to compete among themselves. This incessant testing sloughs off most context work because people quickly see it does not lead to winning. The risk instead is that in its focus on outperforming a competitor, competence culture mistakenly directs its own core down a wrong road simply because that's where the other guy went. Thus the final competence required is the ability to navigate by a higher goal as well, defining core as an alignment between the company's internal competitive motivations with external value-creation activities that serve an end customer.

Control cultures shed context incrementally through quality improvement programs that prune and adapt work flows to accommodate gradual drifts in business processes. Their biggest challenge comes when disruptive technologies enable new market paradigms calling for wholesale deconstruction and reconfiguration of the incumbent value chain. At such points all the inertia and history of the old configuration resists transition to the required new state. The instrument for overcoming this resistance is the business plan. But instead of having it percolate up from the bottom of the organization, as it should in years of incremental change, in times of discontinuous change it must be formulated at the top and driven down through the organization over the objections of middle management.

Under this direction the culture must first plan how it is going to shed context and then execute that plan. The plan itself is built around (1) conducting the core-versus-context exercise at the executive level, (2) identifying the largest chunks of context that can be outsourced, (3) assigning a team and an executive sponsor to each chunk, (4) having them plan the search for, selection of, and transition to an outsourcer, and (5) executing that plan. Once this plan is under way, the rest of the organization that is not being outsourced should also be taught the core-versus-context exercise so that, local to its own planning functions, it can work through it during its next planning cycle.

More than anything else the key to control cultures successfully negotiating shedding of context is for the executive team to really "get" the new core. Mike Vance, a creativity consultant, tells a great story about helping the Mayo Clinic board get over such a hump. They wanted to know what was the key to becoming a more creative and flexible institution. Vance told them the one thing that all creative organizations have in common is that the people who work in them are cool. *Cool,* queried the board? Vance, sensing an uphill battle, was struck by an inspiration. The board had assembled in preparation for a three-day off-site meeting to review and approve the five-year operating plan. Vance proposed that he be allowed to approve the plan on the spot. The chairman, caught a bit off guard, acquiesced. Vance promptly announced, "You've just allowed a complete outsider to come in and approve your five-year plan—*now that's cool!*" The board went on to its off-site meeting, spent three days talking about everything in the Mayo Clinic's future but the five-year operating plan, and the only standard they used to continually challenge each other was, "Yeah, but is that cool?" So for control cultures, when it comes to stepping up to the task of embracing core and shedding context, that is the prescription: Be cool about it.

Finally, *collaboration cultures* shed context and embrace core by continually renewing their focus on the customer to ensure their efforts are adding true value. In stable markets, however, this mechanism can lose touch with the market whenever "the customer" comes to stand for the entity immediately downstream in the value chain. Along this line of thinking, an internal group can determine that its customers are another internal group which in turn could have as its customers yet another internal group, and so on. This leads to more and more energy going into creating customer satisfaction for colleagues or partners, not end customers. It also leads to far too cozy a system in which there is neither motive nor mechanism to pare this context away from core. Thus the first recourse of collaboration cultures must be to redefine customer focus as referring to the *end customer only* and to treat every intermediary in the value chain not as a surrogate customer to whom value is due but rather as a partner who must add value to the end customer or else has no place in the chain. Without this change in frame of reference, collaboration cultures become paralyzed when faced with the need to reengineer value chains to eliminate unnecessary middle men, a key step to ensuring sustainable competitive advantage in maturing markets.

The biggest challenge for collaboration cultures, however, comes when a discontinuous innovation forces the wholesale abandonment of the old value chain. This runs completely counter to the affiliation-based motives of collaboration itself, and there is a tendency among this culture to remain loyal to established relationships long after they have ceased to provide value. The most extreme example of this problem occurs when the disintermediation happens inside the customer organization, so that the old "end customer" is displaced by a new one, as happened in the telephony industry when phone and fax no longer reported to the office manager and was repositioned instead under the IT department.

At such times collaboration cultures must return to their roots by recommitting to true and unwavering customer service. More than any other culture, they are likely to bring the right attitude and the greatest domain expertise to the new challenge. It is simply a matter of reframing their understanding of the market in light of a new end customer who needs a new whole product which will be supplied by a new value chain—in essence, a matter of recrossing the chasm. The challenge is in letting go of the old and letting go of what feels like self-interest (but which in fact is simply inertia headed on a dangerously wrong course). Such radical shifts in momentum, as always, must come from the top down, not the bottom up. There are simply too many local loyalties to overcome piece by piece in anything like the time window available to make the transition.

In conclusion, each of the four cultures offers excellent prospects for shedding context and embracing core, what might be termed in aggregate, *organizational renewal*. In every case, as long as innovation is continuous within existing market frameworks, incremental renewal can be expected to bubble up from below, leveraging the natural attraction to quality as defined within that culture. Here management's primary role is simply to reinforce the natural actions of the culture. But whenever discontinuous innovations arrive, whether they come from outside the organization or, even more challenging, when they come from within, they demand disruptive changes. To navigate such a transition, it must be driven by timely, unambiguous intervention from the top down. In these cases management must make itself highly visible and act courageously outside the organization's familiar norms in order to reposition it onto the next technology wave.

The goal of this book has been to enable that act of leadership. The models and metaphors offer a common vocabulary by which executive leadership interacting with the rest of the management team can accurately describe changes in the marketplace and definitively prescribe actions in response. Specifically, each chapter's contribution is to the following ends:

1. Use the core-versus-context distinction to identify the inertial mass of context work in the organization with a view toward moving it outside the corporation via outsourcing.

2. Use the shareholder value models to connect core with stock price so that every stakeholder in the corporation is motivated to shed context and embrace core. Also use these models to transform the financial markets into a management information system such that everyone in the company can interpret the feedback investors are providing about the company's progress toward securing a stronger competitive-advantage position.

3. Use the competitive-advantage hierarchy as a comprehensive framework for defining the company's and its competition's strengths, weaknesses, opportunities, and threats, specifically in the realm of competitive-advantage elements. These observations become the basis for corporate strategy decisions.

4. Use the fault line model to focus on those competitive-advantage issues that are most pertinent to the current state of the market and to avoid relying on models that are not appropriate to that state.

5. Use the triage exercises to shed context and embrace core. In an era of discontinuous change, use the recrossing-the-chasm prescription to drive renewal through mature organizations to recapture some high ground in the ongoing battle for competitive advantage.

6. Use the culture models to build to last, declaring a unifying global culture so that the company can embrace change optimistically, anticipating the market's demands, and be fully prepared to respond to them as they come on-line.

There has never been a time when there was a greater opportunity for wealth creation. Most of the frustration in business today comes from sensing this opportunity globally and yet feeling paralyzed to capitalize upon it locally. I hope this book creates a sense of urgency in you, partly because its models create new avenues to explore, and partly because this window of opportunity will not stay open forever.

At the end of the day, it may come down to a matter of courage. Specifically, for companies that have thrived on Main Street for decades, that have not seen a discontinuous innovation in management's memory, these new market forces are intimidating indeed. That is why so many companies brought forcefully into in the age of the Internet feel compelled to spin-out a dotcom rather than integrate the Web into their forward-looking plans. Management is scared. But that is as it should be. The thought I would leave you with is a simple one: If we say that leadership requires courage, we should recognize that courage is not required except in the presence of fear. If you are not scared, you are not leading.

Best wishes and Godspeed from
Geoffrey Moore

INDEX